WALT WHITMAN AMONG THE FRENCH

WALT WHITMAN AMONG THE FRENCH

Poet and Myth

Betsy Erkkila

PRINCETON
UNIVERSITY
PRESS
1980

Published by Princeton University Press, Princeton, New Jersey In the United Kingdom: Princeton University Press, Guildford, Surrey

Library of Congress Cataloging in Publication Data will be found on the last printed page of this book

This book has been composed in VIP Electra

Clothbound editions of Princeton University Press books are printed on acid-free paper, and binding materials are chosen for strength and durability

Printed in the United States of America by Princeton University Press, Princeton, New Jersey

Designed by Laury A. Egan

TO

LARRY

MY BEST FRIEND

AND MY HUSBAND

ACKNOWLEDGMENTS

IN COMPLETING THIS STUDY of Walt Whitman's French background and his later impact on French literature from the Symbolist period to the present, I have received help from many sources. A grant from the Fulbright Commission enabled me to spend two years in France, where I had easy access to materials that would have been difficult or impossible to find in the United States. I would like to thank my students in France and the French people in general; the experience of being an American in France and the experience of teaching Whitman to French students aided me in my research.

I am indebted to many Whitman scholars, particularly Gay Wilson Allen and Roger Asselineau, whose many Whitman publications have been invaluable to me. While I was in France, Roger Asselineau took time from his busy schedule as a scholar and teacher at the Sorbonne to read my manuscript and offer useful and supportive commentary. Martin Kanes let me read his personal copy of his unpublished 1953 Sorbonne dissertation, "La Fortune de Walt Whitman en France." Lennis Dunlap generously gave many long hours and great care to proofreading my manuscript. Richard Bridgman read my manuscript and made some incisive suggestions about the phrasing and emphasis of an "influence" study, and Warren Ramsey offered expert commentary on the sections dealing with modern French poetry. A local innovation grant from California State University, Chico, gave me some release time to complete this study.

I owe a particular debt to my mentor and friend, Thomas Parkinson. He did not know me (although I was an admirer from afar) when I first wandered into his office several years ago with a love of Walt Whitman and French literature and a vague notion that I would like to bring them together in a single study. Thomas Parkinson responded with immediate warmth and enthusiasm. Since that time, his passionate commitment to life and letters has been for me a steady source of inspiration and guidance.

Finally, I would like to give special thanks to my husband, Larry, to my family, and to my friends, who have all provided help and support in more ways than they can know.

NOTE ON THE TRANSLATIONS

I have given literal prose translations of all French passages cited. These translations appear at the bottom of the page and are identified by the first and last words of the passage.

CONTENTS

WALT WHITMAN AMONG THE FRENCH

INTRODUCTION

WHITMAN'S RELATIONS with France date back to General Lafayette's tour of America in 1824. Whitman was among the school children who turned out to see General Lafayette lay the cornerstone of the Apprentices Library in Brooklyn. In his biography of Whitman, John Burroughs tells how the French general "took up the five-year-old Walt Whitman, and pressing the child a moment to his breast, and giving him a kiss, handed him down to a safe spot in the excavation." [1] Although the episode may in fact be only another of the myths created and perpetuated by Whitman and his inner circle of friends, this embrace between the young Whitman and the aged Lafayette is in many ways as symbolic as that other famous Franco-American embrace between the young Franklin and the aged Voltaire. The embrace between Whitman, the future poet of Democracy and America, and Lafayette, the past *philosophe* and general, who fought in both the American and the French Revolutions and who was one of the engineers of the *Déclaration des droits de l'homme*, prefigures the long and sympathetic alliance between Whitman and France, which is reflected both in Whitman's thought and art and in the later French response to his work.

Although there have been a few studies of Whitman's use of the French language or his relationship to particular French writers, no one has yet made a thorough study of Whitman's French background and his later influence on French literature from the Symbolist period to the present. An understanding of Whitman's relation to French writers and thinkers is important for a number of reasons. A knowledge of the French roots of some of Whitman's thought, particularly his social and political thought, not only adds to our understanding of the "long foreground" that preceded the appearance of *Leaves of Grass* in 1855, but also enhances our appreciation of Whitman's unique poetic achievement.

The relationship between Whitman and the French is also significant both in the history of Franco-American literary relations and in the history of American cultural influence in general. A knowledge of Whitman's French background illuminates the continental parallels and origins of some of his ideas and themes and thus helps us to understand why the profound "shock of recognition" in response to Whitman was experienced first in Europe and only after, and with much less intensity, in America.

In the course of this study of Whitman and the French, many of the common critical assumptions about Whitman will be called into question, and we will begin to see a different and more cosmopolitan image of the American poet. No longer will we look upon Whitman as an unread American rough, without past and without tradition. Not only did Whitman read widely in the literature of his own and other lands, but he quite self-consciously participated in a tradition. Unlike his American contemporaries, however, Whitman participated in a tradition that was French rather than English in its roots. Whitman's embrace of the French tradition was, in fact, part of his attempt to liberate America from the deeply rooted Puritan sensibility and habits of mind that he associated with England.

In a section of *Specimen Days* entitled "British Literature," Whitman asserts that America, being the offspring of all continents, had been disproportionately influenced by the "British element." He encourages his readers to turn away from Britain and familiarize themselves with the imaginative productions of the continent: "I strongly recommend all the young men and women of the United States to whom it may be eligible, to overhaul the well-freighted fleets, the literatures of Italy, Spain, France, Germany, so full of those elements of freedom, self-possession, gay-heartedness, subtlety, dilation, needed in preparations for the future of the States." [2] Through his reading of Dante and Goethe, as well as through his use of such anthologies as Hedge's *Prose Writers and Poets of Germany* and Ticknor's *Spanish Literature*, Whitman had, in a rather limited way, attempted to follow his own advice. It was mainly in overhauling the thought and writings of France, however, that Whitman defied traditional American loyalties. Unlike most American writers who preceded him and unlike such of his contemporaries as Emerson, Thoreau, Melville, and Hawthorne, who tended to draw upon England and Germany in their own thought and art, Whitman was the first major American writer to find important sources and analogues for his own work in the literature and philosophy of France.

5

Writing in 1866 to Whitman's close friend W. D. O'Connor, Matthew Arnold said:

"As to the general question of Mr Walt Whitman's poetical achievement, you will think that it savours of our decrepit old Europe when I add that while you think it is his highest merit that he is so unlike anyone else, to me this seems to be his demerit; no one can afford in literature to trade merely on his own bottom and to take no account of what the other ages and nations have acquired: a great original literature America will never get in this way, and her intellect must inevitably consent to come, in a considerable measure, into the European movement." [3]

Arnold's criticism of Whitman for his failure to take account of the past suggests that he never got as far into Whitman's work as the 1855 Preface to *Leaves of Grass*, where Whitman asserts: "America does not repel the past or what it has produced under its forms."[4] Arnold's remarks on Whitman are not unique, however. Even sympathetic critics of Whitman, eager to point up his originality and genius, fail to recognize and elucidate his very real connections with the "European movement."

For example, in his book entitled *The American Adam*, R.W.B. Lewis treats Whitman as the archetypal Adamic figure in American literature. His whole argument is based on the premise that

> Whitman began in an Adamic condition which was only too effectively realized: the isolated individual, standing flush with the empty universe, a primitive moral and intellectual entity [5]

By studying Whitman's French background and his later impact on the French writers, I would like to challenge this persistent tendency among critics to regard Whitman as some kind of isolated primitive or eccentric national genius. This study will demonstrate that at least a part of Whitman's uniqueness and originality lay in his ability to absorb and to project poetically certain international currents in thought and art as no other writer before him. Not only did Whitman participate in the international currents associated with the Enlightenment, Romanticism, Positivism, and Symbolism; but he anticipated, if he did not directly inspire, the modernist spirit of Post-Symbolism, Futurism, Cubism, and Surrealism.

CHAPTER I
FRANCE IN WHITMAN

"We grand-sons and great-grand-sons do not forget your grand-sires."
—"Bravo, Paris Exposition"

THROUGHOUT HIS LIFE, Whitman felt a strong political, social, and even temperamental affinity with France. Thinking about the French, Whitman once remarked: "I never had the common Puritan ideas about France: I have long considered the French in some ways the top of the heap. We too generally lack the elemental affinities to judge the Latin races with anything like justice." He expressed surprise that Emerson would be favorable to the French. "Emerson," he says, "was so soaked in and in with English currents of ancestry. I love Emerson—I do not need to say that—but he was somewhat thin on the physiological side. There are things in the French which I do not criticise but which I believe must have been very offensive to Emerson."[1] Whitman's words suggest the French affinities of his own physiological interest, most fully expressed in the "Children of Adam" poems, to which Whitman initially gave the French title "Enfans d'Adam." And this, it might be remembered, was precisely the section that Emerson, in that famous walk on the Boston Common, attempted to persuade Whitman to eliminate from the 1860 edition of *Leaves of Grass*.

Whitman's reference to a certain Puritan antagonism to France among Americans is a fairly accurate description of Franco-American relations in general at that time. In his book *America and French Culture*, Howard Mumford Jones shows that up until about 1770 there was hostility in America to the French because of their close association in the American mind both with Catholicism and with the

Indians. Although there was a brief interlude of American sympathy and alliance with France during the period of the American Revolution and the early period of the French Revolution, the American people generally tended to associate France and the French language with atheism, anarchy, and immorality.[2]

In aggressively stating his profound sympathy with France both in conversation and in writing, Whitman was in a very real sense showing his moral and political colors. To be sympathetic with the French in early nineteenth-century America could never be a politically or morally neutral position, a mere preference for one nationality or country over another. To be pro-French was to be for Jefferson, the Democrats, agrarianism, and the common man; it was to champion social and moral liberty. To be anti-French was to be for Hamilton, the Federalists, aristocracy, and privilege; it was to champion social and moral restraint. Just as in the Revolutionary period in American literature *belles lettres* had tended to reflect the battle between Federalist and Democrat, so Whitman, somewhat in the tradition of Philip Freneau and Joel Barlow, reflected in his own writings the final stages of this political struggle.

Whitman looked to France as a model in his attempt to liberate American sensibility, with its deep roots in the Puritan past, into a new moral and political consciousness. He admired the openness and freedom of the French in human relationships. As early as 1845, in an article written for the *Long Island Star*, Whitman commended the French influence in the fashionable world of New York:

> As for manners, we are assimilating to the Parisian, more and more—and I must confess I like it so. Stiffness and reserve are banished—dignified silence laughed at—all kinds of keeping one's state, sent to Coventry. A dash of familiarity, even with the strangers, (either sex to either sex) you meet at parties, &c. is good breeding now.[3]

Even at this early stage in his career, Whitman's admiration of the freedom and permissiveness of French society was related to his sense that the French way of life, in allowing a "dash of familiarity" between strangers, would provide a more open atmosphere in which to release hiw own Calamus emotions. In French society Whitman saw a model for the kind of sexual freedom he envisioned for the American nation.

He once told Horace Traubel: "I am aware of what our puritans think of the French: it counts for little with me . . . the main difference between us and the French in sex directions is in their frankness as opposed to our hypocrisy."[4]

In addition to his identification with the social and sexual attitudes of the French, Whitman also had a deep sense of political kinship with the French republic. This sense of kinship with France is perhaps best expressed in a note in *Specimen Days*:

> The official relations of Our States we know, are with the reigning kings, queens, &c., of the Old World. But the only deep, vast, emotional, real affinity of America is with the cause of Popular Government there—and especially in France.[5]

Whitman's lifelong sympathy with France was in some ways a result of his belief that the American and the French Revolutions emerged from the same root. Drinking an imaginary toast to France on Bastille Day in 1888, Whitman said: "What America did for the Fourth, France did for the Fourteenth: both acts were of the same stock."[6]

In his poetry, Whitman continually returns to the theme of the French Revolution. One of his earliest free verse poems, "Resurgemus," was in part inspired by the revolution in France in 1848, when Louis Philippe was dethroned and a second French Republic was declared. In the poem "O Star of France," Whitman expresses his sense of identification with the spirit of France and with the French Revolution:

> Dim smitten star,
> Orb not of France alone, pale symbol of my
>   soul, its dearest hopes,
> The struggle and the daring, rage divine
>   for liberty,
> Of aspirations toward the far ideal,
>   enthusiast's dreams of brotherhood,
> Of terror to the tyrant and the priest.
>
> (6-10)[7]

Whitman never lost this fundamental faith in France as the symbol of his hopes for liberty and brotherhood not only in America but throughout the world. Unlike the many people whose support of the

French Revolution did not extend beyond the Reign of Terror, Whitman in "France, The 18th Year of these States" expresses his own belief that the "terrible red birth and baptism" of the Terror was the just retribution for years of oppression and suffering:

> Pale, silent, stern, what could I say to that
> long-accrued retribution?
> Could I wish humanity different?
> Could I wish the people made of wood and stone?
> Or that there be no justice in destiny or time?
> (8-11)

As late as 1889, Whitman again recorded his debt of gratitude to France and to the French Revolution in the poem "Bravo, Paris Exposition." In sending his love and good will to the French people on the occasion of the Paris Exposition, Whitman says: "We grandsons and great-grand-sons do not forget your grand-sires" (4). At the end of his life, as at the beginning, Whitman regarded himself as the offspring of France rather than of England.

I. The French Background

In her book of memoirs entitled *A Backward Glance*, Edith Wharton recalls Henry James's admiration for Walt Whitman. On one occasion, she remembers how "James, in one of his sudden humorous drops from the heights, flung up his hands and cried out with the old stammer and twinkle: 'Oh, yes, a great genius; undoubtedly a very great genius! Only one cannot help deploring his too-extensive acquaintance with the foreign languages.' "[8] Whitman used French words and phrases throughout his writing, and it was probably his extensive and frequently inaccurate use of the French language that provoked James's ironic comment. However, Whitman's use of the French language was neither merely ignorant nor merely arrogant, as is commonly assumed. Not only did his use of the French language come out of some very serious thought about the nature and function of language, but his use of the language, particularly in the titles of his poems, was a way of self-consciously flaunting and celebrating his pro-French sympathies and thus defying traditional American loyalties.

Although some critics have maintained that Whitman had a reading knowledge of the French language, there is no evidence for this assertion. In his biography of Whitman, Richard Maurice Bucke says: "He read no language but English, yet I believe he knew a great deal more French, German, and Spanish than he would own to."[9] Whitman may have known a great many French words and phrases, but his acquaintance with the language was limited to a brief flirtation with the surface. He picked up French words and phrases, which he absorbed and projected in terms of his own poetic program, but he never arrived at any real comprehension of the underlying structure, meaning, or content of the language.

Late in life Whitman would sometimes wait weeks for one of his acquaintances to translate the correspondence and articles that he received from his French admirers. Commenting to Traubel on Jules Laforgue's French translations of some of his poems, Whitman remarked: "I never could have known how they were done, of course, as I have absolutely no conversancy with the language . . . . I try to look at my face in a French glass but somehow it don't work very well."[10] If Whitman's secret knowledge of French was as great as Bucke would have us believe, it is strange that he could not even begin to transcribe some of the letters and articles he had received from France; and it is even more strange that he would be unable to recognize his own face in the French glass of Laforgue's translations.

With such a limited knowledge of the French language, Whitman was probably unable to read anything in the French original. His reading was limited to those works already translated into English and available in America. Thus, even though Whitman's artistic theory and practice often coincide with or anticipate the Symbolist and Modern periods in French literature, his actual reading did not extend much beyond the writings of the French Romantic period which were available in translation.

Although Whitman had some fragmentary and superficial acquaintance with Medieval and Classical French writers, he tended to lump them together as alien to the natural genius and democratic spirit of the American continent. In one of his early notebooks, Whitman says: "I fancy the classical tragedies of Corneille, Racine, Voltaire &c., must illustrate the vital difference between a native and normal growth (as the Greek tragedies themselves) and all that comes from the mere study of that growth."[11] And in an article written for *Life Illustrated*, he made the following remarks on the "Condition of Writers before the American Era":

> Racine, Boileau, Corneille, Molière, La Bruyere, Fenelon—what had they to eat or drink but the shadows of royalty or the aristocracy? . . . There was only one other choice for litterateurs. Some were devoted to the service of priests . . . . Among the profuse shoals of the writers of those times, not one appeared to speak for man, for mind, for freedom, against superstition and caste.[12]

In the form and artifice of French Classical literature, as well as in the political system by which it was nourished, Whitman found the direct antithesis to the vital, organic, and democratic literature that he envisioned for America.

With the exception of Rabelais and Montaigne, whom he read and admired, the early French writers provided a rather barren field for Whitman in his search for precedents and examples of his democratic and spontaneous art. It was primarily among the French writers of the Enlightenment and Romantic periods that Whitman found worthy models for the outsetting American bard.

II. The French Enlightenment

Throughout his childhood and during his early years as a journalist and politician, Whitman was schooled in the social and political philosophy of the Enlightenment and of the French Revolution. Whitman's early acquaintance with the thought and writings of Tom Paine, Thomas Jefferson, and Frances Wright brought him into contact with some of the more radical and important philosophies of the French Enlightenment. He also had some direct acquaintance with the work of such French *philosophes* as Voltaire, Volney, and Rousseau.

Whitman owned a copy of Voltaire's *Philosophical Dictionary*, and a reference to the *Dictionary* in his early notebooks indicates that he may have read Voltaire before the appearance of the first edition of *Leaves of Grass* in 1855.[13] Since the *Dictionary* gives voice to many of the common Enlightenment ideals upon which Whitman was raised, it would be difficult to make a case for any particular impact that this work had upon Whitman's thought and writing. At times, however, Whitman's prose and poetry echo in phrase and meaning the Voltaire of the *Dictionary*.

In the section entitled "Miracles" in the *Philosophical Dictionary*, Voltaire says: "A MIRACLE, according to the true meaning of the word, is something admirable; and agreeably to this, all is miracle. The stupendous order of nature, the revolution of a hundred millions of worlds round a million of suns, the activity of light, the life of animals, all are grand and perpetual miracles."[14] In his campaign against the superstitions and remarkable providences of organized religion in general and Puritanism in particular, Whitman expresses much the same idea of miracle in his 1855 Preface; he rejects

> Any miracle of affairs or persons inadmissible in the vast clear scheme where every motion and every spear of grass and the frames and spirits of men and women and all that concerns them are unspeakably perfect miracles all referring to all and each distinct and in its place.[15]

Whitman embodies the same idea in the 1856 poem "Miracles":

> Why, who makes much of a miracle?
> As to me I know of nothing else but miracles,
>
> ....
>
> To me every hour of the light and dark is a
> miracle,
> Every cubic inch of space is a miracle,
> Every square yard of the surface of the
> earth is spread with the same,
> Every foot of the interior swarms with the
> same.
>
> (1-2; 17-20)

Although it may be mere coincidence that Whitman's words on miracles both in the 1855 Preface and the 1856 poem echo Voltaire in tone, image, and meaning, we can see how close Whitman's vision of the natural and cosmic universe was to the new and more secular vision of the French *philosophes*.

Unlike many of his American contemporaries who had come into the orbit of New England Transcendentalism, Whitman found his own and America's roots in the similar but much more politically based philosophy of self-reliant individualism practiced by Voltaire and the French rationalists. In an article written in 1856 entitled "Voltaire: A Fragment by Walt Whitman,"[16] he describes Voltaire as "a fit precursor, in one or two points, of the American era" (p. 71). For Whitman, Voltaire represented the assertion of individual freedom and of the rational mind against the superstitions and shams of the past. He says of Voltaire: "He had a clear head, never to be cheated by the traditions, quibbles, shams, and tyrannies of those who made a good thing out of churches and courts. He loved to expose the old shysters. He also loved knowledge in itself" (p. 73).

Whitman also regarded the French Encyclopaedists as precursors of the American era. His article on Voltaire includes an encomium on the French *Encyclopaedia:*

> Out of the times of Buffon, La Motte, Fontenelle, Diderot, Piron, Crebillon the tragic, and Crebillon the gay—of Mademoiselle Clairon, Sophie Arnold, Madame de Pompadour, and Marie Antoinette—rose the Encyclopaedia Francais. Long live free literature! Long live science! The French Encyclopaedia tuned the instruments of the French Revolution and the American Revolution.
>
> (pp. 71-72)

In this tribute to the *Encyclopaedia* as a gathering together of the separate intellectual energies of the French Enlightenment, Whitman again points up the roots of the future republics of France and America in the common ground of the French Enlightenment.

In addition to his early connections with Voltaire and the French Encyclopaedists, Whitman's youthful reading of Count Volney's *The Ruins, or Meditations on the Revolutions of Empires* (1802) left a deep impression. Speaking to Traubel, Whitman described Volney's *Ruins* as "another of the books on which I may be said to have been raised."[17]

In *The Ruins,* Volney expresses the fundamental faith of the Enlightenment in reason, science, civilization, and progress. Motivated by the most important virtue of the enlightened man, social usefulness, Volney undertakes to discover the causes of the ruins of empires in order to improve the happiness of man in a social state. He defines and describes at length the physical and natural laws that govern man and the universe. He expresses the ideal of toleration and good will in religion, order and balance in society, liberty and equality in politics. And he looks forward to the establishment of an international community, with all men existing equally under the same natural law of right and reason.

The early and profound impact that Volney's *Ruins* had upon Whitman's artistic development is revealed in Whitman's first known declaration of literary intentions. In one of the "Sun-Down Papers" written for the *Long Island Democrat* in 1840, Whitman expressed his desire to write a history; his words are reminiscent of Volney's political and social themes:

> I would compose a wonderful and ponderous book. Therein should be treated on, the nature and peculiarities of men, the diversity of their characters, the means of improving their state, and the proper mode of governing nations.[18]

He goes on to say that the principal part of the book will deal with the evils of being rich:

> And one principal claim to a place among men of profound sagacity, by means of the work I allude to, would be an account of a wondrous and important discovery, a treatise upon which would fill up the principal part of my compilation. I have found out that it is a very dangerous thing to be rich.[19]

The theme of riches as corrupting is again suggestive of Volney. Throughout *The Ruins*, Volney shows that cupidity, or the desire for riches, is the source of all man's torments, the source of wars among nations, of the division of society into masters and slaves, and of the overthrow of empires.

Whitman accepted the fundamental premise of Volney's work that

> Man is governed by natural laws, regular in their course, consistent in their effects, immutable in their essence; and those laws, the common source of good and evil, are not written among the distant stars, or hidden in mysterious codes: inherent in the nature of terrestial being, interwoven with their existence, they are at all times, and in all places, present to man.[20]

Whitman's early embrace of Enlightenment theories of natural law confirmed or suggested some of his more important ideas about man and the universe, art and life, materialism and science, equality and liberty, faith and religion, brotherhood and international community, ideas which made their first complete appearance in the 1855 edition of *Leaves of Grass*. From his rejection of "the whole theory of the special and supernatural" in favor of the idea of natural law, the idea that "the vital laws enclose all . . . they are sufficient for any case and for all cases," to his embrace of the idea of amelioration, "the eternal tendencies of all toward happiness," and his celebration of individual power in "a new chant of dilation and pride,"[21] Whitman expresses the fundamental faith not only of Volney but of the Enlightenment in general.

The poetry of the 1855 edition of *Leaves of Grass* sometimes directly recalls Volney in image and in phrase. For example, at the outset of *The Ruins*, the Genius or Apparition of the tombs lifts the narrator into a flight above the earth in order to reveal to him the "science of the ages." The narrator says of the Apparition:

> Then approaching and laying his hand on my head, "Rise, mortal," said he, "and extricate thy senses from the dust in which thou movest." Suddenly a celestial flame seemed to dissolve the bands which fix us to the earth, and, like a light vapor, borne up on the wings of the Genius, I felt myself wafted to the region above.
>
> (p. 31)

Floating through space, the narrator surveys the ruins of the empires and the past and present condition of the earth and its inhabitants. Section 33 of "Song of Myself" contains a similar flight through space. Whitman says:

> My ties and ballasts leave me. . . . I
> travel. . . . I sail. . . . my elbows
> rest in the sea-gaps,
> I skirt the sierras. . . . my palms
> cover continents,
> I am afoot with my vision.
> (*LG* 1855, 712-714)

Then begins the famous long catalog in which Whitman, like Volney, enumerates his vision of life upon earth. At one point Whitman finds himself

> entering by the suburbs some vast and ruined city.... the blocks and fallen architecture more than all the living cities of the globe.
>
> (*LG* 1855, 812)

Although Whitman's comic and cosmic imagination has animated and transformed the episode, the idea of a flight through space was probably originally suggested by Volney.

Whitman's early notebooks include several notes on Volney's *Ruins* that were later incorporated into the poetry of *Leaves of Grass*. For example, in a notebook dated 1847-1855, Whitman recorded the following:

> The most immense part of ancient history is altogether unknown. Previous to ten thousand years ago there were surely empires, cities, states and pastoral tribes and uncivilized hordes upon the earth.... There were busy, populous and powerful nations on all the continents of the earth at intervals through the stretch of time from ten thousand years ago down to twenty six hundred years ago—signs and materials of them remain. Of their literature, government, religions, social customs, and general civilization—silence.[22]

Although Whitman's imaginative feeling for the antiquity of the earth and its inhabitants had been stimulated both by his visits to Dr. Abbott's Egyptian Museum and by his reading of scientific articles in the journals of the time, in writing this note he probably recalled Volney's meditation on the ruins of empires. Volney continually laments the passing of the opulent nations of Syria and Egypt: "Here, said I, here once flourished an opulent city; here was the seat of a powerful empire. Yes! these places, now so desert, were once animated by a living multitude—a busy crowd circulated in these streets now so solitary. Within these walls, where a mournful silence reigns, the noise of the arts and shouts of joy and festivity incessantly resounded" (p. 23). This and similar meditations in Volney may have stimulated Whitman to make notes on the unknown nations of ancient history that he later incorporated into the poem "Unnamed Lands."

In another early notebook, Whitman, under the heading "Religions-Gods," copied directly from Volney's *Ruins*. The notes consist of rather fragmentary listings of the identifying traits of several different religions. One note reads:

> Kneph—"existence"—a Theban god, a human figure dressed in dark blue holding in one had a sceptre and a girdle, with a cap of feathers on his head (to express the fugacity of thought).[23]

This is taken from the following passage in Volney's discussion of the Seventh System of religion, "Worship of the Soul of the World": "Kneph, a human figure, dressed in dark blue, having in one hand a sceptre and a girdle (the zodiac), with a cap of feathers, to express the fugacity of thought, and producing from his mouth the great egg (p. 151)." Whitman later incorporated his notes on the figure of Kneph into the poem "Salut Au Monde!" In enumerating the religions of antiquity, Whitman says:

> I see Kneph, blooming, drest in blue, with
> the crown of feathers on his head.
> (99)

Not only in this particular image, but in the religious and geographical catalogs throughout the poem, Whitman reveals a similar debt to Volney.[24]

In addition to the Kneph image, Whitman may have borrowed some of his pantheistic themes and imagery from Volney's description of the Seventh System of religion, "Worship of the Soul of the World." The following passage suggests an early source not only for the image of the "nebulous float," or fluid soul of the world, that recurs throughout Whitman's poetry, but for some of his characteristic ideas on the divinity of man and creation, and on the transmigration and immortality of the soul:

> Now, as a consequence of this system, every being containing in itself a portion of the igneous and ethereal fluid, common and universal mover, and this fluid soul of the world being the Divinity, it followed that the souls of all beings were a portion of

> God himself, partaking of all his attributes, that is, being a substance indivisible, simple and immortal; and hence the whole system of the immortality of the soul, which at first was eternity. Hence also its transmigrations, known by the name of metempsychosis, that is, the passage of the vital principle from one body to another.
>
> (pp. 151-152)

Volney's discussion of pantheism and spirituality is, like his discussion of the other systems, only a stage in his reasoned attempt to prove that the spirit of religion had no other origin than the sensations and wants of man. Whitman, however, stopped short at the Seventh System, to accept and give credence to the very ideas of soul, spirit, and the divinity of the world that Volney had set out to disprove. Perhaps, as Malcolm Cowley maintains, Whitman "reinvented" the Transcendental ideas of his time after some kind of early mystical experience,[25] but he also reinvented some of the ideas on soul and oversoul, transmigration and immortality, pantheism and cosmic evolution that he found in Volney's *Ruins*.

Unlike Volney, Whitman equated physical and natural law not with a perfectly ordered machine but with the divine flux of the soul. It is this tendency to "spiritualize" his heritage from the Enlightenment that sets Whitman apart from the more purely deist and rationalist conceptions of Voltaire, Volney, and other enlightened thinkers. And yet, Whitman's early and deep roots in the political and cosmopolitan philosophies of the Enlightenment led him to an acceptance of the social and material world and to a faith in science and technology that placed him in sympathetic accord with French Romantic and Modernist literature.

If Whitman found the mind and social conscience of the Enlightenment in such French *philosophes* as Voltaire and Volney, he found the soul and personal sensibility of Romanticism in Jean-Jacques Rousseau. Whitman first became acquainted with the writings of Rousseau during the 1840's. In an article on "Home Literature," written for the *Brooklyn Daily Eagle* in 1846, Whitman refers to the "fascinating melancholy of Rousseau." Although he is critical of the evil influence that foreign authors have had on American literature, he lists Rousseau among the "great intellects of

Europe," to whom he pays a "tribute of admiration and respect."[26] We do not know how familiar Whitman was with the writings of Rousseau at this time, but he had some general acquaintance with *The Social Contract* and *The Confessions*.

In one of his notebooks from the late 1840's, Whitman copied passages from the opening chapters of Rousseau's *Social Contract*. He made several annotations on Rousseaus's idea of the social compact. For example, commenting on Rousseau's ideas on natural liberty and right and the equality and sovereignty of the people, Whitman observes: "Singularly some of the most important provisions of the specific laws of the Public Lands of the United States, are taken word for word, and idea for idea, from Rousseau's 'Contract.' "[27] In the Rousseau of the *Social Contract*, Whitman found another French "grand-sire" of America. Although Whitman recognized Rousseau as "one of the noblest apostles of democracy,"[28] however, he was more interested in the personal sensibility and artistic creed that he found in *The Confessions* than he was in the political and social theories of *The Social Contract*.

A number of biographical notes on historical figures in Whitman's early notebooks seem to indicate that he was planning a series of poems on the deeds of great men. Included among these notes is a long biographical sketch of Rousseau that contains Whitman's first reference to Rousseau's *Confessions*. As Whitman records:

> Rousseau's Confessions (Swinton's translation fall of 1856). In 1766 Rousseau, 54 years old, took refuge in Wooton, Staffordshire, England and wrote this frivolous, chattering, repulsive book that still has a great lesson in its pages, and whose revelations one keeps reading somehow to the end.[29]

In the past, critics have used this note as an indication that if Whitman did in fact read the *Confessions*, it was not until 1856. However, certain verbal parallels between the *Confesssions* and the first edition of *Leaves of Grass* indicate that Whitman had read Rousseau's autobiography before 1855. For example, Rousseau describes himself in the following passage: "I delight in busying myself in the merest trifles—beginning a hundred things and never finishing one—coming or going as the whim takes me—planning something new every moment—following a fly through its fickle and fantastic flight—tipping up a big stone to see what's under it—rushing with eagerness into a ten years' task, and throwing it up in ten minutes—musing the live long day—obeying every caprice of the moment, with a behavior light and lawless as snow flakes."[30]

Not only does Rousseau's picture of himself as a loafer provide an analogue for the curious and capricious persona of the 1855 "Song of Myself"; Whitman practically paraphrases Rousseau's "behavior light and lawless as snow flakes":

> Behaviour lawless as snow-flakes . . . words
> simple as grass . . . uncombed head and
> laughter and naivete.
> ("Song of Myself," 980)

He may have recalled Rousseau's words from a very careful and attentive reading of the *Confessions* before the first appearance of *Leaves of Grass* in 1855.

Further similarities in word and image, theme and idea, suggest that Rousseau's *Confessions* had some impact on Whitman's *Leaves*. For example, throughout the *Confessions* the life of the vagabond on the road is set forth as an example of the condition of freedom, independence, and total contact with creation that one finds outside the artificial restraints of society and civilization. Rousseau says: "Never have I thought so much, existed so completely, lived so thoroughly, been so much of myself, if I may use the expression, as in my solitary journeys on foot . . . the sight of the country, the succession of agreeable aspects, the open air, the capital appetite and good health . . . the absence of everything that makes me feel my dependance . . . all conspire to free my mind, to give me a greater audacity of thought, and launch me, in a manner, into the immensity of beings, combining, choosing, and appropriating them after my fancy, without fear and without restraint."[31] For Whitman too, the vagabond on the open road represented a condition of openness, self-reliance, and continual renewal. In the 1855 "Song of Myself," he informed his readers:

> I have no chair, nor church nor philosophy;
> I lead no man to a dinner-table or library
> or exchange;

But each man and each woman of you I lead
upon a knoll,
My left hand hooks you round the waist,
My right hand points to landscapes of
continents, and a plain public road.
(1202-1206)

This passage provides the germ of the idea that, in 1856, Whitman developed in "Poem of the Road" (changed to "Song of the Open Road" in 1867). The poem echoes Rousseau in phrase and image. For example, Whitman's opening recalls Rousseau's celebration of the life of the vagabond on the open road:

Afoot and light-hearted I take to the open road,
Healthy, free, the world before me,
The long brown path before me, leading wherever
I choose.
(1-3)

If Whitman reread the *Confessions* in 1856, it is quite possible that the prominence of the vagabond motif in Rousseau's work played some role in inspiring him to write a poem on the same theme. Whitman certainly remembered the theme of the road in connection with Rousseau, for in his biographical sketch of the Frenchman he noted that Rousseau was a "sort of vagabond."[32]

In Rousseau's writing, Whitman also found a model for the kind of openness and candor that he envisioned for the literature of the future. In his biographical note, he commented on Rousseau's exposure of the mean and dirty aspects of human nature: "His *Confessions,*" he says, "are a singular opening up of the trivial incidents, some quite disgusting, which find their tally in everyman's life."[33] Whitman's awareness of the precedent set by Rousseau in undraping the soul helped him to discover the more confidential and autobiographically revealing voice of his own poetry. The sadder, more personal and confessional voice that we find in some of Whitman's poetry, particularly in the Calamus series, is often reminiscent of the troubled and ambiguous voice of Rousseau's *Confessions*.

In addition to the vagabond and confessional motifs to which Whitman made specific reference in his biographical note on

Rousseau, there are many general similarities between *Leaves of Grass* and the *Confessions*. These are the product of the basic temperamental similarities between the two artists rather than the result of specific influence. For example, Rousseau makes the following defense of loafing: "The loafing I love is not the sort indulged in by a lazy lounger who sits with his arms crossed in total inaction, thinking as little as he acts. Mine is at once that of a child in incessant but aimless movement, and that of an old codger that likes to wander off in his story."[34] Whitman was also a defender of loafing. In his early journalism days he wrote an article on the philosophy of loafing. And later, in words that frequently echo Rousseau, he generalized his indolent disposition into the personal and cosmic poetic "I" who celebrates the joys of reclining and floating with the universe. In the philosophy of loafing, Rousseau and Whitman found a way of returning to a childlike openness to life and experience. For both writers, the state of indolently leaning, loafing, and reclining with the universe was the necessary precondition to those moments of mystic transcendence and imaginative release that they describe in their writings.

Late in life, when Whitman had lost some of his early reluctance to reveal his literary sources and antecedents, he referred quite openly to the similarities between his own work and that of Rousseau. In 1882, he placed *Specimen Days* in the tradition of literary autobiography represented by Montaigne and Rousseau: "It is a great jumble (as man himself is)—Is an autobiography after its sort—(sort o' synonyms & yet altogether different—'Montaigne' Rousseau's 'Confessions' &c)—is the gathering up, & formulation, & putting in identity of the wayward itemizings, memoranda, and personal notes of fifty years, under modern & American conditions."[35]

Ultimately, Whitman came to see *Leaves of Grass* itself as an autobiography in the tradition of Jean-Jacques Rousseau. Following the publication of *The Complete Poems and Prose* in 1888, R. M. Bucke wrote a letter to Whitman in which he placed the life and work of the American poet in the tradition of Rousseau and Goethe: "It is a gigantic massive autobiography, the first of its kind (though the trick had been tried before by Goethe, Rousseau and others; but even Goethe could not do it)."[36] Regarding autobiography as the ideal form through which to realize his aesthetics of vital life and spontaneous growth, Whitman agreed with Bucke's description. Commenting to Traubel on Bucke's description of *Leaves of Grass*, he said: "That the work all centres upon one point—that its origins, beginnings, inspirations, have emanated, vitalized, all, centrally, from one source: that comes more and more to me." And then, as if reminded of a similar impulse in the work of his confrere in France, he recommends reading Rousseau's *Confessions*: "I have had it," he says; "it is a singular mixture—plenty of the petty, the minor, the mean, the dirty—then surprising streaks of genius—often and often."[37]

The example of Rousseau's *Confessions* also influenced the manner in which Whitman described, retrospectively, his intentions in *Leaves of Grass*. Rousseau opens his *Confessions* with the following statement: "I purpose an undertaking that never had an example and whose execution never will have an imitator. I would exhibit to my fellows a man in all the truth of nature, and that man—myself."[38] Whitman probably had these famous lines in mind when, in *A Backward Glance O'er Travel'd Roads* (1888), he described his own intentions in *Leaves of Grass*. He says:

> "Leaves of Grass" indeed (I cannot too often reiterate) has mainly been the outcropping of my own emotional and other personal nature—an attempt, from first to last, to put *a Person*, a human being (myself in the latter half of the Nineteenth Century, in America,) freely, fully and truly on record. I could not find any similar personal record in current literature that satisfied me.[39]

Although Whitman's words echo Rousseau, it is important to recognize the difference in emphasis in the two passages. Rousseau emphasizes the uniqueness of his confessions; Whitman emphasizes the representative character of his "personal nature." If Rousseau's *Confessions* demonstrates the Romantic concept of the uniqueness and unlimited diversity of the individual personality, Whitman, still adhering to the Enlightenment aesthetic of the general and representative, makes this very diversity and unlimited possibility the distinctive quality of his generic "I." If Rousseau's *Confessions* asserts the subjective and personal *moi* of Romanticism against the objective and representative "I" of the Enlightenment, Whitman's celebration of the "simple, separate person" and the "en masse" bridges the gap between the two.

III. French Romanticism

At a time when many of his American contemporaries were looking to the English Romantics for models, Whitman found models that he felt were more relevant to American experience in the greater historical, social, and political consciousness of the French Romantic writers. The affinity that he felt with many of the French Romantic writers was in part due to similar historical circumstances in France and America at the beginning of the nineteenth century. The political revolutions of the eighteenth century had led to a similar sense of new literary and social beginnings in France and America during the Romantic period. Along with many of the French Romantic writers, Whitman believed that his attempt to liberate the form as well as the content of literature from the tyranny of the past and tradition was the literary counterpart of the political revolution. Like the French Romantics, he attempted to carry on the tradition of the social and political "engagement" of the artist, an engagement which had its roots in the revolutionary period in France and America. He was most attracted to those French writers who, like himself, were able to spiritualize and personalize—that is romanticize—the Enlightenment heritage while relinquishing none of the political idealism, progressive humanism, and scientific materialism that were a part of this heritage. Ardently believing in the artist as a kind of new priest and prophet who has the orphic mission of inspiring and guiding humanity in its march toward the democratic future, Whitman naturally found far greater appeal in the active engagement of a Hugo or a Michelet in France than in the contemplative reverie of a Coleridge or a Wordsworth in England.

As editor of the *Brooklyn Daily Eagle*, 1846-1848, Whitman reviewed a number of books by and about the French. Among the books that he chose to review were several works by the French Romantic historians: Alphonse de Lamartine's *History of the Girondists*, François Guizot's *History of the English Revolution*, and Jules Michelet's *History of France*.[40] Although he found Lamartine's work "too dramatic, perhaps, for the higher purposes of history," he accorded high praise to Guizot's work on the English Revolution: "Here is one of the really valuable books of the age."[41]

Whitman's interest in Guizot continued. Among the papers he studied and collected is an article on "Civilization" that had been translated from Guizot's *Histoire générale de la civilisation en Europe*.[42] Guizot's clear and precise analysis of the meaning of civilization may have aided Whitman in formulating some of his own ideas about art and society in *Democratic Vistas*. In the 1870's the moral and intellectual revolution that Whitman had envisioned for America seemed farther than ever from realization: "With unprecedented materialistic advancement—society, in these States, is canker'd, crude, superstitious, and rotten," Whitman complained. "In any vigor," he went on to say, "the element of moral conscience, the most important, the verteber to State or man, seems to me either entirely lacking or seriously enfeebled, or ungrown" (*PW*, II, p. 369). Whitman's analysis recalls one of the hypothetical societies that Guizot describes in his attempt to isolate the meaning of the term civilization: "Suppose a people whose external life is pleasant and easy; they pay few taxes, they have no hardships; justice is well-administered in all private relations; in a word, material existence, taken as a whole, is well and happily regulated. But at the same time the intellectual and moral existence of this people is carefully kept in a state of torpor and sluggishness."[43] In Guizot's hypothetical society, Whitman probably found a rather accurate characterization of the materialistic prosperity and development of the United States, which was not accompanied by any "really grand religious, moral, literary and aesthetic results" (*PW*, II, p. 370).

Whitman exhibited a similar interest in the French Romantic historian Jules Michelet. In his review of Michelet's *History of France*, he says: "Of the many standard works from his pen, the history of France is in some accounts the best: he appears to have taken pride and pains in making it the fullest and clearest."[44] Michelet's historian provides a suggestive prototype for Whitman's ideal poet. In the Preface to his *History*, Michelet reflects upon the idea of history as a kind of resurrection of the past, as he wanders among France's National Archives, which were then in his charge: "These papers and parchments, so long deserted, desired no better than to be restored to the light of day, yet are they not papers, but lives of men, of provinces and of nations . . . . And as I breathed on their dust, I saw them rise up."[45] Whitman may have remembered Michelet in assigning a similar role to his ideal poet in the 1855 Preface: "Past and present and future are not disjoined but joined. The greatest poet forms the consistence of what is to be from what has been and is. He drags the dead out of their coffins and stands them again on their feet . . . . he says to the past, Rise and walk before me that I may realize you" (*LG*, p. 716).

Of the other works by Michelet that Whitman may have read, *The People* would most have appealed to him. According to Gay Wilson Allen, this book "contains every major idea of Whitman's philosophy of democracy, religion and art."[46] Some of the parallels that Allen points out are suggestive. For example, in the Preface to *The People*, Michelet says: "This is more than a book; it is myself, therefore it belongs to you . . . . Receive, then, this book of *The People*, because it is you, because it is I."[47] Whitman echoes Michelet in the poem "So Long" when he says:

> Camerado, this is no book,
> Who touches this touches a man.
> (53-54)

Although many of the parallels between Whitman and Michelet are the product of their shared intellectual heritage, the direct echoes of *The People* in such passages as the above indicate that Michelet had some impact on Whitman.

In one instance, at least, Whitman lifted an entire passage from his French kinsman. As Adeline Knapp points out in her article "A Whitman Coincidence," his 1876 poem "To the Man-of-War-Bird" is a paraphrase of a passage in the 1869 English translation of Michelet's *The Bird*.[48] The fact that Whitman could take a passage from Michelet, arrange it in verse, and call it his own, reflects not only the stylistic similarities between the rhetorical and cadenced prose of Michelet and the free verse rhythms of Whitman's poetry, but also the extent of the parallels between the two men. In the passage from which he formed his poem, Whitman was probably struck by Michelet's use of the same cluster of images—bird, sea, storm, soul—that appears so often in his own poetry. Michelet's bird imagery symbolically expresses the same themes of expansion, liberation, and renewal that inform Whitman's poetry. Whitman's poetic paraphrase of Michelet's *The Bird*, so close as to invite the charge of plagiarism, is a testament to the close social and literary relations not only between Whitman and the French but between France and America.

Whitman's interest in the French Romantic historians was seconded by his early interest in the French popular writers and romance novelists. In his book reviews for the *Brooklyn Daily Eagle*, he noticed or reviewed the works of such French writers as Alexandre Dumas, Eugène Sue, Frédéric Soulié, and Paul de Koch.[49] Whitman's interest in these writers reflects his desire to break through the hard shell of American Puritanism, which he associated with England, by self-consciously embracing and fostering the supposedly "immoral" and "subversive" novels that were associated in the popular mind with France.

Whitman was particularly fond of the French novelist George Sand. Among the novels by Sand that he had read, *Consuelo* and its sequel *The Countess of Rudolstadt* were his favorites. Speaking of these books in one of his conversations with Traubel, Whitman said: "I have had the books—or my mother—I think since '41—nearly fifty years . . . . I have always treasured it: read, read, read—never tiring. The book is a masterpiece."[50]

In an early notebook, Whitman copied the following passage from *The Countess of Rudolstadt*: "The unknown refused to explain himself. What could I say to you that I have not said in another (my own) language. Is it my fault that you have not understood me? You think I wished to speak to your senses, and it was my soul spoke to you. What do I say! It was the soul of the whole of humanity that spoke to you through mine."[51] These are the words of the poet-prophet Rudolstadt to those who have failed to understand the lofty and inspired music of his violin. Except for his substitution of the phrase "in another (my own) language" for Sand's phrase "in a more beautiful language," Whitman had copied verbatim the words of the poet-prophet in the French novel.

This passage is the basis for Esther Shephard's claim in her book *Walt Whitman's Pose* that the source of Whitman's life and writing is found in the novels of George Sand and that Whitman spent much of his life in a fraudulent effort to conceal his very real debts to the French novelist. Shephard says: "The source of *Leaves of Grass* is, in spite of all Walt Whitman's protestations to the contrary, in the fragment of a book, the epilogue of a French novel. The novel is *The Countess of Rudolstadt*, by George Sand, which Whitman read in translation by Francis G. Shaw."[52] Shephard also discusses

Whitman's possible debts to such other works of the French novelist as *Consuelo, The Journeyman Joiner, Spiridion, The Devil's Pool,* and *The Mosaic-Workers.* Although Shephard does suggest something of the very real impression that the novels of Sand made upon Whitman's imagination, it is unlikely that Whitman's early reading of the French novelist did any more than confirm his own socio-political faith, hope, and vision.

It was probably Rudolstadt's ideas on the nature and function of language in art that initially drew Whitman to the passage that he copied into his notebook. The words of Rudolstadt were concerned with the idea of a language that addresses itself to the soul as opposed to a language that addresses itself to the mind. Rather than finding his whole concept of himself as a poet in the words of Sand's poet-prophet, as Shephard maintains, Whitman found the expression of one of the primary aesthetic concerns of his poetic career: the attempt to create a language of the soul. Although Whitman's alteration of the passage in terms of his own artistic intent may be a kind of literary plagiarism, his recognition of his own artistic concerns in the words of Sand's poet-prophet reveals that he had in common with George Sand a preoccupation with one of the important Romantic pursuits. Like Sand, Rimbaud, and Claudel in French and like Blake, Crane, and Lawrence in English, Whitman was engaged in the common Romantic pursuit of a language of the soul, a language that would express "the well nigh inexpressible."

Although Shephard finds that *Consuelo* "had no influence on Whitman that would be traceable in *Leaves of Grass,*"[53] Whitman's many favorable comments upon Consuelo both in speech and in writing indicate that it was probably Consuelo, and not Albert Rudolstadt, who made the deeper and more lasting impression on his imagination. For example, in one of his early notebooks, Whitman suggests Consuelo as a model for the new style of written and oral expression he is attempting to define. He speaks of "founding a *new school* of Declamation or Composition far more direct, close, animated and fuller of live tissue and muscle than any hitherto—entirely different (of course) from the old style—and acting as Consuelo's free and strong Italian style did in the singing of the respectable village church."[54] In the 1855 *Leaves,* Whitman recalls the same episode in which Consuelo sings in the organloft of the

Church of the Mendicanti. One of his catalogs in "Song of Myself" opens with the lines, "The pure contralto sings in the organloft." Similarly, in his famous description of the effect on him of the opera singer,

> I hear the trained soprano . . . . she
> convulses me like the climax of my love-grip;
> The orchestra whirls me wider than Uranus
> flies,
> It wrenches unnamable ardors from my breast,
> It throbs me to gulps of the farthest down
> horror,
> It sails me . . . . I dab with bare feet . . . .
> they are licked by the indolent waves,
> (602-606)

Whitman suggests the profound and rapturous effect that Consuelo's singing continually exerted upon her listeners.

Whitman also found, both in the person of George Sand and in the character of Consuelo, a model for his own vision of the free and equal woman of the future. When he tells Traubel that Consuelo "suggests an athlete, a soldier, stripped of all ornament, prepared for the fight—absolutely no flummery about her,"[55] we are reminded of the heroic breed of athletic and artistic women that Whitman foresees in such poems as "A Woman Waits for Me":

> On you I graft the grafts of the best-beloved
> of me and America,
> The drops I distil upon you shall grow fierce
> and athletic girls, new artists, musicians,
> and singers.
> (33-34)

Again we see something of the "absorptiveness" of Whitman's imagination, the way he picked up pieces from his extensive reading and projected them in terms of his own poetic vision.

According to W. S. Kennedy, Whitman's "Poem of the Road," which first appeared in the 1856 edition of *Leaves of Grass*, may have been inspired by the passage from *Consuelo* in which Consuelo describes the life of a vagabond and the limitless possibilities of the open road.[56] "Poem of the Road" often recalls Consuelo's meditation on "the artist with light feet," who reflects upon the open road as the "land of liberty," the "symbol and image of an active and varied life," and the "passage of Humanity, the route of the universe."[57] For Whitman, as for Sand, the road represented an open life of self-reliance, freedom, and motion as opposed to a closed life of tradition, restraint, and stasis. Although Sand's thematic and symbolic use of the road theme may have played some inspirational role in the composition of "Poem of the Road," it is quite possible that the similar use of the open road motif in Sand and Whitman is the result of their common roots in Rousseau.

Whitman also identified with Sand's attempt to break away from traditional moral and social attitudes. It is George Sand's free thought that he chose to emphasize and defend in his review of *The Journeyman Joiner* for the *Brooklyn Daily Eagle* in 1847:

> That Madame Sand's works are looked upon by a portion of the public, and of critics, with a feeling of great repugnance, there is no denying. But the talented French woman is nevertheless one of a class much needed in the world—needed lest the world stagnate in wrongs merely from precedent.[58]

It was through his reading of *The Journeyman Joiner*, along with *Consuelo* and *The Countess of Rudolstadt*, that Whitman encountered some of the ideas and theories of the Saint-Simonian socialists Pierre LeRoux and Félicité Robert de Lamennais.[59] It is also possible that Sand's representation of the community of comradeship, work, and love in *The Journeyman Joiner* stimulated Whitman's own "Song for Occupations" in the 1855 edition of *Leaves of Grass*.

In reading the novels of George Sand for the first time in the 1840's, Whitman found a sister spirit who confirmed and imaginatively embodied much of his own political, religious, and artistic vision. In later years, George Sand remained a compelling presence in Whitman's thought and art. In an article entitled "Genius—Victor Hugo-George Sand-Emerson," which he wrote in 1874, Whitman praises the quality of balance and control that he finds in George Sand's writing. Comparing Sand to Hugo and Emerson, he says: "I like Madame Daudevant [sic] much better. Her stories are like good air, good associations in real life, and healthy emotional stimuli. She is not continually putting crises in them, but when crises do come they invariably go to the heart. How simply yet profoundly they are depicted—you have to lay down the book and give your emotions room."[60] In this comment, Whitman once again reveals the profound temperamental and artistic sympathy with George Sand that persisted throughout his life.

In addition to his acquaintance with the French Romantic historians and novelists, Whitman also had a certain familiarity with some of the more important poets of French Romanticism. Some of this knowledge was superficial. For example, in his scrapbook he collected articles on the deaths of Gérard Nerval and Alfred de Musset, but there is no evidence that he had any further acquaintance with these two French poets.

Whitman did have some familiarity with the poetry of Henri Murger. He claimed that "some of the boys at the Camden newspaper offices" had made a translation of Murger's "Ballade du désespéré," and he had "licked it into form."[61] He kept a copy of the poem, translated "The Midnight Visitor," in his "Reading Book." The verse that he was writing during his early period so closely resembled the popular, sentimentalized verse of Murger that the *Philadelphia Public Ledger* and the *Press* attributed "The Midnight Visitor" to Whitman. This error was corrected by a note in the *Camden Post*, which Whitman preserved among his papers. The *Post* says that "Whitman is fond of reciting it ["The Midnight Visitor"], and in this way has established a personal connection with it, but has no more claim to its authorship than Booth to Hamlet."[62]

Through his involvement with a group of Brooklyn artists who gathered at the studio of the sculptor Henry Kirke Browne in the late 1840's, Whitman became acquainted with the work of another French poet, Pierre-Jean Béranger. He tells us that among this group of Bohemian artists, John Quincy Ward was the "one sparkling fellow in particular I fancied: he spoke of Beranger—I was greatly interested." Years later Whitman proudly recalled: "In this crowd I was myself called Beranger: my hair had already commenced to turn grey."[63] He was no doubt pleased by the comparison between himself and the French poet of the people whose *chansons* of liberty and internationalism had earned him the title of national poet of France in his own day. But the comparison had more to it than Whitman's prematurely grey hair! The liberty theme of his early free verse poem

"Europe," which was composed about the same time he was being called Béranger by his bohemian friends, may have been suggested by Béranger's *chansons*. The "songs" of the French national poet may have stimulated Whitman to conceive of himself as the "singer" of the American nation; they may also have encouraged his enduring fondness for including the theme of "song" in both the title and content of his poems. And, finally, Whitman's early association with the French singer of internationalism undoubtedly fostered some of the cosmopolitan sentiment he expresses in the 1856 "Poem of Salutation" (entitled "Salut Au Monde" 1860).

During the 1850's, when Whitman was working on the first three editions of *Leaves of Grass*, he had Béranger very much in mind. In his scrapbook, Whitman preserved no less than four articles on Béranger, clipped from newspapers during the 1850's.[64] In an article entitled "The Moral Effect of the Cable," written for the *Brooklyn Daily Times* in 1858, Whitman refers to Béranger's poem "La Sainte Alliance des peuples" as a prophecy of technological achievement:

> When Beranger, the French Poet of Freedom, wrote the great lyric of his, calling upon the nations to "join hands" in amity and with prophetic vision told them of the day when international quarrels should cease and the lion should lie down with the lamb, he must have had some dim foresight, which for ought we know, is vouchsafed to the bards sublime, of the great triumph of man's ingenuity and skill which has just set our people wild with joy and excitement.[65]

Whitman most remembered Béranger as a kind of poet-prophet of freedom and international brotherhood, and it was in terms of this bard sublime's vision of national and international amity and union that he saw the moral significance of technological progress. "It is the sentiment of *union*," Whitman asserts, "that makes the popular heart beat and quiver. . . . This Telegraph Cable is not alone a material bond for the transmission of the rise and fall of stocks, and of news gossip generally, but that it will subserve a higher purpose—that it will link together nations that in heart and feeling are hereafter to be one."[66] Here we have the interpenetration of material and spiritual, of scientific fact and religious faith, that provides the germ for such poems as "Passage to India."

Whitman's early identification with Béranger is a prelude to his later and much more interesting relationship to Victor Hugo. It was his Washington friend William D. O'Connor who first called his attention to the similarities between himself and the French poet. According to Whitman, "O'Connor always said I was like Hugo—that he saw us sometimes almost like twin brothers."[67] It was also O'Connor who pointed out the physical resemblance between Hugo and a portrait of Whitman done by Gardner in 1860. Whitman enjoyed the comparison between himself and the well-known French poet: "Yes," he once said, "a likeness has been suggested before: I would have no reason for resenting it, though it might make Victor turn in his grave."[68]

Although Whitman may have had some general familiarity with Hugo before 1860,[69] it was during his Washington days that he began self-consciously to identify with Victor Hugo as a kind of literary alter-ego. Among his papers is a Hugo letter that Whitman copied in his own hand:

> To Arthur Monnanteuil
> Hauteville House
> 7th July, 1868
>
> I accept your verses Mr.________. You have drawn them from the true source of noble inspirations. Let us love forever and propagate forever La Liberté. Without wings, no bird. Without Liberty, no poet.
>
> Accept the assurance of all my sympathy,
>
> Victor Hugo

To the letter Whitman appended the following note: "If there be but one left, I shall be that one."[70] In the public as well as the private voice of the celebrated French writer, he found a spokesman for himself.

In Hugo's *Les Misérables*, which Whitman probably read in the 1860's, he recognized his own democratic sympathy for the poor and the criminal. "*Les Miserables*," he remarked to Traubel, "has a good deal to do with horror, convicts—hopeless convicts—with that phase of life. It may be that Hugo exalts, toplofticates, the ragamuffins too much." But Whitman also identified with Hugo's attempt to give the real life of the people, particularly the life of the urban masses, a literary voice: "I am ready to recognize a complaint that I also may be said to have unduly patronized the masses. I have often been accused of undervaluing the leaders—of exaggerating the importance of the *miserable*—of unreasonably exalting the rank and file."[71]

During his Washington days, Whitman acquired some knowledge of Hugo's other works through the personal translations of Obin, a Frenchman of whom he says: "My whole—not exactly that: my best-knowledge of Hugo was derived from that man."[72] And on another occasion Whitman told Traubel he got Obin's "help in Washington, in things I could not help myself to—all the French authors, mainly Hugo, our theme. Obin would sit with me, read, about as I am talking now, easily, clearly, deliberately."[73] Although it is difficult to surmise which works of Hugo that Whitman came to know through the translations of his Washington friend, it is likely that Obin introduced him to some of Hugo's poems and plays that would have been less accessible at the time. The only work to which Whitman specifically referred in discussing Obin's translations was *La Légende des siècles*.

By the early 1870's Whitman had some general acquaintance with the novels, poetry, and plays of Hugo. In the 1874 article in the *Christmas Graphic* in which he praised the genius of George Sand, Whitman spoke with some authority of the works of Hugo. Alluding to the failure of even the greatest artists to keep the balance between passion and control, he observed:

> Victor Hugo, for instance, runs off into the craziest, and sometimes (in his novels) most ridiculous and flatulent literary blotches and excesses, and by almost entire want of prudence allows them to stand. In his poems, his fire and his fine instincts carry the day, even against such faults; and his plays, though sensational, are best of all. But his novels, evidently well meant, in the interest of Democracy, and with a certain grandeur of plots, are frightful and tedious violations of the principle alluded to.[74]

As late as 1888, Whitman told Traubel: "Hugo's immortal works were the dramas, the plays, the poems; least accessible, yet greatest of all—greater than the novels, stories, orations."[75]

Of all Hugo's "immortal works," it was *La Légende des siècles* that provoked Whitman's most concentrated interest. He broadened his knowledge of this work through the personal translations that Anne

Gilchrist did for him during her stay in America in 1876; he preferred these translations to the more standard translations of *La Légende* that had been issued in America. Speaking of Carrington's translation of this work, Whitman said: "Carrington is just such a man as could not translate Hugo—do it justly . . . a clergyman. . . . The best renderings of Hugo were Mrs. Gilchrist's. She put the Legende des Siecles into English: copied it for me—showed it to me—while she was here. It was nobly done . . . the Pan and Deity business . . . rich with ore: finer even than the French to English renderings of my French friend in Washington."[76]

In referring to the "Pan and Deity business" in *La Légende*, Whitman was probably thinking of Hugo's poem "Le Satyre," which describes Pan's revolt against the all-powerful deities of the past. He may have been struck by this particular poem because it contains many of the basic themes and concerns of his own poetry. The poem is essentially an allegory in which the Classical deities represent the despotic power of king, priest, and aristocracy, and the Satyr represents the hitherto repressed energy of common humanity, which will ultimately revolt against the deities of the past and establish the new era of Man. In the rebellious, physical energy of Hugo's Satyr, Whitman would have recognized many of the qualities of his own haughty and sensual "I." In the Satyr's vision of the evolution of man and the universe from Chaos toward the Ideal, in his assertion of the holiness of all things, and in his prophecy of a future time of liberty, love, and union among men, Whitman would have recognized the central faith of his own poetry.

Whitman's interest in *La Légende des siècles* is not surprising, for it is this work that corresponds most closely in scope and purpose to his own work. In writing the modern epic of man, both poets attempted to combine the socio-political vision of the Enlightenment with the lyric and poetic voice of Romanticism. Each poet attempted to unite the private with the public, the lyric with the cosmic, the personal with the historic, the real with the mythic. *La Légende des siècles* is an epic portrait of humanity through the ages, but it also includes a lyric evocation of man, nature, and the cosmos. Similarly, Whitman's *Leaves of Grass* is a lyric evocation of man and his soul that unfolds against a backdrop of the epic march of the individual and of the race toward union and love. Time and space roll through *La Légende* as they roll through *Leaves of Grass*. In expressing the largeness and movement of their theme, both poets use similar recurrent images: the Adamic myth, the journey, the procession, cosmic space, and the sea. To express the amplitude and vista of their theme, both poets also break through the limits of conventional rhyme and meter to create a freer, more relaxed verse, based on a greater attention to the poetic line and on the skillful use of repetition, reiteration, and a more breath-oriented poetic rhythm.

Several poems in *La Légende* closely resemble Whitman's poetry in theme and technique.[77] Because of the many suggestive analogies—temperamental, social, and artistic—between Whitman and Hugo, however, it is difficult to speak of any influence that Hugo may have had on Whitman. What can perhaps be said is that Whitman's familiarity after 1860 with the life and work of Hugo played some role in stimulating certain tendencies already present in his early poetry, but which were to be given greater emphasis or development in later editions of *Leaves of Grass*.

The period of Whitman's most active and enthusiastic interest in Hugo during the 1860's and 1870's corresponded with the period in which he decided to turn his poetry to "thoughts, or radiations from thoughts, on Death, Immortality, and a free entrance into the Spiritual world" (Preface 1876, *LG*, p. 746). "Passage to India," the central poem in the new volume that Whitman projected in the early 1870's, bears a striking resemblance to "Pleine Mer-Plein Ciel," one of the central poems in *La Légende des siècles*. In "Pleine Mer-Plein Ciel," Hugo uses two of man's technological inventions, the Leviathan and the flying machine, to represent stages in man's evolution, both material and spiritual, toward a future of power, harmony, and love. In "Passage to India," Whitman also uses several technological events, the building of the Suez Canal, the transcontinental railroad, and the transatlantic cable, to represent a similar evolution of man and the soul toward liberty and union. Although the analogies between these two poems may be merely coincidental, their similarity not only in conception but in word, tone, and image suggests that Whitman remembered "Pleine Mer-Plein Ciel" in composing "Passage to India."

Whitman's poem radiates the same kind of exclamatory excitement, scientific faith, and cosmic vision as Hugo's poem. At times he directly echoes Hugo. For example, Hugo associates the flying machine with such explorers as Christopher Columbus and Vasco de Gama:

> Oh! franchir l'éther! songe épouvantable
> et beau!
>
> (II, 496)
>
> ....
>
> L'homme est ailé. Peut-être, ô merveilleux
> retour!
> Un Christophe Colomb de l'ombre, quelque jour,
> Un Gama du cap de l'abîme.
>
> (II, 500-502)[78]

The figure of Columbus is a central presence in "Passage to India":

> (Ah Genoese thy dream! thy dream!
> Centuries after thou art laid in thy grave,
> The shore thou foundest verifies thy dream.)
>
> (65-67)

And, like Hugo, Whitman associates the figure of Vasco de Gama with man's material and spiritual advance:

> Again Vasco de Gama sails forth,
> Again the knowledge gain'd, the mariner's
> compass,
> Lands found and nations born, thou born
> America,
> For purpose vast, man's long probation fill'd,
> Thou rondure of the world at last accomplish'd.
>
> (76-80)

Again like Hugo, Whitman sees the communication between man and man, continent and continent, made possible by scientific achievement as a significant event in the movement toward international community and brotherhood. But for Whitman, as for

---

Oh! . . . l'abîme: Oh! to pass through the ether! beautiful and frightening dream!/ . . . Man is winged. Perhaps, O marvellous return!/ A Christopher Columbus of the darkness, someday,/ A Gama of the head of the abyss. ("Open Sea-Open Sky")

Hugo, the scientific advances in communication are ultimately a prelude to the spiritual communion of man with God. The voyage of Hugo's flying machine is ultimately a sacred voyage:

> Oh! ce navire fait le voyage sacré!
> C'est l'ascension bleue à son premier degré;
>   Hors de l'antique et vil décombre,
> Hors de la pesanteur, c'est l'avenir fondé;
> C'est le destin de l'homme à la fin évadé,
> Qui lève l'ancre et sort de l'ombre!
>
> Ce navire là-haut conclut le grand hymen.
> Il mêle presque à Dieu l'âme du genre humain.
>   Il voit l'insondable, il y touche;
> Il est le vaste élan du progrès vers le ciel.
> (II, 675-684)

In much the same way, Whitman's "Passage to India" is a passage to more than India; it is an ascension toward God. "Bathe me O God in thee, mounting to thee,/ I and my soul to range in range of thee" (192-193), Whitman exclaims. And the final words of his poem again echo Hugo:

> Away O soul! hoist instantly the anchor!
> Cut the hawsers—hawl out—shake out
>   every sail!
> Have we not stood here like trees in the
>   ground long enough?
> Have we not grovel'd here long enough,
>   eating and drinking like mere brutes?
> Have we not darken'd and dazed ourselves
>   with books long enough?
>
> Sail forth—steer for the deep waters only,

Oh! . . . le ciel: Oh! this ship is making the sacred voyage!/ It is the ascension blue to the first degree;/ Out of the ancient and vile ruins,/ Out of the heaviness, it is the founding of the future;/ It is the destiny of man finally escaped,/ Who pulls up the anchor and comes out of the darkness!/ That ship on high concludes the great marriage./ It almost merges the soul of mankind with God./ It sees the unfathomable, and touches it;/ It is the vast leap of progress toward the sky.

Reckless O soul, exploring, I with thee,
and thou with me,
For we are bound where mariner has not
yet dared to go,
And we will risk the ship, ourselves and all.
(243-251)

Like Hugo, Whitman envisions the final flight of the soul toward spiritual communion with God in terms of an explorer setting sail for unknown seas. For him, as for Hugo, the ocean represents the mysterious, unknown, eternal element in the universe; for both, the joyous leap into the sea represents an assertion of hope and faith.

In the final years of his life, Whitman not only acknowledged and enjoyed the comparison between himself and Hugo; he actively encouraged the comparison. For example, in 1885 Whitman urged William Sloane Kennedy to include a comparison between himself, Tennyson, and Hugo in his defense of Whitman's poetic style in an article entitled "The New Ars Poetica." Referring to Sloane's manuscript, Whitman wrote: "I would not put it *out by itself*—Such things never strike in so well in the abstract as in illustration, of *some definite, personal, critical, concrete thing*—I suggest to you a criticism on *Tennyson and Walt Whitman* (or if you prefer on *Victor Hugo, T. and* WW) where they should be work'd in—."[79]

In the work of Hugo, Whitman found an example of the kind of vital, contemporary, and inspirational literature that he himself was trying to write for his time. He once remarked: "I always have looked upon Hugo as a man among the first forces in literature—in the literature of aspiration."[80] He frequently defended Hugo against the attacks of uncomprehending critics. At one time he asserted: "They charge Hugo with a lack of decorum—God knows! He was a masculine genius. There are some signs of flare, peculiar Frenchiness, in *Legende des Siecles*, but after that a real sublimity of power."[81] In Hugo's effort to break new ground in literature and society, Whitman found common cause with his own attempt to liberate American sensibility from traditional Puritan taboos. According to Whitman, "We are not able to appreciate, explain, Hugo: from our puritan environment Hugo looks *outré*: we can't grasp the peculiarities in him which make him first a child of France, of his time: just the exact right final sort of a man for the situation—no other planned for, possible."[82] In what Victor Hugo was doing for France, Whitman found a counterpart for what he, a child of America and of his time, was attempting to do for America.

IV. French Positivism

In his later years, as Whitman became more and more concerned with preparing the image of himself and the theory of his book to be passed on to the future, he exhibited considerable interest in the Positivistic philosophy and scientific criticism of France. His interest in French Positivism was an outgrowth of his interest in the philosophies of political community and natural law that consistently attracted him to Enlightenment and to Romantic writers in France. As the celebrator of democratic comradeship and international community and as the poet who had exclaimed, "Hurrah for positive science! long live exact demonstration!," Whitman responded favorably to the Positivistic philosophy of Auguste Comte. Speaking of the importance of the word *solidarity* to *Leaves of Grass*, "not Philadelphia alone, Camden alone, even New York alone, but all together," Whitman recalled the French Positivistic philosopher: "Yes: Comte makes much of it: it is peculiarly a French word: comes naturally from the French. That is a fact I always remember in connection with Victor Hugo . . . their great purpose is human: their purpose is communication, understanding."[83] In the philosophy of Comte, as in that of such other French writers as Volney, Sand, Michelet, and Hugo, Whitman found further confirmation for his own vision of the evolution of society toward a new religion of humanity and a new world of international community.

In addition to his acquaintance with the ideas of Auguste Comte, Whitman also had some general familiarity with the Positivistic philosophy of Hippolyte Taine. He referred to Taine's work several times, and in the early 1870's he wrote an article entitled "Taine's *History of English Literature*: A Lesson for America."[84] Throughout his discussion of Taine's *History*, Whitman refers to the relevance of Taine's theories to American experience. He opens with the following observation:

> This is the first elaborated History, comprehending many centuries, of a concrete and consecutive National Literature, written according to the school of modern criticism born in France of Ste. Beuve, and which, after being accepted by the best intellects of Europe, has already crossed the Channel & settled in the British Islands, though it would seem hardly visible in the literary organs of the United States.[85]

In the scientific approach of Taine as well as in his theory of national literature, Whitman found many of his own ideas on the interdependence of literature and historical milieu, ideas he had expressed in his journalism as early as the 1840's and had just recently elaborated in his own discussion of the nature and function of national literature in *Democratic Vistas* (1871).

Whitman was particularly impressed with Taine's ideas on the formative impact of "la race, le milieu, et le moment" in artistic development. Describing Taine's chapter on Byron as the best in the book, he observes:

> When Taine would fully present a poet, Shakespeare, Dryden, Byron, he not only presents his age, public events, excitements, &c., but the poet's parentage, sometimes even his aunts and uncles, always his inherited peculiarities, physical facts, places, personal manners, and as much as possible of everything about him, education, atmosphere, religion and the like, affecting and permeating him.[86]

Taine's investigation of the life and milieu of the artist may have inspired some of Whitman's new preoccupation in his later years with his own ancestry. According to Roger Asselineau, "C'est sans doute l'exemple de Sainte-Beuve et de Taine qui incita Whitman à consacrer tant de pages de *Specimen Days* à sa famille, et à communiquer tant de renseignements d'ordre biographique à Richard Maurice Bucke pour le *Walt Whitman* que celui-ci fît paraître en 1883."[87]

C'est . . . 1883: It is undoubtedly the example of Sainte-Beuve and of Taine that prompted Whitman to devote so many pages of *Specimen Days* to his family, and to convey so much biographical information to Richard Maurice Bucke for the *Walt Whitman* that he published in 1883.

Not only did Taine's *History* provide philosophic support for Whitman's own idea of the artist and of artistic creation as an embodiment of personal and national experience, but the clarity and precision of his critical system affected the way Whitman would articulate his ideas on national literature in the future. For example, in his article on Taine, Whitman comments on the fact that Taine treats the nation as analogous to a man: "Inside all the literature," he says, "he sees the individual or aggregate living human being or community, yearning to deposit some record of his or its idiosyncratic self."[88] Whitman echoes this thought in the 1872 Preface in outlining his intention to turn away from the songs of the Democratic Individual to the songs "of an aggregated, inseparable, unprecedented, vast, composite, electric *Democratic Nationality*" (1872 Preface, *LG*, p. 744). Taine's theory of national literature, at the very least, reinforced Whitman's desire to give greater attention to the theme of Democratic Nationality in future volumes of *Leaves of Grass*.

In his later efforts to evaluate his own achievement in *Leaves of Grass*, Whitman came increasingly to see his work in terms of Taine's theory of national literature. In *A Backward Glance O'er Travel'd Roads* (1888), he consistently echoes Taine. He describes his ultimate intention in *Leaves of Grass* as

> a feeling or ambition to articulate and faithfully express in literary and poetic form, and uncompromisingly, my own physical, emotional, moral, intellectual, and aesthetic Personality, in the midst of, and tallying, the momentous spirit and facts of its immediate days, and of current America—and to exploit that Personality, identified with place and date, in a far more candid and comprehensive sense than any hitherto poem or book.
>
> (*LG*, p. 563)

In defining his concept of the artist as an absorber and expresser of personal and historical milieu, Whitman may well have had Taine's theories in mind. In words that again recall the French philosopher, he says that "first-class literature does not shine by any luminosity of its own; nor do its poems. They grow of circumstances, and are evolutionary" (*LG*, p. 565). His definition of literary value is also reminiscent of Taine: "In estimating first-class song," he says, "a sufficient Nationality . . . is often, if not always, the first element" (*LG*, p. 566). Finally, he came to see the national war experience as the central event in the evolution and structure of *Leaves of Grass:* "Although I had made a start before," he asserts, "only from the occurrence of the Secession War . . . the final reasons-for-being of an autochthonic and passionate song definitely came forth" (*LG*, pp. 569-70). Taine's theory of the "historic" function of literature not only provided philosophic justification for Whitman's more direct treatment of national and contemporary events in *Drum-Taps;* it may also have prompted Whitman's more purely occasional and historical lyrics in his later work. In his later years, in accord with Taine's ideas, Whitman came to see *Leaves of Grass* less as a "literary" achievement than as a fulfillment of his early desire to leave some kind of vital "historical record."

With all these echoes in A *Backward Glance* of Taine's theory of literature, it is not surprising that at the end of his essay Whitman quotes Taine in support of his idea that *Leaves of Grass* is a "candidate for the future": "'All original art,' says Taine, anyhow, 'is self-regulated, and no original art can be regulated from without; it carries its own counterpoise, and does not receive it from elsewhere—lives on its own blood'—a solace to my frequent bruises and sulky vanity" (*LG*, p. 573). In his final disclaimer of literary intentions at the end of A *Backward Glance*, Whitman expands upon Taine's theory of literature as a living and organic embodiment of the artist and his epoch:

> But it is not on "Leaves of Grass" distinctively as *literature*, or a specimen thereof, that I feel to dwell, or advance claims. No one will get at my verses who insists upon viewing them as a literary performance, or attempt at such a performance, or as aiming mainly toward art or aestheticism.
>
> (*LG*, p. 574)

For Whitman, as for Taine, the end of art was not the creation of abstract curiosities or beautiful objects. Along with the many French writers whom he regarded as models for his own work, Whitman was no practitioner of art for art's sake. Like Taine, he believed that neither art nor the artist could exist in a vacuum, that neither could be separated from the personal and historical milieu from which they had arisen. In Taine, Whitman found theoretical articulation of and justification for his own idea of art as an open form whose relationship to the milieu from which it comes and the audience to whom it is addressed is both vital and organic.

Whitman also had some general knowledge of the works of Taine's literary disciple, Emile Zola. When Traubel asked him what specific works by Zola he had read, Whitman responded vaguely: "Not much—only here and there—it seems to me."[89] Then he goes on to mention a translation by Vizetelly, the major nineteenth-century English translator of Zola. Although we cannot be certain which of Zola's works he read, he had some familiarity with the scientific and materialistic aspects of Zola's work. He once remarked to Traubel: "Zola is only treating of life as a physician treats disease. . . . The time will come—is already here for some—when all these things will be treated so—will enter in that way upon our conversation—even in parlors—among the sexes. . . . Then, perhaps, we will see that Zola is justified—that he was advanced, not retrograde."[90] In the work of Zola, Whitman found further support for his own attempt to break through the unhealthy repressions of the past and open literature to all themes, including the themes of sex and the body. Referring to an attack on Zola by a man named Sims, he said: "I have no desire to see freedom attacked, whether through Zola or any other. . . . As to indecency and all that—am I not judged by the same standards. . . . Obscene? dirty? who but Sims is obscene, dirty? It is the usual plea in deference to conventional opinion, society, Sunday schools, the parsons."[91] Whitman identified with the cause of Zola, and he was pleased to number the well-known French Naturalistic writer among his European admirers. "Zola has been friendly to me," he told Traubel, "is an admirer, reader: so, at least I am told: reads Leaves of Grass, accepts. He sent me word of it three or four years ago."[92]

V. The Pre-Symbolist Aesthetics

Whitman could never have remained totally grounded in the Naturalistic determinism and materialism of French Positivistic philosphy. As he says of the scientists in "Song of Myself":

Gentlemen, to you the first honors always!
Your facts are useful, and yet they are not my
  dwelling,
I but enter by them to an area of my dwelling.
(490-492)

Whitman's achievement in *Leaves of Grass* is in many ways a product of his ability to bring about a consummate union of the divergent and often contradictory strains of realism and idealism within himself. When the union between materialist and idealist remained intact, Whitman's pose as an observer, reporter, and participant in the life of his times was inextricably linked with the spiritual flight of his fluid and expanding soul.

Whitman was consistently attracted to those French writers who, like himself, sought to reconcile science and religion, the material and the spiritual. Even in the more purely rationalistic and positivistic orientation of Volney's *Ruins*, it was the section on the fluid and pantheistic soul of the world that most attracted him. If the Positivistic school of French writing tended to see universal law as a purely natural and deterministic force, Whitman participated in the more mystic tradition of such writers as Rousseau, Michelet, Sand, and Hugo, who regarded natural and universal law as spiritual energy and morally determined force. In this sense, his relationship to the French critic Charles-Augustin Sainte-Beuve, who himself wavered between philosophic Positivism and Romantic spiritualism, is significant. The critical theories of Sainte-Beuve provided a suggestive analogue for Whitman in his attempt to define how the mystic and spiritual dimension of reality could be released through language. His relationship to Sainte-Beuve also anticipates his later relationship to the French Symbolists.

Sainte-Beuve was a major figure in early nineteenth-century French literature, not only in bringing a more scientific and relative perspective to literary study, but in raising criticism to a major form of literary art. In his analysis of such formative influences on an author's life as physiological inheritance, environment, and family, Sainte-Beuve was a precursor of Hippolyte Taine's Positivistic criticism.

Unlike Taine, however, Sainte-Beuve brought a more Symbolist perspective to bear on literary analysis.

Although Whitman may have been familiar with other works of the French critic, we know that he had read one of his series of literary *Portraits*.[93] In a passage that he later deleted from *Specimen Days* entitled "From My Bay Window," Whitman referred to re-reading this work in 1879: "For the ten days of my visit here I re-read for a change Sainte-Beuve's 'Portraits,' Taine's 'English Literature,' and Addington Symond's glowing resumé, 'The Greek Poets" (*PW*, I, 340). As Whitman became more and more concerned with the place that he and his book would occupy in literary history, he exhibited an increased interest in the literary histories of other lands. Along with the critical work of Taine, the critical approach of Sainte-Beuve, his attempt to study the work by examining the man and his milieu, further confirmed Whitman's own belief in the inseparability of the age, the artist, and the creation.

Whitman was most drawn, however, to the more Symbolist aspects of Sainte-Beuve's literary criticism. In 1869, he copied the following words of Sainte-Beuve from an article that appeared in the *North American Review:* "For us the greatest poet is he who in his works most stimulates the reader's imagination and reflection, who excites him the most himself to poeticize. The greatest poet is not he who has done the best; it is he who suggests the most; he, not all of whose meaning is at first obvious, and who leaves you much to desire, to explain, to study, much to complete in your turn."[94] Sainte-Beuve's idea of the poet as one who utilizes the creative power of the word to *suggest* rather than to *state* his meaning is one of the major tenets of the French Symbolist aesthetics. From the very first, Whitman had a similar sense of the role that indirection, suggestion, and the dynamic relationship between poet and reader were to play in releasing the transcendent and spiritual dimension of reality. For example, in the 1855 Preface he describes the "transcendent and new" American poetry in the following words: "It is to be indirect and not direct or descriptive or epic. Its quality goes through these to much more. Let the age and wars of other nations be chanted and their eras and characters be illustrated and that finish the verse. Not so the great psalm of the republic. Here the theme is creative and has vista" (*LG*, p. 712). Of the dynamic relationship between the poet and his audience, Whitman says at the outset of "Song of Myself":

> You shall no longer take things at second
> or third hand . . . . nor look through the
> eyes of the dead . . . . nor feed on the
> spectres in books,
> You shall not look through my eyes either, nor
> take things from me,
> You shall listen to all sides and filter them
> from yourself.
>
> (*LG* 1855, 27-29)

And, finally, in his attempt to create a language of the soul, Whitman had already found an early antecedent in George Sand's ideas on the nature and function of language in art. As early as 1855, then, Whitman had some sense of the indirect and suggestive nature of his poetic language; however, it was not until later that he found in the work of Sainte-Beuve a systematic theory for the Symbolist aspects of his own poetic practice.

In his effort to define theoretically his own intention in *Leaves of Grass* and the general character of the poetry of the future, Whitman echoes Sainte-Beuve's words on the importance in the new poetry of suggestion, imagination, and the creative response of the reader. For example, in defining, in *Democratic Vistas*, the qualities of the democratic poetry of the future, Whitman points up the need for a new language of literature that "tallies life and character, and seldomer tells a thing than suggests or necessitates it" (*PW*, II, p. 424). And in calling for a "new theory of literary composition for imaginative works," he again suggests Sainte-Beuve's theory of the creative role of the reader: "Books are to be call'd for, and supplied," he says, "on the assumption that the process of reading is not a half-sleep, but, in the highest sense, an exercise, a gymnast's struggle; that the reader is to do something for himself, must be on the alert, must himself or herself construct indeed the poem, argument, history, metaphysical essay—the text furnishing the hints, the clue, the start or framework. Not the book needs so much to be the complete thing, but the reader of the book does" (*PW*, II, pp. 424-25).

As Whitman turned away from his early "songs of Body and Existence" to thoughts on "Death, Immortality, and a free entrance into the Spiritual world" in his later poetry, he gave increasing emphasis to Sainte-Beuve's ideas on the dynamics of literary composition. In the Preface to *Two Rivulets* (1876), where he outlines his intention of turning his thoughts to the spiritual world, his description of a new language of the soul that is addressed to the imagination again recalls Sainte-Beuve: "Poetry," he says, "must possess a certain fluid, aerial character, akin to space itself, obscure to those of little or no imagination, but indispensable to the highest purposes. Poetic style, when address'd to the Soul, is less definite form, outline, sculpture, and becomes vista, music, half-tints, and even less than half-tints" (*LG*, p. 753).

That Whitman remembered the ideas of Sainte-Beuve in formulating his own theory of the nature and function of poetry is evidenced by the fact that in describing the qualities of the poetry of the future in his 1881 essay "Poetry Today in America-Shakespere-the Future," he alludes to Sainte-Beuve in support of his own ideas: "The poetry of the future," he says, "aims at the free expression of emotion . . . and to arouse and initiate, more than to define or finish. Like all modern tendencies, it has direct or indirect reference continually to the reader, to you or me, to the central identity of everything, the mighty Ego" (*PW*, II, p. 481). And in support of his idea of the new role of suggestiveness and reader response in modern poetry, Whitman quotes the passage from Sainte-Beuve that he had copied from the *North American Review* in 1869.

In his final description of the principal characteristics of *Leaves of Grass*, Whitman sees Sainte-Beuve's concept of "Suggestiveness" as the primary quality of his own work. He says in *A Backward Glance O'er Travel'd Roads* (1888):

> The word I myself put primarily for the description of them as they stand at last, is the word Suggestiveness. I round and finish little, if anything; and could not, consistently with my scheme. The reader will always have his or her part to do, just as much as I have had mine. I seek less to state or display any theme or thought, and more to bring you, reader, into the atmosphere of the theme or the thought—there to pursue your own flight.
>
> (*LG*, p. 570)

According to Whitman, "Suggestiveness" was among the "point-characteristics which I since see (though I did not then, at least definitely) were bases and object-urgings toward 'Leaves' from the first" (*LG*, p. 570). It was probably Sainte-Beuve's theories on the role of suggestiveness and the creative imagination in the arts that prompted Whitman to recognize in his later years that "Suggestiveness" was, in fact, the primary "object-urging" of his own work.

What is important here is not so much the discovery of another French source of Whitman's thought and art, for Whitman had been practicing Sainte-Beuve's theory long before he had any direct acquaintance with the ideas of the French critic. The affinities between Whitman and Sainte-Beuve reveal once again the curious rapport between Whitman and the French tradition. His belated recognition of his own poetic practice in the theoretical formulations of Sainte-Beuve and his attempt to expand and develop the ideas of Sainte-Beuve in articulating the theory of his own verse explain not only the striking similarities between Whitman's aesthetic formulations and those of the French Symbolists, but also his sympathetic reception among several of the French Symbolist writers. Just as Whitman looked to French criticism for a theory of his practice, so many of the French Symbolists looked to Whitman for the practice of their theory.

By identifying with and advancing major currents of French thought from Rabelais to Sainte-Beuve, Whitman was inadvertently preparing for his later French fame and influence. Contrary to Arnold's assertion, he did not "trade merely on his own bottom"; he did come into the "European Movement." His rather self-conscious participation in the tradition represented by Volney and Rousseau, Michelet and Hugo, Taine and Sainte-Beuve, indicates that Whitman can be considered an artist without a tradition only to the extent that the tradition in which he participated was a "non-English" tradition.

CHAPTER II

WHITMAN AND FRENCH SYMBOLISM

> Poetic style, when address'd to the Soul, is less definite form, outline, sculpture, and becomes vista, music, half-tints, and even less than half-tints. True, it may be architecture; but again it may be the forest wild-wood, or the best effects thereof, at twilight, the waving oaks and cedars in the wind, and the impalpable odor.
>
> —Preface to Centennial Edition of *Leaves of Grass*, 1876

IN AN ARTICLE on Whitman written immediately after the poet's death in 1892, the well-known French critic Teodor Wyzewa commented on Whitman's relationship to the French Symbolists: "Lorsque, dans quelques années, nous serons enfin débarrassés du XIXe siècle, les critiques chargés de procéder à sa liquidation seront stupéfaits d'avoir à constater *l'énorme influence de Walt Whitman sur notre mouvement littéraire contemporain.*" [1] But after this rather sweeping introduction, Wyzewa proceeds to deny the possibility of Whitman's influence on the French Symbolists: "Les critiques du XXe siècle auront là une excellente occasion de se tromper. Car malgré que les

---

Lorsque . . . contemporain: When in a few years, we will finally be clear of the XIXth century, the critics charged with settling the accounts will be stupefied to have to record *the enormous influence of Walt Whitman on our contemporary literary movement.*

Les critiques . . . près: The XXth-century critics will have here an excellent chance of being mistaken. For in spite of the fact that Whitman's poems date from 1855 and that they already seem to exhibit all the characteristics that the works of today's writers exhibit, the truth is that they exerted little or no influence on the contemporary literary movement.

poèmes de Walt Whitman datent de 1855 et qu'ils présentent déjà en apparence, tous les caractères que présentent les oeuvres de nos écrivains d'aujourd'hui, la verité est qu'ils n'ont exercé sur le mouvement littéraire contemporain aucune influence ou à peu près." [2]

Although Wyzewa's conclusions are not justified by the evidence, his words of caution to the twentieth-century critic indicate some of the difficulty in studying Whitman's relation to the French Symbolists. Whitman was himself aware of his affinities with the idealistic and mystic strains of French thought and even acknowledged his connection with such forerunners of French Symbolism as Hugo, Sand, and Sainte-Beuve. Rather than a matter of direct influence, some of the apparent similarities between him and the French Symbolists are probably the result of his long flirtation with the French writers and of a common inclination toward spiritualism and the unseen. Nevertheless, Whitman did have a considerable impact on several of the French Symbolist writers.

I. Charles Baudelaire

At first glance, Charles Baudelaire, the aesthete and craftsman, would seem to be the complete antithesis of Whitman. However, an understanding of the rapport between Whitman and Baudelaire is essential to the study of Whitman's relationship to the French Symbolist writers. *Leaves of Grass* was begun around 1847 and was published in 1855; *Les Fleurs du mal* was begun around 1842 and published in 1857. Not only the closeness of the dates of publication but even a certain similarity in the titles suggests the rather strange connection between these two seminal works in modern literature.[3]

In their assertion of the interior, subjective, and sometimes irrational soul of man against the exterior, objective, rational world of logic, both Whitman and Baudelaire anticipate the later French Symbolists. In both poets the Romantic *culte du moi* is renewed and extended. Just as Whitman regarded the self-reliant and rebellious "Ego" as the center of his poems, so Baudelaire rejected the objectivity and impersonality of the Parnassiens in asserting himself, the individual man and his soul, as the subject and object of his poems. Whitman and Baudelaire looked upon their poems as both a record of individual experience and a mirror of the collective experience of mankind. Both poets open their respective works by implicating the reader in the vision of human life they are about to describe. *Leaves of Grass* opens with the words: "One's-Self I sing, a simple separate person,/ Yet utter the word Democratic, the word En-Masse." And in his major poem, "Song of Myself," Whitman begins:

> I celebrate myself, and sing myself,
> And what I assume you shall assume,
> For every atom belonging to me as good
> belongs to you.
>
> (1-3)

Baudelaire's *Les Fleurs du mal* opens with a "Préface" in which he too addresses the reader: "Hypocrite lecteur, —mon semblable, —mon frère!" [4] But whereas Baudelaire takes the hands of his fellow men at the outset of *Les Fleurs du mal,* to lead them through the horrors of Hell and the possibility of damnation, Whitman takes the hands of his fellow men at the outset of *Leaves of Grass* to guide them to the open road and the certainty of salvation.

Although there is no evidence that Whitman had any direct familiarity with the work of Baudelaire, in his article on "The Poetry of the Future," he quoted the well-known French poet in support of his own ideas on poetry. In his rejection of what he calls the "beauty disease" in modern art, Whitman cites Baudelaire:

> "The immoderate taste for beauty and art," says Charles Baudelaire, "leads men into monstrous excesses. In minds imbued with a frantic greed for the beautiful, all the balances of truth and justice disappear. There is a lust, a disease of the art faculties, which eats up the moral like a cancer."
>
> (*PW*, II, p. 482)

Whitman had copied Baudelaire's words from an article by Sainte-Beuve, which had appeared in one of the journals of the time.[5] The fact that he used Baudelaire to support his own ideas on the vital and life-giving function of art indicates that he had no real familiarity with

---

Hypocrite . . . frère: Hypocrite reader, my fellow, —my brother! ("Preface")

the aesthetic philosophy of the Frenchman, who was himself adamantly opposed to the idea of utility or morality as the end of art. However, in some ways Whitman's citation of Baudelaire is appropriate.

The citation comes from Baudelaire's critique of the formal and plastic art of the Parnassien school in *L'Art romantique* (1852). Just as Whitman wanted to assert "the elevating and etherealizing ideas of the unknown and of unreality" against the "growing excess and arrogance of realism" (*PW*, II, p. 417), so Baudelaire attempted to assert a spiritual and soul-centered vision of the universe against the formalism, rationality, and objectivity of the French Parnassiens. In their attempt to open and suggest the spiritual dimension of the modern world and to invent and to maintain a more mystic and "poetic" way of seeing and knowing life, both poets anticipate the later Symbolist reaction against the edifice of Realism, Naturalism, and Positivism.

It is, however, one of the major poetic strengths of Whitman and Baudelaire that they are at one and the same time both thoroughgoing idealists and thoroughgoing realists. Although we find in each writer a forceful thrust toward the ideal and an attempt to see life under its spiritual association, the vision of both is solidly rooted in the realities of the modern world. Like Whitman, Baudelaire is a poet of the city, a poet of modern life. Not only did both poets introduce the imagery of the contemporary urban landscape into their poems, but they also broke through the limits of conventional propriety in order to open poetry to a more candid treatment of sex, the common, the vulgar, and the ugly. Unlike Whitman, however, whose faithful description of the real led him to a pantheistic embrace of both matter and spirit, Baudelaire made realistic description the basis for his rejection of the nastiness of the material world in favor of the ideal world of spirit. Whereas Baudelaire regarded flesh and matter as a hindrance in his aspiration toward the ideal, Whitman regarded material reality as the glorious means of making contact with the spiritual dimension of the universe.

Unlike Baudelaire, whose dualism led him to emphasize the difference between the material and the spiritual and thus to exclude "Scientism" from the realm of art, Whitman regarded science as one of the central and inspirational themes of his poems. He asserts in the 1876 Preface:

> Without being a Scientist, I have thoroughly adopted the conclusions of the great Savans and Experimentalists of our time, and of the last hundred years, and they have interiorly tinged the chyle of all my verse, for purposes beyond. Following the Modern Spirit, the real Poems of the Present, ever solidifying and expanding into the Future, must vocalize the vastness and splendor and reality with which Scientism has invested Man and the Universe.
>
> (*LG*, p. 752)

It is to the vast reaches of time and space opened up by scientific exploration that Whitman attributed the new "Kosmic Spirit," which he regarded as an underlying impetus to the poetry of modern life. Because his poetry includes the scientific and cosmic spirit, the themes and imagery of his poetry are more truly metaphysical than those of Baudelaire. Whereas Baudelaire remained rather conventionally Romantic in his view of nature, Whitman's embrace of science led him to re-define the use of nature in poetry. He says in *Democratic Vistas*:

> In the prophetic literature of these States . . . Nature, true Nature, and the true idea of Nature, long absent, must, above all, become fully restored, enlarged, and must furnish the pervading atmosphere to poems, and the test of all high literary and esthetic compositions. I do not mean the smooth walks, trimm'd hedges, poseys and nightingales of the English poets, but the whole orb, with its geologic history, the kosmos, carrying fire and snow, that rolls through the illimitable areas, light as a feather, though weighing billions of tons.
>
> (*PW*, II, p. 416)

By enlarging the conventional view of nature, by bringing a more cosmic and metaphysical spirit to verse, Whitman broke significant new ground in modern literature.

In his poetry, Baudelaire was more concerned with good and evil than with metaphysics. Like Whitman, he recognized the intricate involvement of good with evil in the material universe. But whereas Baudelaire's vision of the universe tended to be a more purely Catholic one, in which good and evil were in perpetual opposition, Whitman's vision tended to be a dialectical one, in which evil would be reconciled with good in some future and perfect union. The theme of good coming from evil, or "fleurs du mal," is a major theme in the poems of both, but whereas Whitman saw good coming from evil as a symbolic affirmation of the movement of the world towards the ideal, Baudelaire saw the involvement of good with evil as a symbol of the irony and ambiguity of the human condition.

Technically, both poets anticipated the French Symbolists in their use of symbol and suggestion to express the texture and feel of modern experience and the mysteries of the spiritual world. In an article entitled "L'Art Philosophique," Baudelaire defined modern art in the following words: "C'est créer une magie suggestive contenant à la fois l'objet et le sujet, le monde extérieur à l'artiste et l'artiste lui-même." [6] Not only do Baudelaire's words provide a good definition of literary Symbolism as it was practiced by the French writers in the final decades of the nineteenth century; his definition of the literary symbol also provides an accurate characterization of Whitman's poetic method, particularly in some of his more erotic and confessional lyrics. Whitman's external landscapes, like Baudelaire's, are frequently a symbolic reflection of an inner, sometimes troubled, state of mind.

Whitman and Baudelaire were particularly interested in the analogy between music and poetry, and they both regarded the music of Wagner as an example of the effects they were trying to achieve in their work. As Whitman strove to duplicate in his poetry the effects of great music, particularly opera, so Baudelaire favored the musical analogy of the Symbolist writers rather than the pictorial analogy of the Parnassien poets.

Although Baudelaire's metrics are highly traditional, he, like Whitman, anticipated the French Symbolists in his attempt to find or invent a new language and new forms in which to express the themes of the modern world. Just as Whitman felt that it was necessary to break down the traditional barrier between poetry and prose in order to express the vastness and complexity of modern life, so in his Préface to *Les Petits Poèmes en prose*, Baudelaire voiced the desire for a new,

---

C'est . . . lui-même: It is to create a suggestive magic that contains, at one and the same time, the object and the subject, the world exterior to the artist and the artist himself. ("Philosophic Art")

freer form in which to express the teeming life of the contemporary urban landscape:

"Quel est celui de nous qui n'a pas, dans ses jours d'ambition, rêvé le miracle d'une prose poétique, musicale sans rythme et sans rime, assez souple et assez heurtée pour s'adapter aux mouvements lyriques de l'âme, aux ondulations de la rêverie, aux soubresauts de la conscience?

C'est surtout de la fréquentation des villes énormes, c'est du croisement de leurs inoubliables rapports que naît cet idéal obsédant." [7]

In his attempt to release words from the rigidities of rhyme and meter in order to bring them into an organic relation with the poetic impulse, Baudelaire looked forward to the technical experiments of the French Symbolists. However, the example of Whitman's free verse and organic form, rather than the example of Baudelaire's *Petits Poèmes en prose*, provided the more important model for the French Symbolist writers.

Baudelaire, like Whitman, believed in poetry as an inspired art; but he assigned a greater role to craft and calculation in transforming the inspiration into the perfection of art. Baudelaire transformed the initial impulse into a closed and crafted form; Whitman translated the curve of the impulse into an organic and open form. Whereas Baudelaire regarded poetry as magic and the poet as a kind of sorcerer, Whitman regarded poetry as a form of religion and the poet as a kind of prophet. Thus, Baudelaire would be the central figure to those French writers who, like Mallarmé and Valéry, were concerned with the craft and magic of art; Whitman would be more important to such French writers as André Gide and Paul Claudel, who were concerned with the moral and prophetic function of art.

The similarities between Whitman and Baudelaire suggest the extent to which the ground was prepared for Whitman's reception

---

Quel . . . obsédant: Who among us has not dreamed, in his ambitious days, of the miracle of a poetic prose, musical without rhythm and rhyme, supple enough and halting enough to adapt itself to the lyrical movements of the soul, to the undulations of the dream, and to the jolts of the conscience.

It is especially from frequenting large cities, and from the interconnection of their unforgettable relations that this obsessive ideal is born. (*Little Prose Poems*)

among the French Symbolists. In their spiritualism and subjectivism, in their use of symbol, suggestion, and the musical analogy in poetry, and in their attempt to break through the traditional form and content of poetry, both Whitman and Baudelaire are precursors of the French Symbolist movement. However, the ways in which Whitman differs from Baudelaire—his free verse and organic form, his pantheistic and affirmative vision, his cosmic and scientific themes, his social and prophetic concept of art—suggest the extent to which Whitman's poetic venture was sufficiently original to have a strong impact not only on the French Symbolists but on modern French literature in general.

Once Whitman had penetrated the French literary tradition, his life and work played a major role in stimulating a reaction against the solipsistic and melancholy mood that characterized the early French Symbolists. According to Emile Blémont, an early Symbolist writer and critic, "On peut affirmer que l'auteur de *Brins d'herbe* exerça sur les 'Verslibristes' et autres groupes émancipateurs une influence analogue, mais diamétralement contraire à celle qu'avait exercée E. Poe sur les Parnassiens."[8] Just as in America the tradition of Poe and the tradition of Whitman, though they might merge briefly at significant junctures, have created a dialectic in which the poet as prophet opposes the poet as craftsman, the poet of social and cosmic consciousness opposes the poet as aesthete, and the poet of life and joy opposes the poet of death and pathos, so in France Whitman's impact on the French literary tradition counterpoints rather than complements that of Poe. However, whereas the problem of Poe's relation to the French writers has been studied and re-studied,[9] no one has yet made an adequate study of Whitman's relationship to the French literary tradition.

II. The Critical Reception

Around the same time that Baudelaire's translations of Poe began to receive an audience in France, Whitman's work also came to the

---

On peut . . . Parnassiens: One can affirm that the author of *Leaves of Grass* exerted upon the '*Verslibristes*' and other emancipating groups an influence that parallels, but is diametrically opposed to the influence that E. Poe exerted upon the Parnassiens.

attention of the French literary public. Whitman was first reviewed in France in 1861 in an article by Louis Etienne entitled "Walt Whitman, poète, philosophe, et 'rowdy.' "[10] The title of the article indicates the unsympathetic attitude of M. Etienne, who objected to Whitman's immoral and democratic excesses. Although the article contains the first translations of Whitman into French, the passages are wrenched out of context in order to emphasize the image of Whitman as a base sensualist and democratic rowdy. The article includes, for example, the following passage from "Song of Myself" translated thus:

> C'est Walt Whitman, Américain, un rude, un
>   *Cosmos*,
> Désordonné, charnel, sensuel, mangeant,
>   buvant, engendrant,
> Point sentimental, point au-dessus ni en
>   dehors de la foule des hommes et des femmes
> Pas plus modeste qu'immodeste.
>
> (p. 110)

With such passages in the public mind, it is no wonder that Whitman's name was frequently associated with the "decadent" movement in French literature. He was first introduced into France during the years of the French Empire, when the democratic and libertarian ideals of the French Revolution and the French Republic were regarded as suspect. It is ironic that Whitman's earliest French critics objected to his work because of his celebration of the same kind of democratic and moral liberty that Whitman had consistently associated with the French.[11]

It is important to take note of the image of Walt Whitman that was first presented to the French literary public. He quickly attained the proportions of a literary myth in France, and at times it was the Whitman legend rather than the reality of his life and work that exerted the greater impact on the French writers. From the very first,

---

C'est . . . qu'immodeste: Walt Whitman, an American, one of the roughs, a kosmos,/ Disorderly fleshy and sensual . . . . eating drinking and breeding,/ No sentimentalist . . . . no stander above men and women or apart from them . . . . no more modest than immodest ("Song of Myself" 1855, 499-501).

the Whitman myth, both in France and throughout the world, has had a highly charged political dimension. Since Whitman was a celebrator of the democratic and libertarian ideals of the revolutionary period, his literary reputation and influence often tend to correspond with both the political leanings of his audience and the current political fortunes of the country in which he is being read. Thus it is no surprise that the "democratic rowdy" of the French Empire began to receive a more sympathetic critical response immediately after the establishment of the Third Republic.

With Emile Blémont's series of articles on Walt Whitman in the *Renaissance Littéraire et Artistique* in 1872, Whitman criticism in France entered a new phase.[12] In the first article of this series, Blémont challenged the negative critical assessment of Thérèse Bentzon, whose article "Walt Whitman, Muscle and Pluck Forever"[13] had appeared only a week earlier in the *Revue des Deux Mondes*. Blémont, who looked upon Whitman as a real literary "discovery," expressed disappointment that his review was not the first to introduce Whitman to the French writers:

"Le dernier numéro de la *Revue des Deux Mondes* renferme un remarquable article sur Walt Whitman, le poète américain. L'article sur le même sujet, que publie aujourd'hui *La Renaissance*, était prêt depuis longtemps; mais l'abondance des matières nous a forcés à en retarder jusqu'à ce jour l'apparition. Nous aurions voulu être les premiers à signaler Whitman; mais notre point de vue et celui de la noble *Revue* diffèrent tellement que nous pourrions conserver des prétentions à la découverte de cette nouvelle étoile."[14]

These two articles, one by a hostile critic who continued the earlier polemical attack, the other by a sympathetic critic who was enthusiastic in his praise, together played an important role in making Whitman known to the French writers, particularly the early Symbolists.

Le dernier . . . étoile: The last issue of the *Revue des Deux Mondes* contains a remarkable article on Walt Whitman, the American poet. The article on the same subject that *La Renaissance* publishes today was ready a long time ago; but our abundance of materials forced us to delay its publication until this day. We would like to have been the first to draw attention to Whitman; but our point of view and that of the noble *Revue* are so different that we might still maintain our claim to the discovery of this new star.

In a series of lectures on American literature, delivered after World War I, Jean Richepin, the French writer and critic, pointed up the importance of Blémont's article in making their generation "la première en Europe à connaître et admirer Whitman."[15] Richepin recalled: "C'est un de mes contemporains, Emile Blémont . . . qui, dans une petite revue du Quartier Latin, où nous écrivions alors, a dit le premier que Whitman était un grand poète."[16]

In his own poetry, Richepin himself reveals the effect of his early admiration for Walt Whitman. In *Chansons de gueux* (1876) the vagabond motif recalls Whitman's "Song of the Open Road," and in *Les Caresses* (1877) the sexual themes show the candor and openness of Whitman's "Calamus" and "Children of Adam" poems. Although Richepin was only a minor figure among the first generation of French Symbolists, he provides an early instance of the impact that Whitman would have on the later French writers. As Richepin said of Whitman's poetry: "C'est une littérature qui ne ressemble en rien à notre culture gréco-latine, où la raison, la critique, ordonnent et composent tout."[17] The freedom and extravagance of Whitman's form and content released Richepin and his fellow French writers from their traditional classical loyalties and provided inspiration for the renewal of French literature in the late nineteenth and early twentieth centuries.

III. Arthur Rimbaud

In his famous "lettre du Voyant," written to Paul Demeny in 1871, Rimbaud expressed some of his ideas on the "avenir de la poésie," ideas which he incorporated into *Une Saison en enfer* and *Illuminations*. Like Whitman, Rimbaud saw the necessity of reinventing the form and content of poetry in order to express his vision of the modern world: "Demandons au *poète* du *nouveau*,—idées et formes."[18] In

---

La première . . . poète: The first in Europe to know and to admire Whitman. . . . It is one of my contemporaries, Emile Blémont . . . who, in a little review of the Latin Quarter, where we wrote at that time, was the first to say that Whitman was a great poet.

C'est . . . tout: It is a literature that is not at all like our Greco-Latin culture, where reason and criticism order and compose everything.

Demandons . . . formes: Let us ask the *poet* for the *new*,—ideas and forms.

opening up the visionary mode of modern poetry, Rimbaud found a precedent in Baudelaire: "Baudelaire est le premier voyant, roi des poètes, *un vrai Dieu.*" But in the crafted and formal nature of his verse, Baudelaire did not provide a sufficiently new or adventurous model for Rimbaud, who felt that Baudelaire lived "dans un milieu trop artiste: et la forme si vantée en lui est mesquine. Les inventions d'inconnu réclament des formes nouvelles" (*Correspondance*, p. 59). If Baudelaire did not provide a satisfactory model for Rimbaud, Whitman did.

The Whitman articles by Emile Blémont and Thérèse Bentzon, which Rimbaud probably read in 1872, included translations of passages from such poems as "Starting from Paumanok," "Salut Au Monde," and "There Was a Child Went Forth."[19] These translations did not follow Whitman's verse and stanza divisions; they were rendered into paragraphs, with each verse divided by a dash. For example, a passage from "Starting from Paumanok" is translated:

> Je sonnerai les fanfares les plus fières et les plus fortes qu'on ait encore entendues sur la terre.—J'entonnerai les chants de la passion à laquelle il faut céder.—des chants pour vous, transgresseurs de la loi, car je vous regarde avec des yeux de frère, et vous êtes pour moi autant que les autres.—Je ferai le vrai poème des richesses.—richesses du corps et de l'esprit . . . —Je répandrai à longs flots l'égotisme et le célébrerai comme la base de toutes choses.[20]

In such lines, Rimbaud would have recognized many of his own ideas on the new poetry, which he had recently expressed in his "lettre du Voyant." Like Whitman, Rimbaud discovered the source of the illuminated poetry of the future in the mystic and primitive energy of the self. As Rimbaud wrote to Demeny:

Dans . . . nouvelles: In a too artistic milieu: and the form for which he is so praised is commonplace. The inventions of the unknown require new forms.

Je sonnerai . . . choses: I . . . will now shake out carols stronger and haughtier than have ever yet been heard upon earth./ I will make the songs of passion to give them their way,/ And your songs outlaw'd offenders, for I scan you with kindred eyes, and carry you with me the same as any./ I will make the true poem of riches,/ To earn for the body and the mind . . . ./ I will effuse egotism and show it underlying all. ("Starting from Paumanok," 159-164)

"Le poète se fait *voyant* par un long, immense et raisonné *dérèglement* de *tous les sens*. Toutes les formes d'amour, de souffrance, de folie; il cherche lui-même, il épuise en lui tous les poisons, pour n'en garder que les quintessences. Ineffable torture où il a besoin de toute la foi, de toute la force surhumaine, où il devient entre tous le grand malade, le grand criminel, le grand maudit,—et le suprême Savant!—Car il arrive à *l'inconnu!*—Puisqu'il a cultivé son âme, déjà riche, plus qu'aucun!" (*Correspondance*, p. 53)

At a time when Rimbaud was actively searching for "des formes nouvelles" to express his superhuman vision, the form of the 1872 Whitman translations may have played some role in liberating him from his earlier Parnassien loyalties by suggesting the kind of prose poetry that he would employ in *Illuminations* and *Une Saison en enfer*.

Although Rimbaud's violent, anguished, and frequently nihilistic mood separates him from Whitman, *Une Saison en enfer* and *Illuminations* are sufficiently similar to *Leaves of Grass* in theme and technique to suggest that Rimbaud had the American poet in mind when composing these works. The unifying theme of *Une Saison en enfer* is the assertion of pagan against orthodox, primitive energy against conventional form, pride and joy against submission and penitence. Like Whitman, Rimbaud regarded organized religion, particularly Christianity, as responsible not only for the guilt, sin, and superstition of the past, but also for the political tyranny and oppression mankind had suffered. In his glorification of the primitive and barbaric against the Christian and civilized, Rimbaud often suggests the Whitmanian persona. In "Mauvais Sang," for example, Rimbaud asserts.

> Je reviendrai, avec des membres de fer, la peau sombre, l'oeil furieux: sur mon masque, on me jugera d'une race forte. (p. 215)[21]

Le poète . . . qu'aucun: The poet makes himself a *seer* by a long, immense, and reasoned *derangement* of *all the senses*. All forms of love, suffering, madness; he seeks himself, he exhausts all poisons in himself, so as only to keep the quintessences. Unutterable torture where he has need of all faith, of all superhuman force, where he becomes among all men the infected one, the great criminal, the great damned one,—and the supreme Knower!—For he arrives at *the unknown!*—Since he has cultivated his soul, rich already, more than anyone.

Je reviendrai . . . forte: I will return, with limbs of iron, dark skin, a wild eye: by my mask, men will judge me to be from a strong race. ("Bad Blood")

He recalls these lines from Whitman's "Starting from Paumanok," which Bentzon cited in his article on the American poet:

> Je ne suis pas un délicat *dolce affettuoso*, moi!—barbu, brûlé par le soleil, le cou bruni, le ton austère, j'arrive."[22]

As Daniel de Graaf points out in an article on Rimbaud and Whitman, Rimbaud at times seems to parody the Whitmanian attitude.[23] For example, in his famous declaration, "La science, la nouvelle noblesse! Le progrès. Le monde marche! Pourquoi ne tournerait-il pas?" (*Oeuvres*, p. 214), Rimbaud mocks the kind of Whitmanian optimism that is to be found in Bentzon's citation of "Starting from Paumanok":

> Américains, conquérans, l'humanité marche: en avant!—le siècle marche! Liberté! Masses, à vous le programme de mes chants![24]

But *Une Saison en enfer* ends on an affirmative note that echoes rather than parodies Whitman: "Il faut être absolument moderne," Rimbaud asserts in his final poem, "Adieu" (*Oeuvres*, p. 241). And in the lines,

> Et à l'aurore, armés d'une ardente patience, nous entrerons aux splendides villes,
>
> (*Oeuvres*, p. 241)

Rimbaud expresses the same kind of Whitmanian faith in the city of the future that we find in Blémont's quotation from "Salut Au

---

Je ne suis . . . j'arrive: No dainty dolce affettuoso I,/ Bearded, sun-burnt, gray-neck'd, forbidding, I have arrived. ("Starting from Paumanok," 233-234)

"*La science . . . pas:* Science, the new nobility. Progress. The world marches forward! Why should it not turn back?

Américains . . . chants: Americanos! conquerors! marches humanitarian!/ Foremost! century marches! Libertad! masses!/ For you a programme of chants. ("Starting from Paumanok," 37-39)

Et . . . villes: And at dawn, armed with an ardent patience, we will enter splendid cities. ("Adieu")

Monde": "Toutes les cités où la lumière pénètre, j'y pénètre aussi."[25] Whether or not Rimbaud remembered such lines in his final march toward the "splendides villes" of the future, his attempt to be "absolument moderne" led him, like Whitman, not only to incorporate the urban landscape in his poems, but also to regard the city as the most representative symbol of the new and future world.

It is in *Illuminations*, where Rimbaud more fully expresses the hopeful and affirmative vision he announces at the end of *Une Saison*, that the correlation between Whitman and Rimbaud most clearly emerges. Technically, the prose poems in *Illuminations* are full of Whitmanian enumerations, identifications, repetitions, and parallelisms; thematically, the prose poems reverberate with such Whitmanian motifs as the child, the city, the vagabond, voyaging, science, and the cosmos. For example, in the lines from one of the opening poems, "Enfance,"

> Je suis le savant au fauteuil sombre. Les branches et la pluie se jettent à la croisée de la bibliothèque.
>
> Je suis le piéton de la grand'route par les bois nains; la rumeur des écluses couvre mes pas. Je vois longtemps la mélancolique lessive d'or du couchant.
>
> Je serais bien l'enfant abandonné sur la jetée partie à la haute mer, le petit valet suivant l'allée dont le front touche le ciel,
>
> (*Oeuvres*, p. 257)

Rimbaud reveals a Whitmanian impulse in his impressionistic succession of images, his use of such devices as repetition and identification, and in the themes of the child and the vagabond, which are central to the poem.

Toutes . . . aussi: What cities the light or warmth penetrates I penetrate those cities myself. ("Salut Au Monde!," 221)

Je suis . . . ciel: I am the scholar in the dark armchair. Branches and rain dash themselves against the library window./ I am the pedestrian on the main road by the pygmy forest; the murmur of the sluices covers my steps. For a long time I see the melancholy wash of golden sunset./ I might well be the child abandoned on the jetty parting for the high sea, the little footman following the path with face touching the sky. ("Childhood")

Some of the Whitmanian overtones of *Illuminations* are perhaps the result of a shared ideological and artistic heritage. Both poets reveal affinities with the mystic and religious philosophies of the East. Both poets had common roots in the political and scientific philosophies of the Enlightenment. In *Illuminations*, among the poems that evoke the negative and pessimistic mood of *Une Saison en enfer*, appear such visionary and prophetic poems as "Conte," "A Une Raison," and "Génie," which reveal Rimbaud's Enlightenment heritage in their celebration of a new social order of universal harmony and love. Rimbaud's vision of man's spiritual regeneration was grounded, like Whitman's, in the Enlightenment faith in reason, science, and humanitarian advance. Like Whitman, Rimbaud attempted, by giving reason and natural law a mystic and illuminated dimension, to spiritualize the political rationalism and scientific materialism that he took from the Enlightenment. Similarly, both poets found common models in such French writers as Rabelais, Rousseau, Michelet, and Hugo, who, it should be remembered, also attempted to reconcile matter and spirit, reason and illumination, politics and religion.

There are times, however, when the similarities between Whitman and Rimbaud are less the result of a shared ideological heritage than of Whitman's direct impact on Rimbaud. In composing his poem "Promontoire," for example, Rimbaud may have remembered such lines as the following from "Salut Au Monde," which he would have known from Blémont's article:

> En moi la latitude s'élargit, la longitude s'allonge;—l'Asie, l'Afrique, l'Europe, à l'Est, l'Amérique à l'Ouest! . . . —En moi, zones, mers, cataractes, plantes, volcans, groupes,—Malaisie, Polynésie et les grandes îles des Indes orientales! [26]

In "Promontoire" Rimbaud makes a similar imaginative flight to such diverse regions of the world as Asia, Japan, Arabia, Italy, Germany—and even Brooklyn! In his geographical catalogs, Rimbaud echoes Whitman both in form and content:

En . . . orientales: Within me latitude widens, longitude lengthens,/ Asia, Africa, Europe, are to the east—America is provided for in the west./ . . . Within me zones, seas, cataracts, forests, volcanoes, groups,/ Malaysia, Polynesia, and the great West Indian islands. ("Salut Au Monde!," 14-15; 20-21)

> Des fanums qu'éclaire la rentrée des théories, d'immenses vues de la défense des côtes modernes; des dunes illustrées de chaudes fleurs et de bacchanales; de grands canaux de Carthage et des Embankments d'une Venise louche; de molles éruptions d'Etnas et des crevasses de fleurs et d'eaux des glaciers; des lavoirs entourés de peupliers d'Allemagne; des talus de parcs singuliers penchant des têtes d'Arbre du Japon.
>
> (*Oeuvres*, p. 299)

Central to the poem is the same kind of international sentiment and cosmopolitan vision that characterize "Salut Au Monde!"

The Whitmanian nuances of *Illuminations* are strongest in those prose poems in which Rimbaud celebrates the march of humanity and the coming of a new age. For example, the central images of "A Une Raison" are the tambour and the march:

> Un coup de ton doigt sur le tambour décharge tous les sons et commence la nouvelle harmonie.
>
> Un pas de toi c'est la levée des nouveaux hommes et leur en-marche.
>
> (*Oeuvres*, p. 268)

These images parallel those in Whitman's poem "Beat! Beat! Drums!" (translated in both Bentzon and Blémont as "Battez, battez, tambours!"). Celebrating the spirit of the new age in "Génie," Rimbaud again recalls Whitman. Like all of Rimbaud's prose poems, "Génie" abounds in Whitmanian exclamations, enumerations, repetitions, and parallelisms. And the description of the Génie himself is a virtual embodiment of the dynamic and regenerative powers of the Whitmanian persona:

Des fanums . . . Japon: Temples that are lit by the return of theories, immense views of the ramparts of modern coast lines; dunes made lustrous with warm flowers and bacchanals; long canals of Carthage and embankments of a shady Venice; Etna's gentle eruptions and crevasses of flowers and of glacier waters; wash houses surrounded by German poplars, slopes in strange parks where the tops of the Tree of Japan hang down. ("Promontory")

Un coup . . . en-marche: A tap of your finger upon the drum gives rise to all sounds and begins the new harmony. / One of your steps gives rise to new men and their forward march. ("To Reason")

Sa vue, sa vue! tous les agenouillages anciens et les peines *relevés* à sa suite.

Son jour! l'abolition de toutes souffrances sonores et mouvantes dans la musique plus intense.

Son pas! les migrations plus énormes que les anciennes invasions.

O lui et nous! l'orgueil plus bienveillant que les charités perdues.

(*Oeuvres*, p. 309)

It is also probable that Whitman's free verse suggested the form of the two vers-libre poems, "Marine" and "Mouvement," which were included in *Illuminations*. As Suzanne Bernard says of the poem "Mouvement" in her introduction to Rimbaud's *Oeuvres:* "Ce texte, de même que *Marine*, est écrit en vers libres, et il doit dater de la même époque: il est fort possible que Rimbaud ait été influencé par les poèmes en "versets" de Whitman, dont la *Renaissance littéraire* publiait la traduction en 1872, et qui chantaient l'ère nouvelle, les découvertes modernes et le progrès."[27] "Marine" and "Mouvement," first published in 1886, were among the earliest attempts at vers-libre in France. Both poems provided models for the formal experiments of the French Symbolists. As Dujardin says in his study *Les Premiers Poètes du vers-libre*, "Marine" and "Mouvement" were "le déclic grâce auquel quelques-uns des jeunes gens qui cherchaient leur formule la trouvèrent, ou du moins purent la parfaire."[28] That Whitman's free verse may have provided the inspirational impulse behind these two early vers-libre poems suggests the importance of his

---

Sa vue . . . perdues: His sight, his sight! all the ancient kneelings and afflictions are lifted as he passes. / His day! the abolition of all clamorous and restless suffering in more intense music. / His step! migrations greater than the ancient invasions. / O he and we! pride that is more benevolent than lost charities. ("Genie")

Ce texte . . . progrès: This text, as well as *Marine*, is written in *vers libres*, and it must date from the same period: it is quite possible that Rimbaud had been influenced by Whitman's poems in "*versets*," which the *Renaissance littéraire* published in translation in 1872, and which celebrated the new age, modern discoveries, and progress.

Le déclic . . . parfaire: The trigger that stimulated some of the young people who were looking for an appropriate form to find that form, or at least to be able to perfect it. (*The First Poets of Vers-Libre*)

formal experiments in the origin and development of vers-libre in France.

Rimbaud's major work was introduced to the French reading public in the same year and by the same literary journal that carried the first official translations of Whitman's poems. In the year 1886, under the editorship of Gustave Kahn, the *Vogue* published several translations of Whitman's poems and the major part of *Illuminations*. It is no surprise that, as Marcel Raymond observes, "in the imagination of many readers, the vagabond of America's roads was associated with that other tramp, Rimbaud."[29]

Whether or not Whitman had any significant impact on Rimbaud, the French literary public would continue to associate Rimbaud with Whitman. Both poets represented a new and revolutionary departure, a revolt of the basically illogical flux and flow of things against the orderly, artistic constructs of the past. In their assertion of individual energy and extravagance; in their exhilaration in time, space, and the cosmos; and in their intoxication with the variety, dynamism, and speed of modern life, both Whitman and Rimbaud became seminal figures in the development of modern literature.

IV. Jules Laforgue

Among the French Symbolist writers and critics who came to know Whitman during the 1880's, Jules Laforgue was one of the most influential in making him known to the French literary public. While he was working in the early 1880's as a reader to the Empress of Germany, Laforgue came across Bentzon's Whitman article in the *Revue des Deux Mondes* (the same article that Rimbaud may have read).[30] The article, in which Bentzon moralistically chides Whitman for his artistic and democratic excesses, must have sparked Laforgue's interest in the American poet; for, shortly afterwards, he undertook a series of Whitman translations. In 1886, Laforgue's translations of Whitman's "Inscriptions," "O Star of France," and "A Woman Waits for Me" were published by *La Vogue*, the leading Symbolist revue, which was then being edited by Gustave Kahn.[31]

The first official translations of Whitman in France, these works had a far-reaching effect on Laforgue and on the development of vers-libre in France. With their absence of rhyme and meter, their long and irregular lines, and their organic form, Laforgue's translations were the most advanced and "liberated" example of free verse that had yet appeared in France.

Laforgue planned a complete translation of *Leaves of Grass*. In 1887, Whitman received the following letter from R. Brisbane, who called himself "the interpreter of the little group" in Paris: "I will say for Mr. Laforgue that he is glad of your permission to translate Leaves of Grass and that he expects to make it an interesting volume. We want to publish it with a preface in the shape of a biographical sketch. It would be pleasant to have facts in your life not yet published: your youth, how you gave yourself on the battlefield during the War, etc. . . . In any event you have too many friends on both sides of the ocean ever to be forgotten."[32] If Laforgue's premature death in 1887 had not prevented this project from being realized, Jules Laforgue would have performed the same function for Whitman in France as Baudelaire had earlier performed for Edgar Allan Poe. In any event, the letter indicates that Whitman was already beginning to gain an impressive following in France.

Laforgue's enthusiastic interest in Whitman was reflected in a new departure in his own work. It was during the time that he was studying and preparing for his translations of Whitman that Laforgue decided to turn away from the conventional and philosophical verse of *Les Sanglots de la terre* to "faire l'original à tout prix" in a new volume of poems entitled *Les Complaintes* (1885). Laforgue's innovative use of language and rhythm; his cosmic, scientific, and urban themes; his evocation of the commonplace and the trivial; and even, in the introductory poem, his use of the word "chalumeau" (calamus) suggest the Whitmanian antecedents of this volume. But Laforgue did not imitate Whitman. The inventiveness and irony, the sensibility and the Pierrot figures, are entirely his own. Whitman's message of openness and self-confidence had the same effect on Laforgue that it has often had upon other writers: he freed Laforgue to be himself. In translating Whitman's "Poets to Come,"

> Mais vous, une nouvelle génération, pure, puissante, continentale, plus grande qu'on ait jamais vu,
> Levez-vous! Car vous devez me justifier.
> Moi, je n'écris qu'un ou deux mots indicatifs pour l'avenir;

....

Vous laissant le soin de l'examiner et le définir,
Et attendant de vous le principal,[33]

Laforgue must have been struck by the accuracy of Whitman's prophecy. In a very real sense, Whitman's poetic theory and practice planted the liberating seeds which Laforgue and the new generation of French writers would develop according to their own potentialities and genius.

Whitman's impact is particularly evident in the new technique of Laforgue's later work. At the same time that he was working on his Whitman translations, Laforgue decided to turn away from his earlier *vers-libéré* to the vers-libre of his later period. In August 1886, after his Whitman translations had been published in *La Vogue*, Laforgue, in a letter to the *Vogue's* editor, Gustave Kahn, made this Whitmanian comment on his new verse technique: "J'oublie de rimer, j'oublie le nombre des syllabes, j'oublie la distribution des strophes, mes lignes commencent à la marge comme de la prose. L'ancienne strophe régulière ne reparaît que lorqu'elle peut être un quatrain populaire."[34] Laforgue describes the main characteristics of Whitman's free and organic verse: absence of rhyme and meter, long lines, verse and stanzas which vary in length and structure according to the inspiration.

On August 16, 1886, immediately following the publication of the last of Laforgue's Whitman translations, *La Vogue* carried "L'Hiver qui vient," Laforgue's first vers-libre poem. Although Laforgue continues to make use of rhyme and a relatively short line, the freer verse line and organic stanza form of "L'Hiver qui vient" represent an important technical break with the past. In the irregularity and freedom of its lines and stanzas and in its enumerative and reiterative technique, the poem also reveals a certain debt to Whitman. For

---

Mais . . . principal: But you, a new brood, native, athletic, continental, greater than before known, / Arouse! for you must justify me. / I myself but write one or two indicative words for the future. / . . . Leaving it to you to prove and define it, / Expecting the main things from you. ("Poets to Come," 3-5; 8-9)

J'oublie . . . populaire: I forget to rhyme, I forget the number of syllables, I forget the division of stanzas, my lines start at the margin like prose. The old, regular stanza only reappears when it can be a popular quatrain.

example, Laforgue describes some of the "misère des grands centres" thus:

> Mais, lainages, caoutchoucs, pharmacie, rêve,
> Rideaux écartés du haut des balcons des grèves
> Devant l'océan de toitures des faubourgs,
> Lampes, estampes, thé, petits-fours.
> Serez-vous pas mes seules amours!...
> (*Poésies*, II, 146)[35]

His impressionistic evocation of an urban setting as well as his use of the catalog technique recall Whitman. His attempt to "donner la note" of a seasonal landscape communicates a typically Laforguean mood of nostalgia and pathos. At times, however, particularly in his effort to render the movement and variety of the modern landscape, Laforgue directly suggests Whitman. For example, although the context is very different, the lines,

> Allons, allons, et hallali!
> C'est l'hiver bien connu qui s'amène;
> Oh! les tournants des grandes routes,
> Et sans petit Chaperon Rouge qui chemine!...
> (*Poésies*, II, 144),

echo such lines as "Allons! the road is before us!" from Whitman's "Song of the Open Road." And in the image of "les fils télégraphiques des grandes routes où nul ne se passe" (*Poésies*, II, 145), Laforgue recalls the "electric telegraph stretching across the continent" in Whitman's "Starting from Paumanok."

The poems of *Les Fleurs de bonne volonté* (posthumously, 1890) reveal further thematic parallels. Laforgue wrote many of the poems of this volume at the same time that he was preparing his Whitman

---

Mais . . . amours: But, woollens, galoshes, pharmacy, dream,/ Curtains drawn back at the top of balconies, its shores/ Facing the ocean of suburban roofs,/ Lamps, engravings, tea, fancy cookies./ Won't you be my only loves! . . . ("The Coming Winter")

Allons . . . chemine: Let's go, let's go, on to the end!/ It's old winter in the lead;/ Oh! the curves in the main roads,/ And no little Red Riding Hood tramping along!...

Les fils . . . passe: The telegraph wires along highways where no one passes.

translations; his close contact with the American poet inspired some of the humanitarian mood of these later poems. Even the title of the volume, which is a kind of affirmative response to Baudelaire's *Les Fleurs du mal*, suggests Laforgue's movement away from the lunar landscapes and somber, metaphysical attitude of his early poems to a more Whitmanian impulse to "Paître, dans notre coin, et forniquer, et rire!" ("Petite Prière sans prétensions," *Poésies*, II, 36).

The poems of this volume, in which Laforgue attempts to bridge the gap between reality and the soul, to create "un pont entre Mon Coeur et le Présent" (*Poésies*, II, 12), provide the first important evidence of Whitman's role in turning Symbolism away from the more negative, solipsistic mood of the past toward the more solar, life-embracing mood of the later period. In several of the poems of *Les Fleurs*, Laforgue reveals his closeness to Whitman both in his technical innovation and freedom and in his mood and theme. In the poem "Albums," for example, Laforgue's exclamatory and panoramic vision of life in the Far-West recalls Whitman:

> On m'a dit la vie au Far-West et les
>   Prairies,
> Et mon sang a gémi: "Que voilà ma patrie!..."
> Déclassé du vieux monde, être sans foi
>   ni loi,
> *Desperado!* là-bas, là-bas, je serai roi!...
> Oh! là-bas, m'y scalper de mon cerveau
>   d'Europe!
> Piaffer, redevenir une vièrge antilope,
> Sans littérature, un gars de proie, citoyen
> Du hasard et sifflant l'argot californien!

Paître . . . rire: To graze in our little pasture, and fornicate, and laugh! (*Flowers of Good Will*)

On . . . Pandectes: People have told me about life in the Far-West,/ And my blood has groaned: "If only that were my country!..."/ Without class in the old world, to live without faith or law,/ *Desperado!* over there, over there, I will be king!.../ Oh! over there, to scalp myself of my European brain!/ To swagger, to become once again a virgin antelope,/ Without literature, a boy of prey, citizen/ Of chance and spouting Californian slang!/ A vague and pure settler, stockbreeder, architect,/ Hunter, fisherman, gambler, up above the Pandectes! ("Albums")

Un colon vague et pur, éleveur, architecte,
Chasseur, pêcheur, joueur, au-dessus des
Pandectes!

(*Poésies*, II, 43)

Laforgue's *desperado* is an ironic French version of Whitman's American rough. His appreciation of the humorous aspect of Whitman's pose looks forward to the work of Valery Larbaud, who makes a similarly humorous use of the Whitmanian persona in the figure of A. O. Barnabooth. The French again anticipated the Americans by several years in recognizing and sympathetically responding to the hilarity that is part of the "essential" Whitman.

Laforgue's contact with Whitman is also evident in the dominant theme of *Les Fleurs de bonne volonté:* an exploration of the relationship between men and women. Laforgue's Pierrot figures had always been concerned with the rapports between men and women. But in these poems, the rapports take on a fleshy, carnal, and frankly sexual dimension that may well have been stimulated by Laforgue's recent translation of Whitman's "A Woman Waits for Me," the poem he described as "un des plus Whitman du Volume."[36] In voicing the desires of the body as well as the soul, in extolling the naturalness and self-sufficiency of the love relationship between men and women, and in invoking the female as the equal of the male, Laforgue recalls similar themes in Whitman's "A Woman Waits for Me." For example, in the following description,

Il est le Fécondeur, le Galant Chevalier
De tes couches, la Providence du Foyer!
("L'Aurore-Promise," *Poésies*, II, 77),

Laforgue evokes the same image of the impregnating male and the procreative female that informs Whitman's poem. And, in his desire to make the female the equal of the male by bringing her down from her traditional pedestal and grounding her in the earth,

---

Il est . . . Foyer: He is the Impregnator, the Gallant Knight/ Of your child-bed, the Providence of the Hearth! ("The Promised Dawn")

Je te crierai: "Nous sommes frères!
Alors, vêts-toi à ma manière,
Ma manière ne trompe pas;
Et perds ce dandinement louche
D'animal lesté des ses couches,
Et galopant par les haras!"

Oh! vivre uniment autochtones,
Sur cette terre (où nous cantonne
Après tout notre être tel quel!)
("Dimanches XXXIV,"
Poésies, II, 74-75),

Laforgue probably remembered his translation of Whitman's "A Woman Waits for Me":

Elles ne sont pas moins que moi, en rien;
Elles ont la face tannée par les soleils
radieux et les vents qui passent.

. . . .

Elles savent nager, ramer, monter à cheval,
lutter, chasser, courir, frapper, fuir et
attaquer, résister, se défendre.

. . . .

Je suis pour toi et tu es pour moi, non
seulement pour l'amour de nous, mais
pour l'amour d'autres encore.[37]

Although Laforgue decided not to publish *Les Fleurs de bonne volonté*, he drew upon the poems of this volume in preparing *Le*

Je te . . . quel: I will cry out to you: "We are brothers!/ So, dress yourself like me,/ My style never goes wrong;/ And get rid of that shabby waddle/ Of an animal weighted down by pregnancy,/ And galloping about the stud farm!"/ Oh! to live smoothly autochthonous,/ Upon this earth (that divides us up/ According to our nature such as it is!) ("Sundays XXXIV")

Elles . . . encore: They are not one jot less than I am,/ They are tann'd in the face by shining suns and blowing winds./ . . . They know how to swim, row, ride, wrestle, shoot, run, strike, retreat, advance, resist, defend themselves./ . . . I am for you, and you are for me, not only for our own sake, but for others' sakes. ("A Woman Waits for Me," 15-16; 17; 22)

Concile féerique (1886) and *Derniers Vers* (1886). In preparing these new books, Laforgue retained many of the more Whitmanian selections and themes from *Les Fleurs de bonne volonté.* Laforgue's description in *Le Concile féerique* of the movement away from metaphysical speculation and the lunar landscape toward an acceptance of life and love on earth continues to reveal his Whitmanian antecedents. For example, in the following lines,

> O chairs d'humains, ciboire de bonheur!
> on peut
> Blaguer, la paire est là, comme un et un
> font deux
> (*Poésies*, II, 139),

Laforgue gives a slightly humorous note to the sexual and procreative theme of such lines as "I am for you and you are for me," from "A Woman Waits for Me."

It is in *Derniers Vers*, however, that Whitman's impact on Laforgue is most clearly evident. The volume opens with "L'Hiver qui vient," the poem Laforgue regarded as the "type d'aspect" of his final work.[38] We feel Whitman's presence in the greater technical innovation and freedom of such poems as "L'Hiver qui vient" as well as in those poems in *Derniers Vers* that retain the amative and sexual themes of *Les Fleurs de bonne volonté.* Laforgue's lament in "Solo de lune,"

> J'eusse été le modèle des époux!
> (*Poésies*, II, 172),

echoes his translation of Whitman's affirmative chant in "A Woman Waits for Me":

> C'est de ces femmes que je veux être le solide époux.
> ("Une Femme m'attend," p. 74)

O chairs . . . deux: O flesh of humans, ciborium of happiness! one can/ Joke about it, the pair is there, like one and one make two. (*The Fairy Council*)

J'eusse . . . époux: I would have been a model husband! ("Moon Solo")

C'est . . . époux: I will be the robust husband of those women. ("A Woman Waits for Me," 14)

At times the Whitmanian echoes of Laforgue's verse are more faintly suggested. Laforgue's declaration in "Dimanches III,"

> L'âme et la chair, la chair et l'âme,
> C'est l'esprit édénique et fier
> D'être un peu l'Homme avec la Femme
> (*Poésies*, II, 154),

and his reverie in "Poème IX,"

> Oh! qu'une, d'Elle-même, un beau soir, sût venir
> Ne voyant plus que boire à mes lèvres, ou mourir!...
> (*Poésies*, II, 177),

are reminiscent of Whitman's songs of men and women, body and soul, Adam and Eve, not only in the "Children of Adam" poems but throughout *Leaves of Grass*.

Laforgue was a seminal figure in the renewal of both the form and the content of French verse which began in the late nineteenth century. It is significant that this important innovator among the French Symbolists was also the first official translator of Whitman in France. Not only did Laforgue's Whitman translations inspire a new technical and thematic departure in his own work; his translations did much to expand Whitman's reputation among the young *avant-garde* writers with whom Laforgue was associated.

V. Stuart Merrill and Francis Vielé-Griffin

Along with Jules Laforgue, Stuart Merrill and Francis Vielé-Griffin were important in spreading Whitman's reputation among the French writers. Both Merrill and Vielé-Griffin were native-born American citizens who had spent most of their lifetime in France, where they became major figures in the French Symbolist movement.

Stuart Merrill made the acquaintance of Whitman on the occasion

---

L'âme . . . Femme: The soul and the flesh, the flesh and the soul,/ It's the proud and edenic spirit/ Of being a bit of a Man with a Woman. ("Sundays III")

Oh! . . . mourir: Oh! that one of them, herself, some beautiful evening, could come/ With no other desire but to drink at my lips, or die!... ("Poem IX")

of Whitman's annual Lincoln address in 1887. An ardent admirer of Whitman for many years, Merrill looked upon his trip to America to meet the American bard as a kind of literary and religious pilgrimage. As Merrill later recalled: "We were at that happy age (and for my part I have never gone beyond it) in which literary reverence takes on all the force of a religious emotion. The poster announced that the lecture would take place at a very early hour in the afternoon; it was hoped thus to conserve the energy of 'Old Walt,' as his familiars called him. . . . We knew that, in this chilly theater, silent and dim, we were going to hear the weak voice, feeble and trembling, of an old man . . . the voice of the prophet who strides ahead of his people and his time."[39]

At this time, an enthusiastic interest in the life and work of the American poet had already begun to be more generally felt in French literary circles. Stuart Merrill's response to Whitman indicates some of the proportions of this interest and the kind of cultish following that Walt Whitman as man, poet, and myth was beginning to gather in France.

In paying "homage to the Master" after his Lincoln address, Merrill presented Whitman with a copy of the Laforgue translations that had appreared in *La Vogue*. Merrill remembers Whitman's delight: " 'Ah. How happy I am that someone has translated me into French!' he cried." He went on to ask which of his poems had appeared in French. When Merrill responded that some of the "Children of Adam" poems had been translated, "Walt Whitman gave a smile half satisfied and half waggish in replying . . . 'I was sure that a Frenchman would hit upon that part.' "[40] The French interest in the "Children of Adam" poems probably confirmed Whitman's tendency to associate the French with sexual liberty. Having initially given his poems on amative love the French title "Enfans d'Adam," Whitman was no doubt gratified that these poems had been sympathetically received by the French.

Along with many of his French contemporaries, Merrill regarded Whitman as one of the great social and literary prophets of the new world. He says: "De toutes parts, ont surgi des prophètes d'une ère de justice, de paix et de bonheur, dont il est impossible que les predictions soient vaines; j'en atteste Hugo, Comte, Proud'hon, Lammenais, Emerson, Shelley, Ibsen, Carlyle, Ruskin, Walt

Whitman, Tolstoi et enfin cet admirable William Morris."[41] It was particularly in Whitman's liberated attitude toward sex and the body that Merrill found a momentous prophecy of the future. He praised Whitman as "le glorificateur de la chair, le chantre de l'amour physique, le prophète de la société future."[42] Just as in his later years Whitman had looked to Emile Zola as a perpetuator of his own struggle for a new attitude toward sex and the body, so in an article on the French Naturalist, Merrill recognized Whitman as a precursor of Zola's liberated and modern sexual attitude. According to Merrill, the pioneering efforts of Whitman and Zola opened literature to traditionally taboo topics, with the result that "dans la société future les mères n'auront plus honte de l'acte qui perpétue la race."[43]

Francis Vielé-Griffin, although he never actually met Whitman, wanted to pay a similar kind of homage to the Master. In 1888, Whitman received a letter from him accompanied by a copy of his volume of poems entitled *Les Cygnes* (1887), which was inscribed: "To Walt Whitman—the homage and sympathetic admiration of the author, Francis Vielé-Griffin."[44] Although *Les Cygnes* is full of the melancholy sighs and frustrations which were antithetical to Whitman's poetic mood, Griffin's inscription again indicates the sympathetic following that Whitman was beginning to attract among some of the French Symbolist writers.

Vielé-Griffin wanted to make Whitman known to the French literary public by carrying out Jules Laforgue's plan to do a complete translation of *Leaves of Grass*. As he says in his letter to Whitman:

"Sir and Dear Poet, In admiration of some of your poems, which I read in an edition, ridiculously 'expurgated,' published by Chatto & Windus, in London, I feel constrained to have the Parisian people share the estimation in which I hold your high lyrical talent.

De toutes . . . Morris: From all over, prophets of a new era of justice, peace, and happiness have arisen, and it is impossible that their predictions are for naught; I call to witness some of them like Hugo, Comte, Proud'hon, Lammenais, Emerson, Shelley, Ibsen, Carlyle, Ruskin, Walt Whitman, Tolstoi, and finally that admirable William Morris.

Le glorificateur . . . future: the celebrator of the flesh, the singer of physical love, the prophet of future society.

Dans . . . race: In the future society, mothers will no longer be ashamed of the act that perpetuates the race.

"Would it be too much that you indicate the volume (the edition) which you would prefer having rendered in the French? My friend, Jules Laforgue (who died only too prematurely) has already given to the public two of your poems, and the reception they met with seems to presage a new victory for your works.

"In expectation of your kind reply, Sir and dear poet, permit me to assure you of my sympathy in art and my profound admiration."[45]

Elated by the attention that his work was beginning to receive in France, Whitman mailed off to Vielé-Griffin the David McKay edition of *Leaves of Grass*.[46]

Whitman received no acknowledgment of the receipt of *Leaves of Grass*, but he later came across Griffin's translations of "Faces," "To a Locomotive in Winter," and "The World Below the Brine," which had appeared in the November issue of the *Revue Indépendante* in 1888.[47] Although Vielé-Griffin had some trouble with publishers that prevented him from carrying out his plan to translate the complete *Leaves of Grass*,[48] he continued to do translations of Whitman's poems for some of the Symbolist revues in France,[49] and in 1908 he did a translation of "When Lilacs Last in the Dooryard Bloom'd," which was published as a brochure.[50] Vielé-Griffin's continued interest in Whitman is reflected in the fact that late in life he became president of the "Comité de Whitman," which had been established in honor of Whitman by Sylvia Beach in 1926.[51]

Whitman had the same kind of impact on the work of Merrill and Vielé-Griffin that he had on the work of Laforgue. In such early volumes of poetry as *Les Gammes*, Merrill was writing the kind of musical and melancholy verse characteristic of such first-generation Symbolist poets as Verlaine and René Ghil. It was during the period of Merrill's Whitman enthusiasm, and after his literary pilgrimage to America to meet the poet, that he began to write his first vers-libre poems, which were collected in the volume entitled *Le Jeu des épées* (1887-1897). Whitman's new physical and social attitude, however, rather than his experimental language and form, most attracted Merrill's attention. In a letter to Rudmose Brown, Merrill confessed certain reservations about Whitman's form of expression: "I sometimes dream of a poet who would have been both Whitman and Morris, a Morris leaning less toward things mediaeval, a Whitman with a greater charm of expression. But I would give neither Whitman nor Morris, even as they are, for that poet of my imagination."[52]

The example of Whitman's life and work played some role in turning Merrill away from the more purely aesthetic and technical concerns of his early period toward the pantheistic and humanitarian orientation he announced in an article on poetry in 1893: "Aux plus habiles joueurs de rimes et de rythmes, je préfèrerai ces frères qui cherchent si naivement leur âme en les choses. . . . La nouvelle renaissance commence déjà, l'artiste se sent enfin après l'éxil que lui imposa la caste du Veau d'or, redevenir homme."[53] It was not until his later years, however, when *Whitmanisme* had already become a major force in French literature, that we see the real effects of Whitman on Merrill's work.

Merrill's debt to Whitman is particularly evident in such later volumes as *Les Quatre Saisons* (1900) and *Une Voix dans la foule* (1909). The energetic optimism and pantheism of *Les Quatre Saisons* are reminiscent of Whitman's life-embracing mood. At times, Merrill directly echoes Whitman. For example, in announcing his movement away from the negation of his earlier verse,

> Arrière ô cauchemar du sommeil de la Terre!
> Car ce printemps fait éclore au sein rosé
> des mères
> La bouche des petits enfants qui doucement
> crient,
> Et de la vallée aux lacs luisants à la
> montagne, source des eaux,
> Voici, parmi les brises et les ailes
> légères des oiseaux,

Aux . . . homme: To the most skillful manipulators of rhyme and rhythm, I shall prefer our fellow poets who seek so naively their soul in things. . . . The new renaissance is already beginning, the artist finally feels himself, after the exile imposed on him by the caste of the golden Calf, becoming a man again.

Arrière . . . Vie: Behind O nightmare of the sleep of the Earth!/ For this spring brings to bloom in the rosy breasts of mothers/ The mouth of little babies who cry gently,/ And from the valley with its sparkling lakes to the source of waters in the mountain,/ Here, amid the breeze and the flutter of birds' wings,/ Ring, like the beating of the heart, all the bells of Life! ("Peace")

Sonner, battant comme des coeurs, toutes
  les cloches de la Vie!
("Paix," p. 15),[54]

Merrill recalls "Song of Myself":

Long enough have you dream'd contemptible
  dreams,
Now I wash the gum from your eyes,
You must habit yourself to the dazzle of
  the light and of every moment of your
  life.
(1228-1230)

It was in these same lines that a whole generation of post-Symbolist French writers would find the essence of Whitman's life-giving message.

In *Une Voix dans la foule*, Merrill's social and humanitarian mood are again reminiscent of Whitman. The entire volume reverberates with Whitmanian ideas and themes; and in the final poem, "Le Vagabond," Merrill writes a kind of apostrophe to the Whitmanian persona.

His description of the vagabond,

Mais voici: j'entendis des pas sur le
  chemin
Et je vis, sac au flanc et bâton à la main,
Le vagabond qui suit, malgré l'homme et
  ses ruses,
Le fleuve s'écoulant par-delà les écluses
Vers les cités, les ports de la plage où
  la mer
Déferle en écumant sur les galets de fer.
(p. 195),[55]

recalls Whitman's evocation of himself as the companion of the open road in "Song of Myself":

Mais . . . fer: But here: I heard footsteps on the road/ And I saw, pack at his side and staff in his hand,/ The vagabond who follows, in spite of man and his tricks,/ The river flowing beyond the sluices/ Toward the cities, the beach harbors where the sea/ Breaks into foam upon the iron shingles. ("The Vagabond")

I tramp a perpetual journey, (come listen
all!)
My signs are a rain-proof coat, good
shoes, and a staff cut from the woods.
(1202-1203)

The presence of Whitman is clearly felt not only in the figure of the vagabond, but in the message that he imparts to the poet. The vagabond impells Merrill toward a pantheistic embrace of the universe. In words that echo Whitman in tone and spirit, Merrill exclaims:

Je ris à tous les cieux, je vais vers tous
les êtres!
Je voudrais de mes bras étreindre l'univers.
(p. 199)

The vagabond inspires Merrill with a Whitmanian sympathy and compassion for all things:

A moi vos yeux et le parfum de vos haleines,
Enfants, et vos baisers dans l'ombre, doux
amants,
Et les larmes des vieux accablés de
tourments,
Et leurs cris quand la mort sur le seuil
frappe et gronde!
Car toute ta douleur avec ta joie, ô monde,
Je voudrais l'assumer pour agrandir mon
coeur!
(p. 199)

In both style and image, these words recall such lines as the following from Whitman:

Je ris . . . l'univers: I laugh at all heavens, I approach all people!/ I would like to embrace the universe with my arms.

A moi . . . coeur: I take to myself your eyes and the perfume of your breath,/ Children, and your kisses in the darkness, gentle lovers,/ And the tears of the old, weighted down with torments,/ And their cries when death knocks and rumbles at the door!/ For all your pain with all your joy, O world,/ I would like to absorb in order to enlarge my heart!

The little one sleeps in its cradle,
I lift the gauze and look a long time, and
silently brush away flies with my hands.
The youngster and the red-faced girl turn
aside up the bushy hill,
I peeringly view them from the top.

The suicide sprawls on the bloody floor of
the bedroom,
I witness the corpse with its dabbled hair,
I note where the pistol has fallen.
("Song of Myself," 148-153)

And when Merrill addresses the vagabond in the final lines of his poem,

O vagabond, ayant compris le sens secret
De tes chants, je comprends celui de ton
silence.
C'est à moi de chercher, seul et sans
défaillance,
Le chemin que tu suis vers l'aube de demain
(p. 199),

he must have remembered Whitman's words:

Not I, not any one else can travel that
road for you,
You must travel it for yourself
("Song of Myself," 1210-1211);

or:

You are also asking questions and I hear you,
I answer that I cannot answer, you must find
out for yourself.
("Song of Myself," 1223-1224)

O vagabond . . . demain: O vagabond, having understood the secret import/ Of your songs, I understand the meaning of your silence./ It is up to me to seek, alone and without flinching,/ The road that you follow toward tomorrow's dawn.

In following the road of moral and poetic liberty that Whitman had opened, Stuart Merrill, like Jules Laforgue before him, found his own way. But in discovering a guide in Whitman, Merrill again reveals the primacy of Whitman's example in pointing the way toward the "nouvelle renaissance" that he had announced in 1893.

The effects of this "nouvelle renaissance" are also discernible in the work of Vielé-Griffin. Like Laforgue, Vielé-Griffin had been studying the work of Whitman with the concentrated attention of the translator. It was after he had proposed to Whitman a French translation of *Leaves of Grass* and after the appearance of his first free verse translations of Whitman in 1888 that Vielé-Griffin published his first vers-libre poems in *Joies* (1889). Vielé-Griffin opened his volume with a Whitmanian celebration of liberty. "*Le vers est libre* . . . . nulle forme fixe n'est plus considérée comme le moule nécessaire à l'expression de toute pensée poétique . . . . désormais comme toujours, mais consciemment libre cette fois, le Poète obéira au rythme personnel auquel il doit d'être."[56]

Vielé-Griffin's close study of Whitman's rhythmic verse undoubtedly inspired some of his decision to attempt in his later work a more organic verse, based on a "rythme personnel." The theory that Vielé-Griffin announced in his preface to *Joies*, however, is much more liberated than his actual practice, which retains many of the remnants of rhyme and syllabic regularity.

Whitman also prompted some of Vielé-Griffin's move away from the sadder, more reflective mood of such earlier volumes as *Cueille d'avril* and *Les Cygnes* toward the new embrace of life and the senses in *Joies*. The poems in this volume are close to Whitman in theme and spirit. The song of the bird in the opening poem, "Un Oiseau chantait," recalls the elegiac love theme of "Out of the Cradle Endlessly Rocking," And in "Par La Roseraie," Vielé-Griffin, like Whitman, uses a prepositional style to reinforce a sense of seclusion in nature:

Le vers . . . d'être: Verse is free . . . no fixed form is any longer considered the mold necessary to the expression of a poetic thought . . . in the future, as always, but now consciously free, the Poet will obey the personal rhythm to which he owes his existence. (*Joys*)

Par la roseraie éclose,
Par la saulée apâlie,
Au bord des viviers, sous l'aurore rose,
Au long des étangs où le roseau plie,
Au son d'une chanson trillée,
Jusqu'à la plaine ensoleillée!

Au cours de la rivière lente
Des herbes traînent vertes ou rousses.
(p. 21)

Vielé-Griffin continued to express a similarly Whitmanian mood of physical joy in such later volumes as *Clarté de vie* (1897). For example, his description of the poet's relationship with the sea in "Devant la mer,"

S'en aller à elle et l'étreindre
Et se fondre en sa caresse vive!
Se vêtir d'elle et la ceindre
Et se draper en elle et en vivre
Et rire en sa voix et s'y plaindre
Et la pleurer toute et la suivre
(p. 124),[57]

recalls Whitman's similarly erotic embrace with the sea in "Song of Myself":

You sea! I resign myself to you also—
  I guess what you mean,
I behold from the beach your crooked
  inviting fingers,
I believe you refuse to go back without
  feeling of me,

Par . . . rousses: By the rose garden in bloom,/ By the faded willow,/ At the edge of the fishponds, under the rose-colored daybreak,/ Along the ponds where the reed bends,/ From the sound of a trilled song,/ To the sunny plain!/ Amidst the flow of the slow river/ Grass streams forth green or red. ("By the Rose Garden")

S'en . . . suivre: To depart with her and embrace her/ And melt in her vigorous caress!/ To cloth oneself with her and encircle her/ And drape oneself with her and live in her/ And laugh in her voice and complain/ And weep all to her, and follow her. ("Before the Sea")

We must have a turn together, I undress,
hurry me out of sight of the land,
Cushion me soft, rock me in billowy drowse,
Dash me with amorous wet, I can repay you.
(448-453)

If Laforgue responded to Whitman as the energetic poet of man, and Merrill responded to him as a kind of social prophet, Vielé-Griffin identified with the more private, elegiac poet of nature that he found in Whitman.

Although Vielé-Griffin would later deny his debt to Whitman,[58] his close contact with Whitman's work during the time that he was writing the poems of *Joies* played some role in inspiring the liberated technique and affirmative mood of this volume. The Whitman poems that Vielé-Griffin translated contain many of the new themes of *Joies* and *Clarté de vie:* the theme of common life in "Faces," the evolutionary theme in "The World below the Brine," the embrace with the real in "There Was a Child Went Forth," the dynamic energy theme of "Song of the Broad-Axe," and the elegiac nature theme of "When Lilacs Last in the Dooryard Bloom'd" all correspond to the new themes of Vielé-Griffin's later work.

In his important work on the Symbolist movement, *Message poétique du symbolisme*, Guy Michaud describes *Joies* as "le premier cri d'optimisme que fasse entendre le Symbolisme."[59] At least in part inspired by Whitman, this cry of optimism once again reveals the significant impulse that Whitman's work provided in turning Symbolism away from the more negative, melancholy mood of the early period to the more positive, joyous mood of the later Symbolists.

VI. Stéphane Mallarmé

At the same time that Vielé-Griffin was working on his Whitman translations in the late 1880's, he was regularly attending the meetings of Mallarmé's *Mardist* group. It is likely that Vielé-Griffin spoke with Mallarmé about Walt Whitman, whose experiments in the form and content of poetry would certainly have been of interest to Mallarmé. However, as the master of a poetry of crafted perfection and aesthetic detachment, Mallarmé would have found a spirit very different from his own in Walt Whitman.

The differences between the two poets were accurately described by Georges Duhamel in an article in which he names both Whitman and Mallarmé as the artistic heroes of the nineteenth century. Whitman, he says, "puissant introducteur à la vie poétique, coeur débordant, compagnon généreux de toute souffrance, laisse une oeuvre imparfaite et confuse qui est comme le procès-verbal fidèle d'une vie de cordialité, de dévouement, d'entreprise"; whereas Mallarmé, "philosophe solitaire, voilant d'un sourire incolore les profondeurs tormentées, laisse une oeuvre parcimonieuse et parfaite où la crainte de se confier aux apparences s'exaspère presque jusqu'au refus de toucher les réalités."[60] These differences between Mallarmé and Whitman, the formal perfection and introspective mood of the one and the formal extravagance and life-oriented mood of the other, are significant in that they describe the two major directions that French poetry was to take in the late nineteenth and early twentieth centuries.

In considering the relationship between Mallarmé and Whitman, however, it is also essential to note the similar theoretical assumptions from which they started. For example, in Whitman's Sainte-Beuve-like commentary on poetic style,

> Poetic style, when address'd to the Soul, is less definite form, outline, sculpture, and becomes vista, music, half-tints, and even less than half-tints. True, it may be architecture; but again it may be the forest wild-wood, or the best effects thereof, at twilight, the waving oaks and cedars in the wind, and the impalpable odor
>
> (1876 Preface, *LG*, p. 753),

we find striking analogies with Mallarmé's comments on Symbolist art: "Nommer un objet," says Mallarmé in his critique of the

---

Puissant . . . d'entreprise: Powerful initiator into the poetic life, his heart overflowing, a generous companion of all sufferers, leaves an imperfect and disorderly work that is, like the verbal process, true to a life of cordiality, devotion, and enterprise.

Philosophe . . . réalités: Solitary philosopher, veiling profound anguish behind a colorless smile, leaves a perfect and parsimonious work in which the fear of trusting appearances is almost carried to the point of refusing to touch reality.

Nommer . . . rêve: To name an object is to discard three-forths of the joy of the poem, which consists of guessing little by little; to suggest, that is the dream.

Parnassiens, "c'est supprimer les trois-quarts de la jouissance du poème qui est faite de deviner peu à peu; le suggérer, voilà le rêve."[61] Whitman's reference to the effects of twilight, wind, and impalpable odor in poetry also brings to mind Mallarmé's famous comment that the aim of the poet is to "peindre non la chose mais l'effet qu'elle produit."

Like Mallarmé in his revolt against the Parnassiens, Whitman attempted to oppose a dynamic, suggestive, musical art to the static, descriptive, and pictorial art of the past. Although there is little possibility of influence in the relationship between Whitman and Mallarmé, the similarities in the theory if not in the practice of the two poets again point up the extent to which the ground had been prepared for Whitman's reception among the French Symbolists.

VII. Maurice Maeterlinck and Emile Verhaeren

In his biography of Maurice Maeterlinck, Jethro Bithell points up the influence that Whitman's free verse had on the Belgian poet: "One poet Whitman's lawless line did directly influence; and this was Maeterlinck whose rhymeless verses in 'Serres Chaudes' were written under the inspiration of 'Leaves of Grass.' "[62] The poems of *Serres chaudes* (1889), most of them written in octosyllabic quatrains, continue the negative and pessimistic mood of the early French Symbolists. Seven of the poems, however, are written in a vers-libre form that reveals some of Maeterlinck's technical debt to Whitman. As P. M. Jones points out in "Whitman and the Origins of Vers Libre," Maeterlinck's technical debt to Whitman is particularly evident in the poem "Regards," which Tancrède de Visan, the theorist of Symbolism, regarded as a typical example of the Symbolist mode of expression.[63]

In writing "Regards," Maeterlinck apparently recalled Vielé-Griffin's recent translation of "Faces," which opens with the following lines:

> Flânant par les pavés ou chevauchant par
>   le sentier rustique, ô, ces visages!
> Visages d'amitié, de précision, de
>   cautèle, de suavité, d'idéal;
> Le visage de spirituelle prescience et,

toujours bienvenu, le bon visage du
vulgaire.

("Visages")[64]

The opening lines of "Regards" parallel Whitman in tone and mood:

O ces regards pauvres et las!
Et les vôtres et les miens!
Et ceux qui ne sont plus et ceux qui
vont venir!
Et ceux qui n'arriveront jamais et qui
existent cependant!
Il y en a qui semblent visiter des pauvres
un dimanche;
Il y en a comme des malades sans maison;
Il y en a comme des agneaux dans une prairie
couverte de linges.

(p. 73)[65]

The sympathetic and compassionate content of this poem, as well as its iterative, enumerative, and exclamatory technique are clearly reminiscent of Whitman.

The connection between Whitman and Maeterlinck is of particular importance in the history of the vers-libre movement. In making use of Whitman's long line, in basing his rhythm on a Whitmanian repetition of word and phrase, and in abandoning all use of rhyme and regularity, Maeterlinck created one of the most liberated examples of vers-libre that had yet appeared in French, an example that corresponded very closely with Whitman's model.

Although a study of the Belgian poets is not within the scope of this study, the relationship between Maeterlinck and Whitman also

---

Flânant . . . vulgaire: Sauntering the pavement or riding the country by-road, lo, such faces!/ Faces of friendship, precision, caution, suavity, ideality,/ The spiritual-prescient face, the always welcome common benevolent face. ("Faces," 1-3)

O ces regards . . . linges: O these poor and tired looks!/ Yours and mine!/ And those that are no longer and those that are to come!/ And those that will never arrive and that exist even so!/ There are those that seem to visit the poor on Sunday;/ There are those that are like sick people without a home;/ There are those that are like lambs on a prairie covered with cloth. ("Looks") throws an interesting sidelight on the relationship between Whitman and the Belgian poet Emile Verhaeren, who was part of Maeterlinck's *avant-garde* group. The striking formal and thematic similarities between Whitman and Verhaeren, often remarked by the critics,[66] are particularly evident in such volumes as *Les Vies tentaculaires* (1895), *Les Visages de la vie* (1899), *Les Forces tumultueuses* (1902), and *La Multiple Splendeur* (1906). All of these volumes represent a withdrawal from the more pessimistic and decadent mode of Verhaeren's earlier period. In these later works Verhaeren employs a rhythmic long line that recalls the technique and style of Whitman's free verse. Verhaeren's affirmative vision, his attempt to embrace in his poems the energy and imagery of modern life, is very close to Whitman.

Verhaeren was an admirer of Whitman, but he denied that he had had any acquaintance with Whitman's work before the publication of Bazalgette's complete translation of Whitman's verse in 1909.[67] Although Verhaeren's reluctance to admit an earlier familiarity with Whitman is understandable, he must certainly have had some incomplete knowledge of the American poet before 1909. Through Maeterlinck and his group, and through his close association with such ardent Whitmanians as Stuart Merrill, Vielé-Griffin, Marcel Schwob, and André Gide, Verhaeren probably gained some acquaintance with Whitman's free-verse technique in the early 1890's, before he turned to the totally liberated rhythmic style of his later verse.

VIII. Vers-libre

An understanding of Whitman's relationship to the early French Symbolists is particularly important in discussing the role that Whitman's poetic theory and practice played in the development of vers-libre in France. In his articles on Whitman and the origins of vers-libre, P. M. Jones discusses the several possible sources from which vers-libre may have derived.[68] These include the *vers-libéré* of Verlaine, the two vers-libre poems in Rimbaud's *Illuminations*, as well as the vers-libre poems of Gustave Kahn, Jules Laforgue, and Vielé-Griffin. Jones denies the possibility of Whitman's influence on the development of French vers-libre; and although he gives some credit to the vers-libre experiments of Laforgue and Vielé-Griffin, he concludes that "the *vers-libre* virtually dates from the publication of M. Gustave Kahn's *Palais nomades* (1887)."[69]

Although Gustave Kahn maintained that he was the first to introduce the theory and practice of vers-libre into France, he was preceded by both Rimbaud and Laforgue. And although he would also claim vers-libre as his own personal invention, he must have found a suggestive model in the technical experiments of Whitman, several of whose poems were published in *La Vogue* while he was editor. In fact, Whitman probably played a much more significant role in the development of vers-libre in France than Jones would suggest. The figures who have been put forth as the possible originators of French vers-libre have one common denominator: Walt Whitman. Rimbaud, Laforgue, Kahn, and Vielé-Griffin were all aware of Whitman's poetic theory and practice before any of their own vers-libre appeared.

IX. Gabriel Sarrazin

The French Symbolist critic Gabriel Sarrazin was one of the first major critics to recognize the true stature of Walt Whitman and the significance of his achievement in *Leaves of Grass*. It was in the new form as well as in the new substance of Whitman's poetry that Sarrazin found the essence of Whitman's achievement. As he says in an article on Whitman, which was published in the *Nouvelle Revue* in 1888: "Dans ce chant d'une lumière continue et presque aveuglante, point d'hésitations, ni de désespérances; le présent et le passé, l'univers et l'homme, libres de tous voiles, affrontaient avec une sérénité supérieure le mauvais sourire de l'analyste. . . . L'homme qui s'annonçait ainsi, lui et sa race, apportait, en même temps qu'une parole absolument nouvelle, une forme instinctivement audacieuse, novatrice, en dehors des préjugés et conventions littéraires."[70] It

---

Dans . . . littéraires: In this song of a perpetual and almost blinding light, there is no hesitation, no despair; the present and the past, the universe and man, free from all concealment, confront the wicked smile of the analyst with a superior serenity . . . The man who thus announced himself and his race brought, at the same time, an absolutely new utterance and an instinctively audacious and innovative form, beyond the bounds of literary convention and prejudice.

was particularly in Whitman's new attitude—his simultaneous embrace of matter and spirit and his pantheistic, life-giving mood—that Sarrazin discovered Whitman's real contribution to modern literature.

For Sarrazin, Whitman represented the introduction of a constructive, affirmative impulse into the more decadent mode of the early Symbolists. He praises Whitman's "joie énorme et sacrée qui rit dans toute l'oeuvre, joie telle qu'on évoque à son propos l'image des ébats de quelque innocent colosse antédiluvien, battant de sa queue les vagues resplendissantes et soufflant d'énormes trombes à la face des premiers soleils" (p. 169). But Sarrazin does not make the usual critical mistake of regarding Whitman as an unread rough: "Non seulement il n'était point un illettré," Sarrazin asserts, "mais il avait lu tout ce que nous avons lu nous-mêmes" (p. 165). In fact, Sarrazin's article is a key document in the history of Whitman criticism because he was the first to see Whitman's work as vital synthesis: of past, present, and future; matter and spirit; good and evil. According to Sarrazin, Whitman "reliait l'enseignement de Jésus à celui de Spinoza, rapprochait les Brahmes des Encyclopédistes, Lucrèce de Fichte, Darwin de Platon, fondait en un l'extase et la science" (p. 171). It was particularly to the French that Whitman looked in his attempt to reconcile "Brahmin and the Encyclopaedists," and thus it is no surprise that a Frenchman should be the first to recognize the importance of this synthesis for modern art.

Sarrazin's article on Whitman took its place alongside the work of Laforgue, Merrill, and Vielé-Griffin in making Whitman known to the French literary public. He gave sympathetic critical exposure to Whitman's work, and he also presented a legendary image of the man

---

Joie . . . soleils: Mighty and sacred joy that laughs throughout the work, the same joy that is evoked, in its way, by the image of the gambols of some innocent, antidiluvian colossus, beating the resplendent waves with its tail and blowing, from huge water spouts, in the face of the first suns.

Non . . . nous-mêmes: He was not only not illiterate, but he had read all that we ourselves have read.

Reliait . . . science: Joined the teaching of Christ to that of Spinoza, he brought together the Brahmins and the Encyclopaedists, Lucretius and Fichte, Darwin and Plato; he brought ecstasy and science together as one.

to the French public. His article ends with a eulogistic portrait of Whitman, much of which is a direct quotation from R. M. Bucke's biography. No longer does Whitman appear as a decadent or democratic rowdy, but rather as a robust figure of humane and prophetic stature. Sarrazin's laudatory description of Whitman was the first in a long series of French portraits in which Walt Whitman, the man, would be presented as a legendary figure, whose epic work was no more than a direct transcription of his heroic life. Sarrazin's assertion, "Whitman n'est pas un artiste: il est au-dessus de l'art" (p. 172), signals the initiation of the Whitman cult in France. In the post-Symbolist period, the example of Whitman's life sometimes took precedence over the example of his work in his influence on the French writers.

Like Laforgue, Merrill, and Vielé-Griffin, Sarrazin was in communication with the American poet. Sarrazin sent him a copy of his Whitman article, which in January, 1889, Whitman promptly arranged to have William Sloane Kennedy translate.[71] When Whitman read Kennedy's translation, he immediately recognized the importance of the Sarrazin piece: "I don't think anything nobler has been anywhere said about *Leaves of Grass*," he told Traubel.[72] To Whitman, Sarrazin seemed "fundamentally to have entered into the ideals, methods, upon which, if upon anything, we have built, staked our fortunes."[73] As with the letter from Emerson, which represented the start of Whitman's career in America, Whitman arranged to publish Sarrazin's article.[74] Although the article would be printed and distributed among Whitman's inner circle of friends, however, it was not until after his death that a translation of the article by Harrison Morris would be published in *In Re Walt Whitman* (1893).

As a gesture of gratitude, Whitman sent Sarrazin a copy of *Leaves of Grass*. Sarrazin immediately responded with a letter of thanks, which Whitman preserved in translation among his papers. "It is a very dear gift to me," says Sarrazin, "and I shall peruse the new pages with the same admiration I bore to the ancient ones, with all my love for one I considered, from my first reading of him, as one of the best and the greatest men of all time."[75] A few months later, Sarrazin sent

---

Whitman . . . l'art: Whitman is not an artist: he is above art.

Whitman an inscribed copy of *La Renaissance de la poésie anglaise* (1889), which closes with a reprint of his Whitman article.

Whitman was particularly pleased that Sarrazin, a Frenchman, was the first to recognize the significance of *Leaves of Grass*. In expressing his pleasure, Whitman reveals all his old enthusiasm for France: "Have been reading Sarrazin in full," he wrote to Bucke; "it is both immense & definite—have we had anything up to it yet?—& to think it comes from Paris!"[76] Still fond of the French language, Whitman imagined the article must be even better in the original: "You know," he told Traubel, "I consider Sarrazin's piece our Koh-i-noor—unsurpassed—the very topmost, wonderful for its daring, its explicitness. Oh! I think there is a marvellous lightness of touch in parts of it that, in the French, must be delicious, appetizing, beyond our alien conceptions."[77]

It was through Sarrazin that Whitman learned that his cosmopolitan spirit was beginning to spread among the new generation of French writers. As Whitman commented:

> There's a new school in Paris, of which Sarrazin is one—very catholic—very Hegelian—acknowledging other places than Paris, other men than Parisians. Among the old fellows, even so great a man as Victor Hugo seemed to start out with the assumption that there was no city in the world but Paris. But these new men have come to the conclusion—the conviction, in fact—and a deep conviction it is—that there is a wider audience, a vaster area of action . . . populaces, ideals, what-not.[78]

Making this comment shortly before his death, Whitman perhaps suspected that the new school in Paris would mean another victory for his own work. It was the new international spirit of this very same school that would lead, indeed had already led, many of the French writers to find a vital source in the life and work of Walt Whitman.

The French Symbolist writers and critics were primarily responsible for introducing Whitman into France. In this initial period of Whitman's French reception, we find in broad outline the three major ways that he had affected and would continue to affect the

French literary tradition. First, the example of Whitman's free verse form provided and would continue to provide a valuable precedent in the development of the theory and practice of vers-libre in France. Second, the affirmative and life-oriented mood of Whitman's verse helped to release some of the French Symbolist writers into a new embrace of the physical and social universe, which would find further development in the post-Symbolist and Modern period. And, finally, in this initial period we see the first signs of the Whitman myth, which would make Walt Whitman, the man, an important cultural and social influence in France.

CHAPTER III

WHITMAN AND POST-SYMBOLISM

Long enough have you dream'd contemptible
dreams,
Now I wash the gum from your eyes,
You must habit yourself to the dazzle
of the light and of every moment of
your life.

—"Song of Myself"

BEGINNING around 1890, French Symbolism tended to break into a number of separate schools that represented either a reaffirmation of or a reaction against the spirit of the early French Symbolists. Romanism, naturism, jammism, intimism, and unanimism were only a few of the many "isms" that began to proliferate during the post-Symbolist period. Except for the *école romane* of Jean Moréas and Charles Maurras, which represented a return to the Classic tradition of Greece and Rome, all of these new schools had one thing in common: a desire for renewal in both literature and life. In their pursuit of renewal, many French writers found an inspiring model in the life and work of Walt Whitman.

In the initial period of Whitman's reception and influence in France, his work had provided a vital impulse in the liberation and ultimate breakdown of the French alexandrine and in the evolution of Symbolism away from the earlier mood of darkness, pessimism, and escape toward a celebration of life, optimism, and engagement. In the post-Symbolist period, Whitman continued to provide a suggestive example and precedent in the renewal of the form and substance of French literature. In the Symbolist period, his most significant impact on the French artists was in the area of technical and formal innovation; in the post-Symbolist period, on the other hand, it was the content of his life and work that would have the greatest impact on the French writers.

At the same time that the post-Symbolist French writers were finding new energy in the foreign source of Whitman, they were also renewing themselves in the native tradition of Rabelais and Hugo. They found important precursors among many of the French writers with whom Whitman most closely identified. In their affirmative vision and in their utilitarian concept of art, the post-Symbolist writers represented a renewal of the humanitarian dreams and aspirations of such writers as Michelet and Sand, Hugo and Zola. The post-Symbolists also revived the same spirit of hope and faith that had animated the French Enlightenment writers on the eve of the French Revolution and the French Romantic writers on the eve of the 1848 revolutions. Whitman had also found both precedent and inspiration for his own artistic creed in the revolutionary and humanitarian spirit of the Enlightenment and Romantic periods in France. With the revival of a similar spirit in the post-Symbolist period, it is no surprise that the new generation of French writers would virtually claim Whitman as one of their own.

I. The Renewal of Substance

In reaction against the solipsism, unreality, and artifice of early Symbolist writing, the post-Symbolist writers sought to renew the substance of French literature by bringing it back into vital contact with the natural, the human, and the social world. The Naturist group, along with such writers as Paul Fort and Francis Jammes, Marcel Schwob and André Gide, were instrumental in turning French literature away from the formalism and impersonality of art for art's sake. By returning to a celebration of self and other, the joys of physical nature, the warmth of human contact, and the splendors of life on the open road, these writers made literature touch earth again. And in this movement to renew the substance of French literature, Whitman would once again provide an inspirational source.

A. *Naturism*

Among the many new schools that began to develop in the 1890's, *naturisme* represented one of the strongest and most significant reactions against the more negative and decadent mood of the early French Symbolists. *The école naturiste* was founded by the poet Sainte-Georges de Bouhélier; the theorist of the movement was Maurice Le Blond, who defined the Naturist doctrine in an article written in 1895: "Les jeunes gens désertent les musées, les parlotes et les bibliotèques pour l'enseignement divin et sentimentale de la Nature et de la Vie. . . . Qu'est-ce donc être naturiste? C'est ne pas cultiver son Moi, et c'est, sans cesser de conformer à l'harmonie de son Destin, se courber pieusement au joug de la Nature."[1]

The extent to which Whitman's poetic program corresponded to, if it did not directly influence, both the Naturist doctrine and the general direction of French literature in the late nineteenth and early twentieth centuries is perhaps best indicated by Le Blond's comment in his *Essai sur le naturisme* (1896): "Nos aînés ont préconisé le culte de l'irréel, l'art du songe, le frisson nouveau; ils ont aimé les fleurs vénéneuses, les ténèbres et les fantômes, et ils furent d'incohérents spiritualistes. Pour nous, l'au-delà ne nous émeut pas, nous croyons un panthéisme gigantesque et radieux. C'est dans l'étreinte universelle que nous voulons rajeunir et magnifier notre individu. Nous revenons vers la Nature. Nous cherchons l'émotion saine et divine. Nous nous moquons de l'art pour l'art."[2]

In their movement from art back to life, in their pantheism and individualism, in their announcement of sun and health, of the present and the real, the Naturists directly echo the poetic ideals that Whitman opposed to a similarly morbid and Poesque tradition in America.

Les jeunes . . . Nature: The young people are deserting the museums, debating societies, and libraries for the sublime and tender teaching of Nature and of Life . . . So, what does it mean to be a naturist? It is not to cultivate the Self, and it is, without ceasing to conform to the harmony of one's Destiny, to bend oneself piously to the yolk of Nature.

Nos . . . l'art: Our elders advocated the cult of the unreal, the art of dreams, the latest chill; they liked poisonous flowers, darkness and phantoms, and they were incoherent spiritualists. For us, the beyond does not move us; we believe in a gigantic and radiant pantheism. It is by embracing the universe that we want to rejuvenate and magnify our individual self. We return to Nature. We seek healthy and sublime emotion. We laugh at art for art's sake. (*Essay on Naturism*)

As singers of life, joy, and the dynamic flow of the universe, the Naturists found a precursor in Vielé-Griffin, whom Le Blond called "le petit-fils de Walt Whitman."[3] It was precisely Whitman's embrace of the natural world and his attempt to embody poetically the physical energy of the universe that most attracted Vielé-Griffin. Like Whitman, and unlike Vielé-Griffin, however, the Naturists identified with the tradition of Zola and the French Naturalists; and thus their turn back to life included an embrace of science, progress, and the urban landscape.

Although they were not officially part of the Naturist group, such figures as Francis Jammes, Paul Fort, Marcel Schwob, and André Gide are frequently associated with this movement back to life and nature in late nineteenth-century French literature. All of these writers also reveal connections with Walt Whitman.

B. *Paul Fort and Francis Jammes*

The poetry of Paul Fort, which is collected in several volumes entitled *Ballades françaises*, is reminiscent of Whitman in both form and content. Although many of Fort's ballads deal with scenes from the past or legend, in the nature lyrics of such volumes as *Naissance du printemps* and *Vivre en Dieu*, the simplicity and immediacy of expression and the sense of physical joy and wonder reveal Fort's possible Whitmanian antecedents. For example, in the following passage from *Naissance du printemps* (1910),

> Tout mon corps est poreux au vent frais du printemps. Partout je m'infinise et partout suis content . . . je suis heureux d'Hier, d'Aujourd'hui, de Demain, me croyant dieu et sans commencement ni fin
>
> ("Le Bonheur"),[4]

Fort recalls Whitman's cosmic nature,

> Within me latitude widens, longitude
> lengthens
> ("Salut Au Monde," 14)

Tout . . . fin: All the pores of my body are open to the fresh wind of spring. I extend myself everywhere, and everywhere I am content . . . I am happy with Yesterday, Today, Tomorrow, believing myself a god, without beginning or end. ("Happiness") and his sensual fervor for life,

> I have instant conductors all over me whether
> I pass or stop,
> They seize every object and lead it harmlessly
> through me.
>
> I merely stir, press, feel with my fingers,
> and am happy.
> ("Song of Myself," 615-617)

Many of the poems of *Vivre en Dieu* (1910) display a similarly Whitmanian zest for life and celebration of the god-like powers of the individual. Fort announces the message of *Vivre en Dieu* in words that recall the underlying themes of *Leaves of Grass:*

> Reste libre, c'est là ta première noblesse.
> Regarde dans ton âme et vois croître ce Feu!
> Laisse rêver tes sens—homme—et tu es ton
> dieu.

At times Fort directly echoes Whitman in idea and image. The following passage, "Mes yeux s'envolent sur-le-champ, oui, s'envolent bien loin, car dans les vapeurs mauves je grimpe à ce poirier qui domine, isolé, cette colline et tout le cirque des monts roses. Allez, je me repose; volez, mes yeux ailés," recalls Section 33 of "Song of Myself," in which Whitman uses a similar image of flight through space ("I am afoot with my vision") to evoke the imaginative powers of the individual as he "stands or sits." Finally, Fort's poems, even when they are regular in rhyme and meter, are arranged in prose paragraphs that recall the form of Whitman's rhythmic verse.

In an equally Whitmanian mood, Francis Jammes founded a school upon himself in "Un Manifeste littéraire de monsieur Francis Jammes: le jammisme" (1897).[5] Jammes's definition of the simple, common, and natural ideals of Jammism recalls Whitman's poetic

---

Reste . . . dieu: Stay free, this is your first nobility./ Look in your soul and see this Fire grow!/ Let your senses dream—man—and you are your own god. (*To Live in God*)

Mes yeux . . . ailés: My eyes take flight in the country, yes, they fly faraway, for in the purple haze I climb the pear tree that dominates, alone, this hill and the entire range of rose-colored mountains. Go, while I rest; fly away, my winged eyes.

program. In such collections of poems as *De l'Angelus de l'aube à l'angelus du soir* (1898), the pantheistic love of nature and the naïveté and sympathy in the description of all things, even the most ordinary, are reminiscent of Whitman. In the poem "J'allais dans le verger," for example, Jammes describes his relation to his native land with the same sense of childlike wonder and simplicity as Whitman in "There Was a Child Went Forth":

> Près des montagnes je suis né, près des
> montagnes.
> Et je sens bien maintenant que dans mon âme
> il y a de la neige, des torrents couleur de
> givre
> et de grands pics cassés où il y a des oiseaux
> de proie qui planent dans un air qui rend ivre,
> dans un vent qui fouette les neiges et les
> eaux.
> ....
> Oui je sens bien que je suis comme les
> montagnes.
>
> (*Oeuvres*, p. 33)[6]

In "Ce sont travaux," Jammes's sympathy for the common people and his long catalogs of their occupations,

> Ce sont les travaux de l'homme qui sont grands:
> celui qui met le lait dans les vases de bois,
> celui qui cueille les épis de blé piquants et
> droits,
> celui qui garde les vaches près des aulnes
> frais
>
> (*Oeuvres*, p. 35),

Près . . . montagnes: Near the mountains, I was born, near the mountains./ And now I strongly feel that in my soul/ there is snow, frost-colored torrents/ and large broken peaks where there are birds/ of prey that soar in an intoxicating air,/ in a wind that lashes the snows and waters./ . . . Yes I strongly feel that I am like the mountains. ("I Went to the Orchard")

Ce sont . . . frais: These are the works of man that are great:/ he who puts the milk in the wooden pots,/ he who picks the sharp and straight blades of wheat,/ he who watches the cows near the cool alder trees. ("These Are the Works") recall similar catalogs in such Whitman poems as "Song of Myself" and "A Song for Occupations." In "Cette Personne," Jammes expresses a feeling for nature in language and imagery that are again suggestive of Whitman:

> Cette personne a dit des méchancetés:
> ....
> Alors j'ai été révolté.
>
> Et j'ai été me promener près des champs
> où les petits brins d'herbes ne sont pas
> méchants,
> avec ma chienne et mon chien couchants.
> ....
> Je pensais: oiseaux, soyez mes amis.
> Petites herbes, soyez mes amies.
> Soyez mes amies, petites fourmis.
> (pp. 241-42)

And, finally, in the poem "Le Poète et l'oiseau," Jammes makes use of a talking bird who teaches the poet the same lesson of sympathy, love, and faith in the continuity of things that the solitary bird utters to the outsetting bard in Whitman's "Out of the Cradle Endlessly Rocking."

The Whitmanian parallels in the verse of Fort and Jammes suggest some of the impulse, direct or indirect, that Whitman provided in the Naturist reaction against the first generation of French Symbolists. In Whitman's relationship to Marcel Schwob and André Gide, the two poets who most importantly embody the ideals of the Naturist movement, we see the full extent of Whitman's impact on the renewal of the substance of French literature in the late nineteenth century.

C. *Marcel Schwob*

Unlike many of the other French Whitmanians, Marcel Schwob was fluent in English, and thus he was able to read Whitman's work at a young age. Among his early writings are translations of Whitman's

---

Cette . . . fourmis: This person said wicked things:/ . . . So I was upset. / And I went for a walk near the fields/ where the little leaves of grass are not wicked,/ with my she-dog and he-dog lying down./ . . . I thought: birds, be my friends./ Little grass, be my friends./ Be my friends, little ants. ("This Person")

"The Artilleryman's Vision," "To Think of Time," and the 1855 Preface.[7] The darker mood of "To Think of Time" and "The Artilleryman's Vision" would have corresponded with the negative and pessimistic mood of Schwob's early years. Like many of the French Symbolist writers of the 1890's, however, Schwob was also trying to renew contact with the world, and the more positive mood of Whitman's 1855 Preface to *Leaves of Grass* suggested a way to renewal.

In defining and expressing in his writing a new and more life-oriented mood, Schwob had closely in mind the example of Whitman's poetic theory and practice. In the Preface to *Coeur double* (1891), Schwob describes the dual impulse that animates his stories in words that recall Whitman: "Le coeur de l'homme est double; l'égoisme y balance la charité; la personne est le contre-poids des masses . . . les pôles du coeur sont au fond du moi et au fond de l'humanité."[8] Schwob must have remembered from the 1855 Preface his recent translation of such lines as the following: "The soul has that measureless pride which consists in never acknowledging any lessons but its own. But it has sympathy as measureless as its pride and the one balances the other and neither can stretch too far while it stretches in company with the other" (*LG*, p. 716). Schwob goes on to point up the significance of Whitman's balance between pride and sympathy, self and other, for the new generation: "Mais la fin du siècle sera peut-être menée par la devise du poète Walt Whitman; *Soi-Même et En-Masse.* La littérature célébrera les émotions violentes et actives. L'homme libre ne sera pas asservi au déterminisme des phénomènes de l'âme et du corps. L'individu n'obéira pas au despotisme des masses, ou il les suivra volontairement. Il se laissera aller à l'imagination et à son goût de vivre."[9]

Le coeur . . . l'humanité: The heart of man is double; within it, egoism is balanced with charity; the person is the counterweight of the masses . . . the poles of the heart are in the depths of the self and in the depths of humanity. (*Double Heart*)

Mais . . . vivre: But the end of the century will perhaps be led by the motto of the poet Walt Whitman: *One's-Self* and *En-Masse.* Literature will celebrate violent and active emotions. The free man will no longer be enslaved by the deterministic phenomena of the soul and the body. The individual will not obey the despotism of the masses, or he will follow them voluntarily. He will let himself go with his imagination and his taste for life.

In placing his generation under the ensign of Whitman's,

> One's-Self I sing, a simple separate person,
> Yet utter the word Democratic, the word
>   En-Masse
>
> ("One's-Self I Sing," 1-2),

Schwob again indicates some of Whitman's importance as both precursor and model for the late nineteenth-century French writers. Schwob's "borrowing" from the American poet also shows how Whitman's use of the French language tended to aid his reception in France. The French writers frequently gave their most concentrated attention to those very poems which were heavily sprinkled with borrowings from the French.

As the writer who has been described as the "literary conscience" of French Symbolism, Schwob helped to spread Whitman's reputation among the new generation of artists. He was frequently seen with a copy of Whitman in his pocket, and he often did oral translations for the group of French writers with whom he associated. The *Journal* of the Goncourt brothers contains the following note: "Schwob, avec sa tête de gras rongeur et une chemise sale, nous arrive aujourd'hui, avec, dans sa poche, le poète américain Whitman, qu'il est en train de traduire. Il nous traduit, au courant de la lecture, 'La Maison des Morts de la Cité,' un morceau étrangement poétique sur un cadavre de prostituée, un morceau d'un lyrisme fantasque d'où sort tout entier Maeterlinck."[10] The subject of the poem, the death of a prostitute, may have appealed to the Goncourt brothers' naturalistic taste for authentic description; but it was probably Whitman's sympathetic feeling for the prostitute that drew Schwob to the poem.

The effects of Schwob's infatuation with Whitman are seen throughout his work. Schwob's major work, *Le Livre de Monelle*, embodies much of the solipsistic and pessimistic vision of the early Symbolist period; but the main character, Monelle, expresses an urge toward sympathy and renewal that frequently recalls Whitman. At

---

Schwob . . . Maeterlinck: Schwob, with his plump rodent's head and a dirty shirt, arrives today carrying in his pocket the works of the American poet Walt Whitman, whom he is translating. He translates, in the course of reading, "The City Dead-House," a strangely poetic piece about a prostitute's cadavre; the piece has a whimsical lyricism that sounds very much like Maeterlinck.

times the Whitmanian echoes are direct. For example, in advising her followers to submerge themselves in the present moment, "Ne crains pas de te contredire; il n'y a point de contradiction dans le moment,"[11] Monelle directly echoes the famous dictum from "Song of Myself,"

> Do I contradict myself?
> Very well then I contradict myself,
> (I am large, I contain multitudes.)
> (1324-1326),

where Whitman similarly expresses a lesson of confidence in earthly process and change.

Schwob was most attracted by the new moral attitude he found in Whitman, and thus his interest extended beyond the work to the life of the American poet. In one of his final works, a collection of essays entitled *Spicilège*, it is in the example of Whitman's life that Schwob finds an inspirational model: "Les biographes du poète américain Walt Whitman disent que personne ne le vit rire une seule fois dans sa vie. C'était un homme doux et gai, qui comprenait toutes choses. Les anomalies n'étaient pas pour lui des miracles de l'absurde. Il ne se croyait supérieur à aucun être."[12] For Schwob, as for many of the artists of the post-Symbolist generation, Whitman came to represent as much a way of living as a way of writing.

Schwob's response to Whitman indicates the greater interest that his generation showed in Whitman's ethical philosophy rather than in his formal innovations. Since an ethical position could be expressed in prose as well as in poetry, Whitman's influence extended beyond the poets to the prose writers in the post-Symbolist period. Marcel Schwob was the first in a long line of French writers who would bring Whitman's new moral vision to prose.

D. *André Gide*

It was through Marcel Schwob that André Gide gained his first acquaintance with Whitman. In a letter to S. A. Rhodes, André Gide

---

Ne crains . . . moment: Do not be afraid of contradicting yourself; there are no contradictions in the moment. (*The Book of Monelle*)

Les biographes . . . être: The biographers of the American poet Walt Whitman say that no one saw him laugh a single time in his life. He was a gentle and gay man, who understood all things. Anomalies were not, for him, miracles of the absurd. He did not think himself superior to any other being. (*Observations*) acknowledged Whitman's influence on both Schwob and himself: "Ce que je crois c'est que Marcel Schwob et moi souffrions également de l'atmosphère factice et uniquement livresque de la littérature d'alors, et éprouvions un égal désir de nous en échapper. La grande connaissance que Marcel Schwob avait de la littérature anglaise l'y aidait et peut-être serait-il juste de parler d'une influence commune: celle de Walt Whitman qui Marcel Schwob, l'un des premiers, m'apprenait à aimer."[13] Like Marcel Schwob, Gide in his early years was a frequenter of Symbolist circles, and such works of his first period as *Les Cahiers d'André Walter* (1891) and *Traité du Narcisse* (1891) reflect the "atmosphère factice et uniquement livresque" of the first generation French Symbolists. As he had done for Schwob, Whitman helped Gide to re-establish contact with himself and the world.

The effects of Gide's acquaintance with Whitman, whom he came to know in the 1890's, are reflected in a new departure in his life and work. Gide had had a strict religious upbringing, which provoked an anguished conflict between the body and the soul, his biological impulses and his spiritual aspirations. This troubled period in his personal life corresponded to the Symbolist phase of his early writing. In Whitman, Gide found a confidence and an affirmation which freed him to be himself in both his life and his writing.

The renewal that Whitman prompted in Gide's personal life is reflected in Gide's decision to leave for Africa in 1893 with his companion Paul-Albert Laurens. Years later, in *Si le grain ne meurt* (1926), Gide described his personal transformation and his decision to depart; his words clearly echo Whitman's call to the open road: "La réclamation de mon coeur devint . . . j'appelais ce camarade dont l'exaltation fraternelle eût gémellé la mienne, et je me racontais à lui,

---

Ce que . . . aimer: What I believe is that Marcel Schwob and I suffered equally from the artificial and totally bookish atmosphere of literature at that time, and we experienced the same desire to escape from it. The great knowledge that Schwob had of English literature aided him in doing this, and perhaps it would be fair to speak of a common influence: that of Walt Whitman, whom Schwob was one of the first to teach me to like.

La réclamation . . . routes: The protest of my heart grew . . . I called to this comrade whose fraternal exaltation was the twin to my own, and I revealed myself to him, and spoke to him in a loud voice, and sobbed to not feel him by my side. I decided that it would be Paul Laurens . . . and had an extraordinary presentiment that we would depart like this, the two of us together, alone, giving ourselves up to the chances of the road. (*If It Die*) et lui parlais à haute voix, et sanglotais de ne le point sentir à mon côté. Je décidai que ce serait Paul Laurens . . . et pressentis extraordinairement qu'un jour nous partirions ainsi, tous deux ensemble, seuls, au hasard des routes."[14] Gide's discovery of Whitman in the early 1890's stimulated his acceptance of the body, his desire for fraternal contact, and his pursuit of life on the open road. Henceforth, this new attitude would become an integral part of Gide's life and writing.

Gide first expressed his sense of personal and artistic renewal in *Les Nourritures terrestres*, which he wrote in 1897. In the Préface to the 1927 edition, he says: "Les Nourritures terrestres sont le livre sinon d'un malade, du moins d'un convalescent, d'un guéri—de quelqu'un qui a été malade. Il y a, dans son lyrisme même, l'excès de celui qui embrasse la vie comme quelque chose qu'il a failli perdre."[15] And he goes on to say of the Symbolist milieu of his early years: "J'écrivais ce livre à un moment où la littérature sentait furieusement le factice et le renfermé; où il me paraissait urgent de la faire à nouveau toucher terre et poser simplement sur le sol un pied nu" (*Oeuvres*, II, 227-228). As the above comments suggest, it is also in *Les Nourritures terrestres* that Whitman's impress appears most clearly.

The narrator of *Les Nourritures terrestres* says that he was initially educated into the glories of man, the earth, the body, and the senses by a Whitmanian figure named Menalque, who is a veritable embodiment of Whitman's vagabond and companion of the open road. In words that echo Whitman's "Song of the Open Road," Menalque declares: "A dix huit ans . . . je partis sur les routes, sans but, usant ma fièvre vagabonde. . . . Je traversai des villes, et ne voulus m'arrêter nulle part. Heureux, pensais-je qui ne s'attache à

Les Nourritures terrestres . . . perdre: Fruits of the Earth is the book of someone who, if not sick, was at least convalescing, recently cured—of someone who was sick. There is, even in the book's lyricism, the excess of someone who embraces life as something he has almost lost.

J'écrivais . . . nu: I wrote this book at a time when literature had the strong scent of the artificial and the enclosed; then it seemed urgent to me to make it touch earth once again and to place one bare foot simply upon the ground.

A dix . . . mobilités: At eighteen years of age . . . I departed on the road, without a goal, exhausting my vagabonding fever. . . . I passed through cities and didn't want to stop any place. Happy is he, I thought, who is not attached to anything on the earth, and who carries an endless fervor through life's constant mobilities.

rien sur la terre et promène une éternelle ferveur à travers les constantes mobilités" (*Oeuvres*, II, 113). Throughout *Les Nourritures terrestres* we hear the voice of Whitman as Gide relates to Nathaniel, the imaginary figure to whom the book is addressed, Menalque's lesson of life, love, and fervor.

At the very outset, Gide announces the identity of himself and his work ("Je m'y suis mis sans apprêts, sans pudeur") in words that recall Whitman's similar avowal ("Camerado, this is no book,/Who touches this touches a man"). There is the same balance between self and other ("Que mon livre t'enseigne à t'intéresser plus à toi qu'à lui-même,—puis à tout le reste plus qu'à toi")[16] that we find in Whitman's balance between pride and sympathy, the individual and the "en-masse." In Gide's pantheistic vision ("Ne souhaite pas Nathaniel, trouver Dieu ailleurs que partout"), we find the same impulse that impregnates Whitman's poetry ("I hear and behold God in every object").[17] Throughout *Les Nourritures terrestres* we also find a thrust toward the open air ("Il y a des habitations merveilleuses; dans aucune je n'ai voulu longtemps demeurer. Peur des portes qui se referment, des traquenards. Cellules qui se reclosent sur de l'esprit")[18] that recalls the similar opposition between indoors and outdoors, books and experience in Whitman's poetry. And in his final exhortation to Nathaniel, "Nathaniel, à présent, jette mon livre. Emancipe-t'en. Quitte-moi. Quitte-moi; maintenant tu m'importunes. . . . Ne crois pas que ta vérité puisse être trouvée par quelque autre, plus que de tout, aie honte de cela" (*Oeuvres*, II, 223), we hear echoes of "Song of Myself," in which Whitman similarly exhorts his readers to discover their own road:

Je m'y suis . . . pudeur: I put myself into it without affectation, and without shame.

Que . . . toi: Let my book teach you to take more interest in yourself than in another,—then in all the rest more than yourself.

Ne souhaite . . . partout: Do not hope, Nathaniel, to find God any place other than everywhere.

Il y a . . . l'esprit: There are marvellous houses; I did not want to live for long in any of them. Fear of doors that lock one up, traps. Cells that close upon the spirit.

Nathaniel . . . cela: Nathaniel, at this moment, throw away my book. Emancipate yourself from it. Leave me. Leave me; now you are pestering me. . . . Do not believe that your truth can be found by another; more than anything, be ashamed of that.

Not I, not any one else can travel that road
for you,
You must travel it for yourself.
(1210-1211)

. . . .

You are also asking me questions and I hear
you,
I answer that I cannot answer, you must find
out for yourself.
(1223-1224)

Aside from the general Whitmanian overtones of *Les Nourritures terrestres*, there are times when Gide echoes Whitman directly in idea, word, and image. In expressing his desire for intimacy with the reader, "Je voudrais m'approcher de toi plus encore" (*Oeuvres*, II, 89), Gide echoes Whitman's expression of a similar desire in "Crossing Brooklyn Ferry":

Closer yet I approach you.
(86)

In expressing his desire to renew his vision, "J'attendais une seconde puberté. Ah! refaire à mes yeux une vision neuve, les laver de la salissure des livres, les rendre, plus pareils à l'azur qu'ils regardent" (*Oeuvres*, II, 71), Gide recalls the following lines from "Song of Myself," in which Whitman evokes the same image of eyes being cleansed:

Long enough have you dream'd contemptible
dreams,
Now I wash the gum from your eyes,
You must habit yourself to the dazzle of the
light and of every moment of your life.
(1228-1230)

Je voudrais . . . encore: I would like to get even closer to you.

J'attendais . . . regardent: I awaited a second puberty. Ah! to renew the vision of my eyes, to cleanse them from the soil of books, to make them more like the azure that they look upon.

This Whitmanian image of renewed vision would become one of the central symbols for the post-Symbolist and Modern French writers.

Gide must also have remembered Whitman's description of harvest-time in "Song of Myself":

> The big doors of the country barn stand
> open and ready,
> The dried grass of the harvest-time loads
> the slow-drawn wagon.
> (167-168)
>
> . . . .
>
> I am there, I help, I came stretch'd atop
> of the load.
> I felt its soft jolts, one leg reclined
> on the other.
> (171-172)

In *Les Nourritures terrestres*, Gide describes a harvest-time in which he too comes "stretch'd atop" a hay wagon:

> Les chariots sont rentrés chargés de
> moissons odorantes.
> Les greniers se sont emplis de foin.
> Chariots pesants, heurtés aux talus,
> cahotés aux ornières; que de fois
> vous me ramenâtes des champs, couché
> sur les tas d'herbes sèches, parmi
> les rudes garçons faneurs!
> (*Oeuvres*, II, 154)

And, finally, in the following reflection on death and the continual renewal of things,

> Le plus petit instant de vie est plus fort
> que la mort, et la nie. La mort n'est que

Les chariots . . . faneurs: The wagons have returned, laden with the sweet-smelling harvest./ The granaries are full of hay./ Heavy wagons, knocked against the embankments, jolted over the ruts; how many times did you carry me back from the fields, lying stretched atop the load of dried grass, among the roughs who make the hay.

la permission d'autres vies, pour que tout
soit sans cesse renouvelé
(*Oeuvres*, II, 74),

Gide echoes in word, tone, and image these lines from Whitman:

The smallest sprout shows there is really
no death,
And if ever there was it led forward life,
and does not wait at the end to arrest
it,
And ceas'd the moment life appear'd.
All goes onward and outward, nothing
collapses.
("Song of Myself," 126-129)

The striking parallels between *Les Nourritures terrestres* and *Leaves of Grass* suggest that Gide had Whitman very much in mind when he composed his own testament to life.

Gide also reveals a certain stylistic debt to Whitman in *Les Nourritures terrestres*. In the poetic prose of the narrative, Gide makes use of a rhythmic, repetitive, enumerative style that is frequently reminiscent of Whitman:

Il y a des sources qui jaillissent des
rochers;
Il y en a qu'on voit sourdre de sous les
glaciers;
Il y en a de si bleues qu'elles en ont l'air
plus profondes.
(A Syracuse, la Cyané, merveilleuse à cause
de cela).

Le plus . . . renouvelé: The smallest instant of life is stronger than death, and negates it. Death is no more than the permission of other lives, so that all will be perpetually renewed.

Il y a . . . terre: There are sources that gush forth from the rocks;/ There are some that one sees spring from under glaciers;/ There are some that are so blue that they seem deeper./ (In Syracuse, the Cyane, is marvellous because of this)./ . . . In Zaghouan, from the Nymphaea, gush the waters that supplied Carthage./ In Vaucluse, water springs from the earth. . . .

....

A Zaghouan, de la Nymphée jaillissent les
eaux qui abreuvaient Carthage.
A Vaucluse, l'eau sort de la terre. . . .
(*Oeuvres*, II, 166-167)

The parenthetical style and geographical catalogs of the passage are particularly reminiscent of Whitman. In the rondes and ballades which appear throughout the narrative, Gide reveals a similar stylistic debt to Whitman. For example, in the following lines from "Ballade des Biens Immeubles,"

Il y avait des paysans qui firent monter
leurs troupeaux sur les collines;
D'autres qui emportèrent dans un bateau
leurs petits enfants;
Il y en a eut qui emportèrent de la
bijouterie,
Des mangeailles, des papiers écrits, et
tout ce qui pouvait flotter d'argent
(*Oeuvres*, II, 135),

Gide recalls Whitman not only in his use of a rhythmic, vers libre line, but also in his use of such Whitmanian techniques as initial repetition, parallelism, and enumeration.

Like Whitman, Gide wanted to unfix rather than fix, diffuse rather than fuse the attention, and he was particularly fond of using Whitman's catalog technique to communicate this diffuse and ambulatory mode of perception. At one point in the narrative of *Les Nourritures*, he comments on his enumerative technique in words that exactly describe Whitman's mode of poetic incantation: "Je voudrais être né dans un temps où n'avoir à chanter, poète, que, simplement en les dénombrant, toutes les choses. Mon admiration se serait posée successivement sur chacune et sa louange l'eût

---

Il y avait . . . d'argent: There were peasants who took their herds up into the hills;/ Others who took their little children away in a boat;/ There were others who carried off jewelry,/ Victuals, written documents, and any money that could float. ("Ballad of Real Property")

démontrée; c'en eût été la raison suffisante" (*Oeuvres*, II, 181). Like Whitman, Gide aspired to a kind of Adamic state in which to name a thing would be to celebrate its essence.

In attempting to get the flux of reality into his writing, Gide also reveals a fondness for such Whitmanian techniques as simultaneity and the ensemble. Like Whitman, he wanted to render the diverse and disordered impressions of life as it is being perceived: "Par une attention subite, *simultanée* de tous les sens, arriver à faire (c'est difficile à dire) du sentiment même de sa vie, la sensation concentrée de tout l'attouchement du dehors. . . . Et tout cela *ensemble*, etc., en un petit paquet;—c'est la vie" (*Oeuvres*, II, 182). Again, Gide's words are an exact description of Whitman's poetic procedure. Just as in the Symbolist period Whitman's verse provided an important practical example for the theorists of vers-libre, so in the post-Symbolist period his poetic practice provided a suggestive model in the development of the theory of an art of spontaneity and immediacy, which would find its fullest realization in the Cubist poetry of Guillaume Apollinaire, Blaise Cendrars, and André Salmon.

Although Gide could not have read Whitman in the original at the time that he wrote *Les Nourritures terrestres*, he had probably read some of the Whitman translations that had appeared in the French reviews; he also must have listened to and read the personal translations of Schwob as carefully as Whitman listened to and read the Hugo translations of Anne Gilchrist. After the appearance of *Les Nourritures terrestres*, Schwob accused Gide of having plagiarized *Le Livre de Monelle.*[19] However, the similarities between these two representative works in the post-Symbolist movement back to a repossession of man and the world are probably explained by the fact that both works, as Gide himself suggested, had a common source in Walt Whitman.

Je voudrais . . . suffisante: I would like to have been born at a time when a poet could sing simply by enumerating all things. My admiration would have focused on each thing in succession, and my praise would have evoked the thing itself; this would have been its own justification.

Par . . . vie: By a sudden, and simultaneous attention of all the senses, succeed in creating (it's difficult to say) the impression of life itself, the concentrated sensation of all contact from outside. And all that *together*, etc., in a little package; that is life.

In the works that followed *Les Nourritures terrestres*, Gide continually returned to Whitmanian themes. In 1899, he published an account of his adventures in North Africa under the Whitmanian title *Feuilles de route*. In such fictional works as *L'Immoraliste* (1902), he carried on his celebration of the joys of the earth, the body, and the senses, which Whitman had helped him to rediscover. It was particularly Whitman's sexual attitude that continued to exert a powerful influence on Gide's personal and literary life. Gide was one of the first artists to recognize fully the homo-erotic impulse in Whitman's verse, and it was in part through Whitman that he learned to accept and acknowledge his own Calamus yearnings. In *Les Nourritures terrestres* and the works that followed, sexuality, physical desire, and the problem of sexual inversion became persistent themes in Gide's writing.

Gide had both a personal and a literary interest in stressing the homo-erotic impulse in Whitman's verse. When Bazalgette published his *Walt Whitman: l'homme et l'oeuvre* in 1908 and when his complete translation of Whitman's poetry, *Feuilles d'herbe*, appeared in 1909, Gide was critical of Bazalgette's attempt to "heterosexualize" Whitman.[20] Gide responded to Bazalgette's falsification by making Whitman one of the central figures in *Corydon*, a series of imaginary dialogues on pederasty, which Gide circulated among his friends in 1911 but which was not officially published until 1922.

In these dialogues the narrator speaks for heterosexuality, and Doctor Corydon, who is known for his questionable morals, defends pederasty. It is probably no coincidence that the doctor is also an admirer of Walt Whitman. At the very outset we are told that a picture of the American poet appears on Doctor Corydon's work table: "Sur sa table de travail, le portrait d'un vieillard à grande barbe blanche, que je reconnus aussitôt pour celui de l'Américain Walt Whitman, car il figure en tête d'une traduction que M. Bazalgette vient de donner de

Sur . . . l'entretien: Upon his work table, the portrait of an old man with a great white beard, that I immediately recognized as that of the American Walt Whitman, because he is pictured at the beginning of a translation that Mr. Bazalgette has just done of his work. Mr. Bazalgette had also published a biography of this poet, a voluminous study that I had recently come to know, and which served as a pretext to begin the conversation. (*Corydon*) son oeuvre. M. Bazalgette venait de publier également une biographie de ce poète, volumineuse étude dont j'avais récemment pris connaissance, et qui me servit de prétexte pour engager l'entretien."[21]

The first dialogue begins with a discourse on Bazalgette's treatment of Whitman's sexuality. Doctor Corydon is critical of Bazalgette's reasoning:

> L'homosexualité, pose-t-il en principe, est un penchant contre nature.
>
> *Or*, Whitman était de parfaite santé, c'était, à proprement parler, le représentant le plus parfait, que nous ait offert la littérature, de l'homme naturel....
>
> —*Donc*, Whitman n'était pas pédéraste.
>
> (p. 19)

The Doctor counters Bazalgette's argument with the syllogism:

> Whitman peut être pris comme type de l'homme normal.
> *Or* Whitman était pédéraste.
> —*Donc*, la pédérastie est un penchant normal.
>
> (p. 19)

Gide projects himself into the figure of Doctor Corydon. Like the doctor, Gide consistently looked to Whitman as a model of the kind of sexual freedom and health he envisioned for himself and his fellow men.

Gide was particularly critical of Bazalgette's attempt to play down Whitman's homo-eroticism by falsifying the text of Whitman's poems. Throughout his translation, Bazalgette consistently translates the love between men with the word *affection* and the love between men and women with the word *amour*. Similarly, the word lover is translated *ami* when it is a question of adhesive love and *amant* when

---

L'homosexualité . . . pédéraste: Homosexuality, he lays down as a principle, is a tendency that is contrary to nature. Now, Whitman was perfectly healthy; he was, to speak exactly, the most perfect representative that literature has offered of the natural man....—*Thus*, Whitman was not a pederast.

Whitman . . . normal: Whitman may be taken as a typical normal man. Now, Whitman was a pederast. —*Thus*, pederasty is a normal tendency.

it is a question of amative love. Gide comments on this aspect of Bazalgette's translation in *Corydon*: "M. Bazalgette aura beau traduire par 'affection' ou 'amitié' le mot 'love' et 'sweet' par 'pur' dès qu'il s'adresse au 'camarade.'. . . Il n'en restera pas moins que toutes les pièces passionnées, sensuelles, tendres, frémissantes, du volume, sont du même ordre que vous appelez 'contre nature' " (p. 19). Bazalgette's inability to recognize that Whitman's most lyrical and passionate poems were addressed to men leads Gide to conclude: "Je connais peu de traductions qui trahissent mieux leur auteur" (p. 20).

As part of his campaign for a freer sexual attitude, Gide planned to correct Bazalgette's errors by publishing a selection of Whitman's poems, of which the central section would be a translation by Louis Fabulet of several of the Calamus poems. Although Gide began planning this translation around 1913,[22] it was not until 1918 that the book, *Walt Whitman: oeuvres choisies*, was published by the *Nouvelle Revue Française*. This book is significant in the history of Whitman's French reception; it includes translations by some of the major French writers who had taken an interest in the American poet. In addition to Gide's translations of "Song of Myself" and several poems from *Children of Adam* and *Drum-Taps*, the book includes some of the translations by Jules Laforgue and Vielé-Griffin that had already appeared.[23] The Preface was written by Valery Larbaud, who also translated "The Sleepers" and some selections from Whitman's prose. Initially, the volume was to include several translations by Paul Claudel; but, having discovered Gide's sexual anomaly, Claudel refused to collaborate in the project.

In addition to editing *Walt Whitman: oeuvres choisies*, Gide continued to make use of Whitmanian themes in the works of his post-war period. *La Symphonie pastorale* (1919) contains the same hymn to life and joy that had initially attracted Gide to Whitman. In *Si le grain ne meurt* (1926), there is a confessional and autobiographical impulse and a further exploration of the sexual themes Gide

---

M. Bazalgette . . . nature: Mr. Bazalgette may well translate the word love as "affection" or "friendship," and the word "sweet" as "pure" whenever he speaks of a "comrade." . . . It will nevertheless remain true that all the selections of passion, sensuality, tenderness, and feeling in the volume are of the same sort that you call "contrary to nature."

associated with the American poet. And, finally, in *Les Nouvelles Nourritures*, which appeared in 1935, Gide returned to the Whitmanian themes and inspiration of his earlier work. Whitman is still present not only in the form and content of this later work, but also in the fact that Nathaniel's name has now been changed to the more Whitmanian "Camarade."

II. The Renewal of Form

In the post-Symbolist period, Whitman not only contributed to the renewal of the substance of French literature, but he continued to provide a model for the formal experiments of the French poets. In the Symbolist period, the example of Whitman's verse aided in the breakdown of the alexandrine and the development of a more organic verse; but none of the early vers-librists found the total liberation of Whitman's long, unrhymed, rhythmically based line, nor did they make extensive use of such Whitmanian techniques as repetition, parallelism, exclamation, and the catalog. In the post-Symbolist period, French vers-libre evolved toward a technique and form that more closely approximated Whitman's free verse. In the formal experiments of Paul Claudel, André Spire, and Charles Péguy, French vers-libre found its fullest development in a rhythmic and organic *verset* that closely resembles the technique and form of Whitman's verse. It is particularly in the work of Paul Claudel that we see the role Whitman played in the development of the French *verset*.

A. *Paul Claudel*

Of the French poets, Paul Claudel most closely resembles Whitman in the form, substance, and vision of his work. Critics often point up the striking similarities between the two poets, although they often seem more intimidated than interested by the resemblance.[24] In his introduction to Claudel's *Oeuvres poétiques*, for example, Stanislas Fumet cites the lines from *Cinq Grandes Odes* in which Claudel expresses his desire to write

> Le grand poème de l'homme enfin par delà
> les causes secondes réconcilié aux forces
> éternelles.

La grande Voie triomphale au travers de la
Terre réconciliée pour que l'homme soustrait
au hasard s'y avance!

Fumet points up the resemblance of this poem to Whitman's work, at the same time that he expresses a certain learned reservation about the American "barbarian": "Ce poème . . . aurait pu être l'oeuvre de Walt Whitman si l'Américain aux longs cheveux et à la barbe fleurie avait disposé d'une metaphysique."[25] Despite the reservations of the critics, however, some of the writers who were closest to Claudel have suggested his Whitmanian antecedents. In an interview with P. M. Jones, André Gide, who was one of Claudel's closest friends during the formative years of Claudel's literary career, commented upon Claudel's debt to Whitman. Jones reports: "M. André Gide, with whom I discussed the matter, seems to have been convinced of Claudel's indebtedness to the *Leaves*. Usually, however, it is the Bible, the dramas of Aeschylus and Shakespeare and Rimbaud's *Illuminations* that are cited as his models."[26] Claudel himself admitted his admiration for Whitman, but he did not feel that the American poet had greatly influenced the form and content of his poetry. He said in a letter to Charles Saunders in 1916: "Je connais et j'admire de longue date Walt Whitman. C'est, je crois, mon ami Marcel Schwob qui le premier m'a fait lire les *Leaves of Grass*. Je ne me rends pas compte cependant qu'il a exercé une grande influence ni sur mes idées, ni sur ma technique, toute instinctive, et qui à ce moment était déjà fixée puisque j'avais écrit *Tête d'Or* et un autre drame depuis brûlé."[27]

Le grand . . . avance: The great poem of man reconciled finally, beyond secondary causes, with eternal forces./ The great triumphal Way traversing the Earth, reconciled, so that man, released from chance, can move forward upon it. (*Five Great Odes*)

Ce poème . . . metaphysique: This poem . . . could be the work of Walt Whitman if the American, with long hair and a blossoming beard, had a metaphysics at his disposal.

Je connais . . . brûlé: I know and I have admired Walt Whitman for a long time. It is, I believe, my friend Marcel Schwob who was the first to have me read *Leaves of Grass*. I am not aware, however, that he has exerted a great influence on either my ideas or my technique, which was quite instinctive, and which, at that time, was already determined, since I had written *Tête d'Or* and another drama that has since been burned.

As Claudel suggests, it was during the 1890's, when he attended meetings at the house of Marcel Schwob, that he first read Whitman in the original. However, it is also probable that Claudel had some fragmentary acquaintance with Whitman's formal innovations before he invented the *verset*, which he employed for the first time in *Tête d'Or* (1890).[28]

Like his friends Marcel Schwob and André Gide, Claudel attended Mallarmé's "Tuesdays" in the 1880's. It was during this period that Claudel probably gained some fragmentary acquaintance with Whitman's work by frequenting Symbolist circles as well as by reading the translations of Whitman that appeared in the Symbolist reviews. We know, for example, that in 1886 Claudel discovered Rimbaud's *Illuminations* in *La Vogue*,[29] and in the same year he may have come across Laforgue's translations of Whitman, which were also being published by *La Vogue* at this time. In any event, Claudel's critics assume that he had some knowledge of Whitman in the 1880's. As the French critic Henri Guillemin observes in his book *Claudel et son art d'écrire*: "Et comment croire que Whitman, dont il avait lu dans *La Vogue*, en 1886, de beaux textes en versets, lui est demeuré indifférent."[30]

Although Claudel's early writing reflects the influence of Mallarmé and his group, he quickly realized that the ordered, classic orientation not only of Mallarmé, but of French verse in general, was contrary to his artistic needs: "L'erreur la plus grossière de l'alexandrin," according to Claudel, "c'est qu'il fausse le principe essentiel de la phonétique française en attribuant à chaque syllabe une valeur égale."[31] The example of Whitman's verse may have played some role in prompting Claudel to abandon the balanced alexandrines of his early verse for the baroque rhythms of the *verset* in his attempt to find a rhythmic rather than a syllabic base for French language and verse. And although Claudel maintained that the *verset* was his own personal invention, Whitman's free verse probably seconded the

---

Et comment . . . indifférent: And how is one to believe that Whitman, whose pages of beautiful *versets* he had read in *La Vogue*, in 1886, could not have affected him. (*Claudel and His Art of Writing*)

L'erreur . . . égale: The biggest error of the alexandrine is that it falsifies the essential principle of French phonetics in attributing an equal value to each syllable.

example of Rimbaud's rhythmic prose, Shakespeare's blank verse, and the biblical Psalms in the development and elaboration of the Claudelian *verset*.

As Claudel pointed out in his letter to Saunders, he first employed his experimental *verset* in the poetic drama *Tête d'Or*, which was written in 1889 and published in 1890. Speaking of *Tête d'Or* in his book *Le Livre des masques*, the Symbolist critic Remy de Gourmont suggests Claudel's debt to Whitman: "Ce que cette littérature forte et large doit aux tragédies grecs, à Shakespeare, à Whitman, on le sent plutôt qu'on ne peut le déterminer."[32] Although both the characters and the action of *Tête d'Or* express a sense of the physical force and energy of the universe that is reminiscent of Whitman, it is particularly in the form of this play that we "feel" Whitman's presence. Claudel reveals his Whitmanian antecedents in the long-lined, breath-oriented rhythms of the *verset* and the enumerative and reiterative style of such lines as the following:

Il y a des gens dont les yeux
Fondent comme des nèfles fendues qui laissent
couler leurs pépins.
Et des femmes où le cancer s'est mis comme
l'amadou sur un hêtre.
Et des nouveau-nés monstrueux, des hommes
ayant un mufle de veau!
Et des enfants violés et tués par leurs pères.
Et des vieillards dont les enfants comptent
les jours un à un.
Toutes les maladies veillent sur nous,
l'ulcère et l'abcès, l'épilepsie et le

Ce que . . . déterminer: One can sense but not define what this expansive and vigorous literature owes to the Greek tragedies, to Shakespeare, and to Whitman. (*The Book of Masks*)

Il y a . . . pisser: There are people whose eyes/ Dissolve like split medlars whose seeds flow out./ And women to whom cancer clings like the amadou to a beech tree./ And new-born monsters, men having the snouts of calves!/ And children raped and killed by their fathers./ And old people whose children count the days one by one./ All diseases hang over us, the ulcer and the abscess, epilepsy and Parkinson's disease, and in the end comes gout and gravel, which prevent one from pissing. (*Head of Gold*)

> hochement de la tête, et à la fin vient la
> goutte et la gravelle qui empêche de
> pisser.[33]

Although Claudel's vision is more negative than that of Whitman, the technique of these lines recalls Whitman's impressionistic evocation of the modern, human landscape in "Faces," which Claudel may have read in Vielé-Griffin's 1887 translation.[34] As the above lines might suggest, when Claudel wrote *Tête d'Or* he was still in "la grande nuit métaphysique" of Baudelaire, Mallarmé, and Poe, which he described as "la sympathie avec la Nuit, la complaissance au malheur, l'amère communion entre les ténèbres et cette infortune d'être un homme."[35] It was not until after his conversion to Catholicism in 1890 that Claudel experienced the literary renaissance that led him to say: "Adieu pour toujours, ô pauvre armoire à glace de Stéphane Mallarmé, professeur au lycée Condorcet."[36] At this time, he would renew contact with the world and thus enter into the Whitmanian currents of the French 1890's in both the substance and the form of his writing.

Shortly after his religious conversion, Claudel extended his acquaintance with Whitman through Schwob and his group, and in 1894 he bought his own copy of *Leaves of Grass.*[37] During the years following his conversion, when Claudel struggled to reconcile his religious calling with his active life and his literary aspirations, he found instructive guidance in the work of Whitman.

Claudel treated the conflict between the man of action, the religious man, and the poet in his play *Les Villes*, which he composed in 1890.[38] The impact that Whitman had on Claudel in the years following his conversion is reflected in the revisions that Claudel made in the role of Coeuvre, the poet, in a later version of the play. Whereas in the first version of the play, Coeuvre appears as a rather decadent figure, in the second version of the play, which Claudel completed in 1898, Coeuvre's role has been renewed and expanded

---

La sympathie . . . homme: The sympathy with the Night, the satisfaction with unhappiness, the bitter communion between darkness and the misfortune of being a man.

Adieu . . . Condorcet: Good-bye, forever, O poor mirror-wardrobe of Stephen Mallarmé, professor at the *Lycée Condorcet.*

into a Whitmanian figure of compassion and love. In both word and action, Coeuvre embodies Whitman's idea of the poet. For example, Coeuvre describes the prophetic role of the poet in words that are reminiscent of Whitman:

> O mon fils! lorsque j'étais un poète entre
> les hommes,
> J'inventai ce vers qui n'avait ni rime ni
> mètre,
> Et je le définissais dans le secret de mon
> coeur cette fonction double et
> réciproque,
> Par laquelle l'homme absorbe la vie et
> restitue, dans l'acte suprême de
> l'expiration,
> Une parole intelligible.
> (Act III, *Théâtre*, p. 488)

The essence of Whitman's poetic procedure is contained in these lines: poetry without rhyme and meter, the poet as the absorber of the universe, the breath-oriented rhythm of verse. The similarities between Whitman and Claudel in such passages suggest the role that Whitman played not so much in the invention of the *verset*, but in Claudel's elaboration of the theory and substance of his art in his later works.

It was in *L'Art poétique* (1907) that Claudel first defined his aesthetic philosophy. In discussing his ideas on the nature and function of language and art, Claudel expanded upon the Whitmanian concept of the poet that he had earlier embodied in the figure of Coeuvre. Although *L'Art poétique* reflects much of the Symbolist preoccupation with cognizance, language, and the magical power of the word, one wonders if, in formulating his theory of art, Claudel had not also found certain antecedents in Whitman. Enmeshed as it sometimes is in Symbolist terminology, Claudel's artistic theory is an

---

O mon . . . intelligible: O my son, when I was a poet among men,/ I invented this verse that had neither rhyme nor meter,/ And I defined, in the secrecy of my heart, this double and reciprocal function,/ Whereby man absorbs life and restores, in the supreme act of expiration,/ An intelligent word. (*The Cities*) exact description of Whitman's poetics. Like Whitman, Claudel conceived of the universe as an immense and dynamic unity of matter energized by spirit. Like Whitman, he also regarded the inward and outward motion of inspiration and expiration, advance and retreat, as the central rhythm of the universe. For Claudel as for Whitman, it was the function of the poet to duplicate the natural rhythm of himself and the universe in the language and rhythm of his poetry.

In the 1876 Preface to *Leaves of Grass*, Whitman says that his poetry is "a radical utterance out of the abysms of the Soul, the Emotions, and the Physique . . . and in its very nature regardless of the old conventions, under the great Laws, following only its own impulses" (*LG*, p. 751). It was in the sea that Whitman found an image of the natural motion, the inward and outward "breath" of the universe, that he wanted to repeat in the language and rhythm of his poetry. After cataloguing some of the world's "greatest bards" in "Had I the Choice," Whitman says:

> These, these, O sea, all these I'd gladly
>   barter,
> Would you the undulation of one wave, its
>   trick to me transfer,
> Or breathe one breath of yours upon my verse,
> And leave its odor there.
>
> (6-9)

Similarly, Claudel regarded the *verset* as an attempt to write from life rather than from literature, to duplicate the energetic and harmonious pulse of the universe in his verse and thereby communicate this pulse to the reader. As he says: "Le poète qui a le magistère de tous les mots, et dont l'art est de les employer, est habile, par une savante disposition des objets qu'ils représentent, à provoquer en nous un état d'intelligence harmonieux et intense, juste et fort." Like Whitman, Claudel also found an important rhythmic base for poetry in the physiology of the body. It was in the movements of the breath and the beat of the heart, "la respiration, le battement de coeur, l'aigu et le

---

Le poète . . . fort: The poet, who has the magistracy over all words, and whose art it is to use them, is skillful in provoking in us, by a knowledgeable ordering of the objects that they represent, a harmonious and intense, just and strong state of intelligence.

grave, les brèves et les longues, l'iambe fondamental de tout langage,"[39] that Claudel found the basic rhythm of his *verset*.

Finally, in describing the rhythmic, quantitative basis of his prosody, Claudel exactly defines Whitman's poetic method. Claudel's *verset* is based on his idea that "le français est composé d'une série d'*iambes* dont l'élément long est la dernière syllabe du phonème et l'élément bref un nombre indéterminé pouvant aller jusqu'à cinq ou six de syllabes indifférents qui le précèdent."[40] The similarity between Claudel's theory and Whitman's practice has been pointed out by the influential French scholar of Whitman, Roger Asselineau. After discussing the rhythmic, accentual basis of Whitman's verse in *The Evolution of Walt Whitman*, he says: "In short, we have here Paul Claudel's 'iambe fondamental.' What counts for Whitman as well as for Claudel is the return at *more or less* regular intervals of stressed syllables separated from each other by a variable number of unstressed syllables (from one to four)."[41] The similarities in the prosodic method of Whitman and Claudel are more than mere coincidence. In developing the theory and practice of the Claudelian *verset*, Claudel had found an instructive model in Whitman's free verse.

It was in *Cinq Grandes Odes* (1910) that Claudel, following his religious conversion in 1890, fully realized the renewal in the substance as well as the form of his writing. Claudel regarded the odes as "un chant de delivrance." He says: "Après plusieurs années de captivité, je revenais enfin à la lumière et à la vie. Quelle joie . . . elles marquent l'ouverture de ma fidèle carrière littéraire. Tout ce qui les précède n'est guère que balbutiement."[42] Having renewed contact with the world, Claudel experienced the literary renaissance that brought him into full rapport with the "Whitmanism" of the pre-war years in France.

La respiration . . . langage: The respiration, the heartbeat, the acute and the grave, the short and the long, the fundamental iamb of all language.

Le français . . . précèdent: French consists of a series of *iambs* in which the long element is the last syllable of the phoneme and the short element is an indeterminate number, which can range from five to six, of unweighted syllables that precede it.

Après . . . balbutiement: After several years of captivity, I finally returned to light and to life. What joy . . . these odes mark the opening of my true literary career. All that precedes them is nothing but stammering.

Claudel's odes to life and joy, his celebration of man, God, and creation, are close to Whitman in technique, spirit, and feeling. In *Cinq Grandes Odes* Claudel moved away from the consistent use of enjambment in the *versets* of his earlier works toward an end-stopped line that more closely approximates Whitman's verse unit. Technically, Claudel makes use of the repetitions and parallelisms, enumerations and identifications, parentheses and exclamations, prepositions and participles that are so characteristic of Whitman's style. In the following geographical catalog,

> Connaissant ma propre quantité,
> C'est moi, je tire, j'appelle sur toutes mes
> racines, le Gange, le Mississippi,
> L'épaisse touffe de l'Orénoque, le long fil
> du Rhin, le Nil avec sa double vessie
> ("L'Esprit et l'eau"),[43]

Claudel's technique and vision are clearly reminiscent of Whitman. Claudel may have remembered Whitman's similar use of the geographic catalog in "Salut Au Monde":

> I see the long river-stripes of the earth,
> I see the Amazon and the Paraguay,
> (84-85)
>
> ....
> I see the falling of the Ganges over the
> high rim of Saukara.
> (92)

In addition to echoing the public voice of Whitman, Claudel also makes use of a more confidential tone, the addresses to the soul, and the exhortations to the reader that are again reminiscent of Whitman. For example, in the following addresses,

---

Connaissant . . . vessie: Knowing my own abundance,/ It is I, drawing from, summoning through all my roots, the Ganges, the Mississippi,/ The dense cluster of the Orinoco, the long thread of the Rhine, the Nile with its double bladder. ("The Spirit and the Water")

Ecoute, mon enfant, et incline vers moi la
tête, et je te donnerai mon âme.

Je vous salue, mon frère bien-aimé
("L'Esprit et l'eau," *OP*, pp. 247-248),

Claudel may have remembered such Whitmanian addresses as "Come my children" or "Do you see O my brothers and sisters," which are scattered throughout *Leaves of Grass*.

In addition to these stylistic similarities, there are also similar patterns of imagery in Whitman and Claudel. Like Whitman, Claudel makes frequent use of the march and the procession to represent his optimistic, progressive, and unitary vision of the world; he also makes recurrent use of the departure for the open road or the flight into sea or space as a means of representing and affirming his faith in God and the cosmos. For Claudel, as for Whitman, the sea is a central image. Just as Whitman associates water with spirit,

I fly those flights of a fluid and swallowing
soul
("Song of Myself," 800),

so Claudel associates the water with "cet élément fluide, l'esprit ou l'eau, dont toutes choses sont pénétrées" ("L'Esprit et l'eau," *OP*, p. 234). In his poems Claudel, like Whitman, uses the sea to image an experience of cosmic joy and freedom. In "Passage to India" Whitman rejoices,

We too take ship O soul,
Joyous we too launch out on trackless seas,
Fearless for unknown shores on waves of
ecstasy to sail
(176-178),

Ecoute . . . âme: Listen, my child, and incline your head toward me, and I will give you my soul.

Je vous . . . bien-aimé: I salut you, my belovéd brother.

Cet élément . . . pénétrées: This fluid element, the spirit or the water, that runs through all things.

and in "L'Esprit et l'eau" Claudel similarly declares:

> Et l'eau même, et l'élément même, je joue,
> je resplendis! Je partage la liberté de
> la mer omniprésente!
> L'eau
> Toujours s'en vient retrouver l'eau,
> Composant une goutte unique.
> (*OP*, pp. 236-237)

In "Passage to India" Whitman addresses his soul,

> Sail forth—steer for the deep waters only,
> Reckless O soul, exploring, I with thee, and
> thou with me,
> For we are bound where mariner has not yet
> dared to go
> (248-250),

and Claudel again echoes him when he exclaims:

> Je me suis embarqué pour toujours! Je suis comme le vieux marin qui ne connaît plus la terre que par ses feux, les systèmes d'étoiles vertes ou rouges enseignés par la carte et le portulan.
> ("L'Esprit et l'eau," *OP*, p. 236)

Like Whitman, Claudel uses the launching out to sea to represent an assertion of faith and an immersion in spirit.

In *Cinq Grandes Odes* Claudel consistently uses images of night, space, and the astronomical universe that are also suggestive of Whitman. In "Song of Myself," for example, Whitman associates the potentially terrifying astronomical spheres with the familiar image of an orchard in bloom:

Et l'eau . . . unique: And the water itself, and the element itself, I play, I am resplendent! I am part of the freedom of the omnipresent sea!/ Water/ Always comes to meet water/ Forming a unique drop.

Je me . . . portulan: I have set sail forever! I am like the old sailor who only knows the earth by its lights, the network of green and red stars pointed out by the map and the portulan.

I visit the orchards of spheres and look at
the product,
And look at quintillions ripen'd and look at
quintillions green.
(798-799)

Similarly, in "L'Esprit et l'eau" Claudel associates the stars with the fertility of an orchard:

O fortes étoiles sublimes et quel fruit entr'
apercu dans le noir abîme! ô flexion sacrée
du long rameau de la Petite-Ourse.
(*OP*, p. 244)

Before the vastness of space and the astronomical night, Whitman and Claudel experienced neither fear nor despair, but rather an exhilarated sense of the perpetual renewal of life and the eternal presence of spirit. In "Song of Myself" Whitman avows:

I open my scuttle at night and see the far-
sprinkled systems,
And all I see multiplied as high as I can cip-
her edge but the rim of the farther systems.
(1183-1184)

Claudel again recalls Whitman when he exclaims in "Magnificat":

Que m'importent vos fables! Laissez-moi seule-
ment aller à la fenêtre et ouvrir la nuit et
éclater à mes yeux en un chiffre simultané
L'innombrable comme autant de zéros après
le I coefficient de ma nécessité!
(*OP*, p. 252)

Like Whitman, Claudel wanted to abolish the fear of death and the

---

O fortes . . . Petite-Ourse: O large, sublime stars and what fruit fleetingly glimpsed in the black abyss! O sacred bending of the long branch of the Little Bear.

Que . . . nécessité: Of what importance are your fables to me! Only let me go to the window and open it upon the night and flashing before my eyes, in a simultaneous number, is/ The innumerable like as many zeros after the coefficient I of my necessity. ("Magnificat")

terror and loneliness of the soul in the face of the metaphysical night by asserting his confidence in the perpetual unity and continuity of the universe. As Claudel says in the final poem of *Cinq Grandes Odes:*

> Maintenant je puis dire, mieux que le vieux
> Lucrèce: Vous n'êtes plus, ô terreurs de
> la nuit!
> Ou plutôt comme votre saint Prophète: *Et*
> *la nuit est mon exaltation dans mes*
> *délices!*
> ("La Maison fermée," *OP*, p. 282)

In his poetry, Claudel seconded Whitman in using the joyous embrace of night, space, and the astronomical universe as a kind of symbolic response to Poe, Mallarmé, Valéry, and other poets of the metaphysical night, who were still haunted by Pascal's fear: "le silence éternel de ces espaces infinis."

In *Cinq Grandes Odes* Claudel also presents a cosmic image of the poet that has clear anteeedents in Whitman. Claudel may have remembered the Adamic image of Whitman cataloguing, absorbing, and containing the universe when he addresses the poet in the opening poem, "Les Muses":

> Ainsi quand tu parles, ô poëte, dans une
> énumération délectable
> Proférant de chaque chose le nom,
> Comme un père tu l'appelles mystérieusement
> dans son principe, et selon que jadis
> Tu participes à sa création, tu coopères à
> son existence!
> (*OP*, p. 230)

Maintenant . . . délices: Now I can say, better than the old Lucretius: You no longer exist, O terrors of the night!/ Or rather like your Saint Prophet: *And the night is my exaltation in my delight!* ("The Closed House")

Le silence . . . infinis: The eternal silence of this infinite space.

Ainsi . . . existence: Thus when you speak, O poet, in a delectable enumeration/ Uttering the name of each thing,/ Like a father you mysteriously name it according to its essence, and as formerly/ You participate in its creation, you cooperate in its existence! ("The Muses")

In "Song of Myself" Whitman asserts,

> I have instant conductors all over me
> whether I pass or stop,
> They seize every object and lead it
> harmlessly through me
> (615-616),

and Claudel echoes with:

> Je suis au monde, j'exerce de toutes parts
> ma connaissance.
> Je connais toutes choses et toutes choses se
> connaissent en moi.
> ("L'Esprit et l'eau," *OP*, p. 238)

Claudel's poet laughs with the same kind of cosmic joy as Whitman. "I am satisfied—I see, dance, laugh, sing" (59), Whitman affirms in "Song of Myself"; and in "L'Esprit et l'eau" Claudel similarly declares: "Celui qui connaît la délivrance, il se rit maintenant de tous les liens, et qui comprendra le rire qu'il a dans son coeur?" (*OP*, p. 247).

Throughout *Cinq Grandes Odes* we find the same cosmopolitan spirit and international sentiment that are characteristic of Whitman's writing. At times the echoes are direct. In the following lines, for example, Claudel probably remembered Whitman's "Salut Au Monde":

> Salut donc, ô monde nouveau à mes yeux, ô
> monde maintenant total!
> ("L'Esprit et l'eau," *OP*, p. 240)

Like Whitman, Claudel also uses the flight motif to suggest the cosmic vision of the poet. "I am afoot with my vision," Whitman proudly asserts before his flight through time and space in "Song of

---

Je suis . . . moi: I am in the world, I exercise my knowledge everywhere./ I know all things and all things know themselves in me.

Celui . . . coeur: He who knows deliverance, laughs at all bonds, and who will understand the laughter that he has in his heart?

Salut . . . total: Salut, then, O world new to my eyes, O world now complete!

Myself"; and Claudel similarly declares: "Le monde s'ouvre et, si large qu'en soit l'empan, mon regard le traverse d'un bout à l'autre" ("L'Esprit et l'eau," *OP*, p. 240).

For Claudel, as for Whitman, the poet is a celebrator of the universe. "Magnifying and applying come I," Whitman asserts in "Song of Myself," and Claudel echoes with "Mon âme magnifie le Seigneur" in the opening lines of "Magnificat." Unlike Whitman, however, who celebrates a new religion of man, Claudel celebrates a renewed worship of God. Thus, whereas Whitman absorbs the religions of the past, "buying drafts of Osiris, Isis, Belus, Brahma, Buddha . . . to fill out better in myself" ("Song of Myself," 1030; 1035), Claudel rejects all idols in the name of God:

> Soyez béni, mon Dieu, qui m'avez délivré
> des idoles,
> Et qui faites que je n'adore que Vous seul,
> et non point Isis et Osiris.
> (*OP*, p. 251)

Since he utilized the same images of Isis and Osiris we find in Whitman, Claudel may have intended the passage to be a kind of response to the "un-Catholic" vision of Whitman and his followers in France.

Although Claudel and Whitman begin with different assumptions about the origin and nature of the universe, they share similar views on the nature and function of the poet and poetry. For Claudel, as for Whitman, the poet is the voice of the people. In "Song of Myself" Whitman says:

> These are really the thoughts of all men
> in all ages and lands, they are not
> original with me,
> If they are not yours as much as mine they
> are nothing, or next to nothing.
> (355-356)

Le monde . . . l'autre: The world opens, and however broad the expanse may be, my glance will span it from end to end.

Mon . . . Seigneur: My soul magnifies the Lord.

Soyez . . . Osiris: Blesséd be my God, who has delivered me from idols,/ And who makes me worship only Him alone, and not Isis and Osiris.

And in "La Muse qui est la grâce," Claudel recalls Whitman's words:

> Les mots que j'emploie,
> Ce sont les mots de tous les jours, et ce
> ne sont point les mêmes!
> Vous ne trouverez point de rimes dans mes
> vers ni aucun sortilège. Ce sont vos
> phrases mêmes. Pas aucune de vos phrases
> que je ne sache reprendre!
> (*OP*, p. 265)

Just as Whitman associates his poems with the commonness and universality of grass,

> This is the grass that grows wherever the
> land is and the water is,
> This the common air that bathes the globe
> ("Song of Myself," 359-360),

so Claudel associates the words of the poet with the similarly universal and fertile image of the harvest: "Faites que je la produise [la parole] de la meilleur substance de mon coeur comme une moisson qui va poussant de toutes parts où il y a de la terre (des épis jusqu'au milieu de la route)" (*OP*, p. 283).

For Claudel as for Whitman, the poet is not only the singer of man but also the celebrator of the urban landscape and the modern technological world. As Claudel declares in "La Muse qui est la grâce":

> Je chanterai le grand poème de l'homme
> soustrait au hasard!
> Ce que les gens ont fait autour de moi avec
> le canon qui ouvre les vieux Empires,
> ....

Les mots . . . reprendre: The words that I use,/ They are everyday words, and yet they are not at all the same!/ You will find no rhyme in my verse, nor any trickery. These are your own phrases. Not one of your phrases that I cannot revive! ("The Muse Who is Grace")

Faites . . . route: Make me bring it forth [the word] from the best substance of my heart like a harvest that grows in all places where there is earth (ears of corn even in the middle of the road).

Avec les ports touts bordés intérieurement de
pinces et d'antennes et le transatlantique
qui signale au loin dans le brouillard,
Avec la locomotive qu'on attelle à son
convoi, et le canal qui se remplit quand
la fille de l'Ingénieur en chef du bout de
son doigt sur le coup-de-poing fait sauter
à la fois la double digue,
Je le ferai avec un poème . . . .

(*OP*, p. 267)

In this passage, as throughout *Cinq Grandes Odes*, we find themes and images that Claudel may have remembered from Whitman's "Passage to India." Claudel makes use of the unity theme of "Passage to India" as well as the same technological achievements—the train, the transatlantic, the canal—to express this theme. Just as Whitman's poet was to continue the unifying function of the explorers and engineers,

After the seas are all cross'd, (as they
seem already cross'd,)
After the great captains and engineers have
accomplish'd their work,
After the noble inventors, after the
scientists, the chemist, the geologist,
ethnologist,
Finally shall come the poet worthy that name,
The true son of God shall come singing his
songs

(101-105),

so Claudel's poet was to second the accomplishments of the great captains and engineers in discovering, connecting, and unifying the earth.

Je chanterai . . . poème: I shall sing the great poem of man released from chance!/ What men have done around me with the cannon that opens old Empires,/ . . . With ports all lined inside with pincers and antennae and the translatlantic that signals from afar in the fog,/ With the locomotive that one couples to its train of cars, and the canal that fills up when the daughter of the chief Engineer, touching the grip with her finger tips, makes the double dike burst forth all at once,/ I will do with a poem. . . .

In representing the poet as a kind of discoverer and explorer, Claudel, like Whitman, was particularly attracted to the figure of Christopher Columbus. As he says in "La Maison fermée":

> Mon désir est d'être le rassembleur de
> la terre de Dieu! Comme Christophe
> Colomb quand il mit à la voile,
> Sa pensée n'était pas de trouver une terre
> nouvelle,
> Mais dans ce coeur plein de sagesse la
> passion de la limite et de la sphère
> calculée de parfaire l'éternel horizon.
> (*OP*, pp. 280-281)

Claudel probably remembered Whitman's "Prayer of Columbus," in which Whitman similarly represents and identifies with the unifying function of Christopher Columbus: "By me the hemispheres rounded and tied, the unknown to the known" (33). Years later, Claudel again recalls Whitman when in his play *Le Livre de Christophe Colomb* he makes a similar use of Christopher Columbus as the "réunisseur de la Terre Habitée."

André Gide must have recognized the close ties between Whitman and Claudel when, a few years after the publication of *Cinq Grandes Odes*, he asked Claudel to participate in the translation of Whitman that he planned for the *Nouvelle Revue Française*. Claudel responded with interest, writing to Gide in February of 1913: "J'ai bien les *Leaves of Grass* mais à Paris ou à la campagne et ce sera toute une histoire de les retrouver. Si je traduisais quelque chose de Whitman ce serait les

---

Mon désir . . . horizon: My desire is to be the assembler of God's earth! Like Christopher Columbus when he set sail,/ His idea was not to find a new world,/ But in his heart, full of wisdom, he was driven by a passion for limits, from the known sphere to round off the eternal horizon.

J'ai . . . sabotée: Yes I have *Leaves of Grass*, but it is in Paris or the country, and it will be very complicated to get it. If I translated something of Whitman's, it would be the pieces on the South: "O South, my South" (I no longer remember the title), or that other piece that is also fairly short, where he speaks of the voices of singers, tenor contralto. I hope that Griffin's translation of "When Lilacs Last in the Dooryard Bloom'd" is not going to be the one that he did in alexandrines (why not in Latin verse?). It is a masterful piece that must not be sabotaged.

pièces sur le Sud: 'O South, my South' (je ne me rappelle plus le titre), ou cette autre pièce également assez courte où il parle des voix des chanteurs, ténor contralto. J'espère que la traduction de Griffin du 'Thrène du Président Lincoln' ne sera plus celle qu'il a donnée en alexandrins (pourquoi pas en vers latins?). C'est une pièce maîtresse qui ne doit pas être sabotée."[44]

The poems that Claudel chose to translate indicate some of the basis of his interest in the American poet. As a career diplomat who had spent most of his life in foreign lands, Claudel would have identified with the lyric evocation of place and locality inspired by exile from one's native land that he found in Whitman's "O Magnet-South." In this poem, he would also have found the impressionistic vision, the enumerative technique, and the rich and sumptuous imagery that corresponded with his own poetic style.

Although Claudel's mention of a short piece on contralto and tenor singers is too vague to pinpoint the reference,[45] his attraction to Whitman's poems on music again suggests the similar interests of the two poets. Like Whitman, Claudel was a great lover of music, particularly opera, and he seconded Whitman's attempt to simulate in the structure of his poems the thematic composition of music. Describing his *Odes*, Claudel once said that they develop "non pas en suite continue à la manière littéraire, mais orchestralement, par thèmes entrelacés et décomposés."[46] Claudel's interest in the musical analogy of Whitman's verse is further suggested by his reference to "When Lilacs Last in the Dooryard Bloom'd," since it is this Whitman poem that most closely approximates a musical piece in its organization and progression. Having found a suggestive precedent in Whitman for his own formal experiments, Claudel would quite naturally regard as a complete travesty Vielé-Griffin's attempt to fit Whitman's rhythmic, organic verse into an ordered progression of French alexandrines.

Unfortunately, Claudel's translations of Whitman were never completed. During the period when he was working on these translations, Claudel discovered a passage on homosexuality in Gide's *Les Caves du Vatican* that led him to distrust Gide's zealous interest in

---

Non . . . décomposés: Not in continuous succession in the literary manner, but orchestrally, by themes that are interwoven and then broken down.

Whitman. In March 1914, Claudel wrote to Jacques Rivière: "Je suis, avec un malaise croissant, le roman de Gide, et finalement, je me trouve arrêté page 478 par un passage pédérastique, qui éclaire pour moi d'un jour sinistre certains ouvrages précédents de notre ami . . . . Faut-il donc décidément me resigner à croire . . . que lui-même soit un participant de ces moeurs affreuses . . . . Est-ce pour cela qu'il est tellement désireux de voir attribuer les mêmes moeurs à Arthur Rimbaud, et sans doute à Walt Whitman?"[47]

Having come to suspect that Gide's translation was part of his effort to proselytize for homosexuality, Claudel flatly refused to participate. Only a few days after his letter to Rivière, Claudel wrote to Gide: "Je ne puis pas collaborer à votre *Whitman*. C'est impossible."[48]

Despite Claudel's refusal to participate in Gide's projected translation, his admiration for the American poet continued. In an article he wrote in 1927, Claudel singled out Whitman as the only nineteenth-century artist who had fully immersed himself in the modern technological world: "Toute l'oeuvre positive du XIXe siècle a été pour les artistes comme si elle n'était pas. Examinez combien peu ont été intéressés par le présent, sympathiques à ce qui changeait et se transformait sous leurs yeux, à ce qu'on apportait avec lui de nouveau par exemple le chemin de fer. Cela, il n'y a eu que les économistes et les socialistes pour essayer de le dire tant bien que mal dans leur patois, et personne n'a compris (sauf Whitman) ses frères sur toute la planète qu'on mettait à notre disposition."[49]

Je suis . . . Whitman: I am following Gide's novel with growing uneasiness, and finally I find myself stopped short by a passage on pederasty on page 478, which illuminates for me, on a fateful day, certain preceding works of our friend. . . . Is it thus absolutely necessary to resign myself to believe . . . that he may be a participant in these shocking morals. . . . Is it for this reason that he is so anxious to see the same morals attributed to Arthur Rimbaud, and undoubtedly to Walt Whitman.

Je ne puis . . . impossible: I am unable to collaborate in your *Whitman*. It is impossible.

Toute . . . disposition: The artists acted as if all the positive work of the XIXth century did not exist. Think about how few of them were interested in the present, and sympathetic to that which was changing and transforming before their eyes; the new things that the train, for example, brought with it. There were only the economists and the socialists who tried somehow to express all this in their lingo, and nobody (except Whitman) understood how we were put in touch with our brothers all over the planet.

In Whitman, Claudel found an early precursor of his own effort to embrace and penetrate the "oeuvre positive" of the twentieth century. Whitman's American admirers must have recognized Claudel as a disciple of Whitman's cosmopolitan and futuristic vision when, after the foundation of the Whitman Society in 1927, Claudel was invited to give a discourse on the American bard.[50]

The early impression that Whitman made upon Claudel continued into old age. On the last page of the journal he kept during the First World War, Claudel attached a picture of Walt Whitman and the words "Hélas! encore plus aujourd'hui. 7 juillet 1940" just opposite some "vers applicables à la guerre actuelle," which express the need for faith amid disaster and humiliation.[51] During the difficult years of World War II, Claudel no doubt found both consolation and inspiration in Whitman's message of faith, reconciliation, and international goodwill. Even in Claudel's final years, Whitman remained a vital presence in Claudel's life. Only a few years before his death, in an article entitled "L'Enthousiasme," Claudel still remembered the cosmic joy and exhilaration, "le feu sacré," that he had found in Whitman's work as a very young man.[52]

B. *André Spire and Charles Péguy*

Charles Péguy and André Spire seconded the attempt of Paul Claudel to renew the form of French verse. Like Claudel, these two poets experimented with a rhythmic and organic *verset* that closely resembles Whitman's free verse.

André Spire, one of the theorists of vers-libre, reveals in his major work, *Versets* (1908), a style and vision that are close to Whitman. Spire acknowledges his relation to Whitman by making a line from "Song of the Open Road" an epigraph to the poem "Migraines": "Dorénavant . . . je ne postpose plus" (Henceforth . . . I postpone no more).[53] The poem has an organic form, a simple and unadorned language, and a feeling for the robustness and resources of the human body that are suggestive of Whitman:

Hélas! . . . 1940: Alas, even more so today. 7 July 1940.

J'ai voulu vivre
De tout mon corps, de mes bras, de mes
muscles,
Tant que tu étais jeune, joyeux,
O mon corps.
(p. 64)

Throughout the volume, Spire expresses a similarly Whitmanian vision: the glorification of loafing in "Paix sociale,"

Sur la rivière, sur la belle rivière,
Je flânais, je musais. . . .
(p. 40),

the love of the natural and revolt against artifice in "Dilettantes,"

Regardez le ciel, mes amis!
Regardez les champs, et les arbres;
Et puis regardez, regardez
Vos mains, vos vases et vos robes!
(p. 125),

and the open road theme of such poems as "Seul" and "Vagabondage."

Although there is no evidence that Charles Péguy had any direct acquaintance with Whitman's work, the rhythmic and Biblical style and the social and mystic themes of his writing have sometimes provoked comparison with the American poet.[54] In his attempt to renew the language and subject matter of verse, Péguy, like Claudel and Spire, participated in the attempt to revive the tradition of Hugo in France; and Whitman's work provided an important impetus in this revival. Most of Péguy's major works appeared after 1910, when Whitman's innovative style and vision had already been absorbed into

---

J'ai . . . corps: I wanted to live/ With all my body, my arms, my muscles,/ As long as you were young, joyous,/ O my body. ("Migraines")

Sur . . . musais: On the river, on the beautiful river,/ I loafed, I idled. . . . ("Social Peace")

Regardez . . . robes: Look at the sky, my friends!/ Look at the fields, and the trees;/ And then look, look at/ Your hands, your jars and your clothes. ("Dilettantes")

the mainstream of French literature. Even without direct antecedents in Whitman's work, Péguy's prose poems, along with the *versets* of Claudel and Spire, were a part of the current of Whitmanism in France in the late nineteenth and early twentieth centuries.

III. The Renewal of Life

In his book *Propos critiques* (1912), Georges Duhamel placed the new generation of French writers, which included the Abbaye writers René Arcos and Charles Vildrac as well as such Abbaye associates as Jules Romains, Georges Chennevière, and Luc Durtain, under the aegis of Walt Whitman. Opening his study with Gide's well-known comment on Charles-Louis Philippe, "Le temps de la douceur et du dilettantisme est passé. Maintenant il faut des barbares,"[55] Duhamel goes on to name Whitman as one of the "barbarians" who is most important for the new French writers. Whitman had himself identified with Michelet's cult of the barbarian: with the revival of a similar spirit at the turn of the century, it is no surprise that Whitman's "barbaric yawp" would find enthusiastic auditors among those French writers who were seeking a renewal in both literature and life.

A. *The Abbaye*

For the writers associated with the Abbaye, as for Whitman, a return to the barbaric meant breaking through the formalism and convention of civilization to re-establish a more intimate contact between man and man and between man and nature. Commenting on the new generation of writers, the Abbaye poet Charles Vildrac observed: "Enfin, dans des genres différents et avec des personnalités différentes, les plus récents écrivains novateurs révèlent, tous plus ou moins comme le fait Whitman, une tendance généreuse à déplacer, renouveler, et émouvoir les rapports de l'homme à l'homme, et de l'homme à la nature."[56] In their attempt to renew contact with man

---

Le temps . . . barbares: The time of gentleness and dilettantism is over. Now we must have barbarians. (*Critical Propositions*)

Enfin . . . nature: Finally, in different genres and with different personalities, the most recent, innovative writers reveal, all more or less like Whitman, a generous tendency to alter, renew, and arouse the relations between man and man, and between man and nature.

and nature in both literature and life, the Abbaye writers represented a continuation and reaffirmation of that movement away from the formal elegance and shadowy substance of Symbolist writing toward the kind of direct, real, and human art that had been advocated by the Naturist group. As Bidal says of these writers in her book *Les Ecrivains de l'Abbaye*: "Plus de beautés de detail affectionnées par les Symbolistes; plus d'art savamment ouvragé. Plus de 'clairs-obscurs' propices à la rêverie: le but n'est plus de provoquer des états d'âme sans les orienter, mais de toucher l'homme, et de décupler son ardeur de vivre."[57] In their effort to touch man and to liberate him into a new ardour for life, the Abbaye group, like so many of the French writers of the new generation, found inspiration in the life and writings of Whitman.

The Abbaye was in many ways an attempt to put into practice the fraternal and communal ideals that Whitman expressed in his poetry. Neither a political nor an aesthetic school, the Abbaye was rather an artistic community modeled on the example of Rabelais' Abbaye de Thélème. In 1906, a group of artists, which included the writers Georges Duhamel, René Arcos, and Charles Vildrac, the painter Albert Gleizes, and the musician Henri Doyen, bought an old house in Creteil. By printing and selling books, these artists hoped to make their living at the same time that they preserved their artistic independence. Although the Abbaye failed as a financial venture in 1908, the fraternal spirit of the group continued to link the artists in their personal lives and in their works.

It was Léon Bazalgette who did most to spread Whitman's humanitarian and fraternal message among this group of writers.[58] Speaking of the Abbaye, Duhamel says: "C'est à Bazalgette que nous devons d'aimer Whitman."[59] In both Bazalgette's work and in his person, the Abbaye writers found something of Walt Whitman. As Duhamel says of Bazalgette's introduction into the Abbaye group:

Plus . . . vivre: No more beauty of detail so loved by the Symbolists; no more learnedly wrought art. No more "lights and darks" so propitious to reverie: the goal is no longer to induce moods of the soul without orienting them, but to touch man and to increase his ardor for living. (*The Abbey Writers*)

C'est . . . Whitman: It is to Bazalgette that we owe our love for Whitman.

"Léon Bazalgette, présenté par je ne sais plus lequel de nous, fut accueilli fraternellement. Il venait de publier au Mercure de France la traduction des *Feuilles d'Herbes*. Dans son regard, dans sa franche poignée de main, dans sa voix chaleureuse, il nous semblait retrouver quelque chose de l'humanité whitmanienne et nous n'avions pas tort."[60]

In an article on modern poetry, the Abbaye writer René Arcos pointed up the importance of Léon Bazalgette's translation of Whitman not only for the Abbaye group, but for the whole new generation of French writers: "Quelques-uns, parmi les nouveaux poètes, ont certainement été touchés par la poésie robuste et si humaine de Whitman qui leur a été révélée par l'admirable traduction que nous en a donnée Léon Bazalgette. Il y a dans Whitman une pureté et une violence originelles."[61] As Arcos' comment might suggest, with the publication of Bazalgette's *Feuilles d'Herbe* in 1909, Whitman fully entered the mainstream of French poetry.

Although the Abbaye was not a literary school, the writers shared a common poetic creed: "Que le poème soit une introduction à la vie poétique."[62] For the writers of the Abbaye, as for Whitman, the end of art was the renewal of life; art came from and led back to the "poetic" life. It was in their attempt to make poetry an initiation into the poetic life that the Abbaye writers found a most instructive model in Whitman. According to Duhamel, "Il n'y a sans doute pas, dans le temps actuels, de plus grand introducteur à la vie poétique que Whitman. Il a devancé tous les efforts contemporains dans ce sens. Son exemple est intimidant et généreux."[63] The Abbaye writers were

---

Léon . . . tort: I no longer remember which one of us introduced Léon Bazalgette, but he was welcomed fraternally. He had just published his translation of *Leaves of Grass* in the Mercure de France. In his glance, in his frank handshake, in his warm voice, it seemed to us that he recovered something of Whitman's humanity, and we were not mistaken.

Quelques-uns . . . originelles: Some of the new poets were affected by the robust and very human poetry of Whitman, which was revealed to them by the admirable translation that Léon Balzalgette gave to us. In Whitman, there is an original purity and force.

Il n'y a . . . généreux: At the present time, there is, without a doubt, no greater initiator into the poetic life than Whitman. He has surpassed all the contemporary efforts in this direction. His example is intimidating and generous.

particularly inspired by the Adamic and childlike stance of such poems as "There Was a Child Went Forth." Echoing Duhamel's words on Whitman, Charles Vildrac declares:

"Plus que jamais ce semble être le rôle du poète d'initier, d'introduire à la vie poétique. Walt Whitman y parvient pleinement; et nous nous plaisons à trouver une définition du poète dans cette page où il dit:

" 'Il y avait une fois un enfant qui sortait.' N'est pas qui veut cet enfant-là. Mais tout le monde peut apprendre de lui ce consentement et cette ferveur sans lesquels on ne sait même pas s'éblouir du soleil."[64]

It is only natural that the Abbaye writers were attracted by Whitman's Adamic vision; for this vision, along with the cult of the barbarian, had roots in the sense of rebirth and of a new age of man aroused by the Revolutionary period in both France and America.

In their fundamental concern with moral and humanitarian renewal, the Abbaye group sometimes accorded greater importance to Whitman's life than to his writings. This emphasis is in part due to Bazalgette's laudatory biography of Whitman, which appeared before his translation of the works. Speaking of Bazalgette's Whitman biography, Duhamel says: "Le même homme qui a mené à bien la plus pieuse, la plus respectueuse des traductions, a compris qu'il ne fallait pas ignorer la vie d'un écrivain qui voulut que ses actes demeurassent ses plus beaux poèmes. L'histoire que, grâce à Bazalgette, nous en connaissons est bien celle d'un héros."[65]

Like Bazalgette, the Abbaye writers regarded Whitman's life as his most heroic and poetic creation. As Duhamel says: "Whitman eût, sans en tirer avantage d'ailleurs, d'autre motifs d'orgueil que ses

---

Plus . . . soleil: More than ever, the role of the poet seems to be to initiate into, to introduce to the poetic life. Whitman fully succeeds; and we are pleased to find a definition of the poet on the page where he says: "There Was a Child Went Forth." It is not a question of who wants to be this child. But from him, all the world can learn this consent and this fervor without which one cannot even be dazzled by the sun.

La même . . . héros: The same man who brought out the most reverent and respectful translation, understood that one could not ignore the life of a poet who wanted his acts to remain his most beautiful poems. The history that, thanks to Bazalgette, we know is certainly that of a hero.

Whitman . . . titre: Whitman had, without turning it to his account, more reasons to be proud than just his admirable poetic impulses: for this reason, he is most dear to us.

admirables élans poétiques: il nous est, à ce titre, grandement cher."[66] And in an article entitled "La Leçon de Walt Whitman," Vildrac seconds Duhamel's estimation: "Il est d'abord un homme et voilà son plus beau titre."[67] It is in Whitman's "leçon de beauté agissante" that Vildrac finds Whitman's greatest contribution to the new generation of French writers. If it was Whitman's form that most attracted the early Symbolists and his substance that most attracted Gide and the Naturist group, it was Whitman's "poetic" life that most inspired the Abbaye writers.

Since the Abbaye writers made little distinction between art and life, slipping with relative facility from one into the other and back again, the primary lesson of life and living, of "beauté agissante," that they learned from Whitman was quickly transformed into a significant Whitmanian impulse in their work. Vildrac suggests the nature of this impulse when he says of himself and his fellow writers:

"L'oeuvre du barde de Manhattan s'implante chez nous comme un grand arbre du nouveau monde . . . quelle salutaire senteur de nature, quel joyeux amour, quelle grandeur et quel renouveau. Tout y est fait pour nous conquérir: gaîté, bonté, héroisme, indépendence, et aussi ce robuste optimisme qui fait partie de notre santé morale. C'est dans l'heureuse destinée de notre race d'aimer et d'assimiler de tels apports, d'exalter de telles richesses et de les recréer avec son génie propre."[68]

It is precisely in their lyrics of nature and love, their mood of humanity and good will, gaiety and optimism that the writers of the Abbaye assimilated and recreated Whitman according to their own genius.

B. *René Arcos*

In the poetry that René Arcos was writing during his years of association with L'Abbaye, Arcos' embrace of evolution and natural

---

Il est . . . titre: He is first of all a man, and that is his most beautiful title. ("The Lesson of Walt Whitman")

L'oeuvre . . . propre: The work of the Manhattan bard implants itself here like a large tree from the new world . . . what a wholesome scent of nature, what joyous love, what grandeur and what renewal. Everything is made to overpower us: gaiety, kindness, heroism, independence, and also this robust optimism that is part of our moral health. It is in the happy destiny of our race to love and to absorb such contributions, to exalt such riches, and to recreate them according to our own genius.

law is frequently reminiscent of Whitman. For example, in *La Tragédie des espaces*, which was published by the Abbaye in 1908, Arcos expresses the idea that the poët should write in accordance with universal law:

Notre art?
Nous le voulons en rapport avec l'évolution
latente de toutes les choses.
(p. 13)[69]

These words echo Whitman's idea that the poet is to write in accordance with "the laws that pursue and follow time" (1855 Preface, *LG*, p. 716).

In expressing in *La Tragédie des espaces* and later volumes his mystic sense of the individual's continuity and communion with all things, Arcos may have remembered certain images and motifs from Whitman. For example, *Ce qui naît*, which appeared in 1911, opens with an epigraph, "Vous êtes là, mes doux amis, et je vous vois"; and a "Dédicace,"

J'ai chaud de vos coeurs
qui brûlent ensemble
à l'entour,[70]

in which Arcos, like Whitman, confidentially addresses the reader. Throughout *Ce qui naît* Arcos expresses his sense of continuity with time and his robust confidence in self and world in the same mood of boisterous "giantism" that is so characteristic of Whitman's pose. In "Une Lourdeur sentie à peine," he boasts:

Je suis tout ce qui dure
Le temps c'est moi.

Notre . . . choses: Our art?/ We would like it to be in rapport with the latent evolution of all things. (*The Tragedy of Space*)

Vous êtes . . . vois: You are there my gentle friends, and I see you. (*What is Born*)

J'ai . . . l'entour: I am warmed by your hearts/ that burn together/ all around. ("Dedication")

Je suis . . . moi: I am everything that lasts/ Time is me./ I am larger each minute./ My unlimited size is a number of days/ and each new day makes me a new being,/ even each moment makes me another self. ("A Scarcely Felt Heaviness")

Je suis plus grand chaque minute.
Ma taille illimitée est un nombre de jours
et chaque nouveau jour me fait un nouvel être,
même chaque moment me fait un autre moi.

In voicing his joyous optimism, Arcos was particularly drawn to Whitman's Adamic stance. He expresses a Whitmanian mood of gay, Adamic confidence in "Oh! la dernière nuit":

Il m'est donné d'être naif jusqu'à aimer
....
Je marche en riant,
mon pas se retient de danser.
La terre sous mon pas vibre comme un
tremplin.
....
Si je suis tout ce que je sais,
je contiens tout ce que je vois.
(Ce qui naît)

Again, we hear the voice of Whitman in such poems as "There Was a Child Went Forth" and in such lines as the following from "Song of Myself":

The press of my foot to the earth springs
a hundred affections.
(253)

A few years later, in his article on the modern poets, Arcos would include this passage among the several passages from *Leaves of Grass* which he cited to illustrate Whitman's humanitarian sense of sympathy and identification with all things.[71]

Although Arcos cultivated Whitman's optimistic and life-embracing mood in his own writings, he also reveals some of the tenacity of France's classical heritage when, in his article on the modern poets, he objects to the unbridled form of Whitman's verse.

Il m'est . . . vois: I am gifted with being innocent enough to love/ . . . I walk smiling,/ my step holds back from dancing./ The earth under my feet vibrates like a trampoline./ . . . If I am all that I know,/ I contain all that I see. ("Oh! The Last Night")

Citing Boileau's dictum, "Qui ne sut se borner ne sut jamais écrire," Arcos finds fault with Whitman: "Il semble bien que Walt Whitman ait trop méprisé l'art."[72] Arcos himself wrote in vers-libre, but his verse is tighter and more crafted than Whitman's free verse. At times, however, Arcos employs a long line that is reminiscent of Whitman. For example, in such lines as the following from *Ce qui naît*,

> Dans le balancement, qui ne cesse, des flots;
> les îlots à fleurs d'eau . . .
> ("Dans le balancement, qui ne cesse, des flots"),

the muscular and organic rhythm parallels Whitman's similar evocation of the sea in "Out of the Cradle Endlessly Rocking."

Although Arcos' Whitmanian antecedents are most evident in *La Tragédie des espaces* and *Ce qui naît*, in the volume of poems entitled *Le Sang d'autres* (1918), which he wrote after the war, Arcos may again have remembered Whitman. These war poems express a human sympathy and compassion and an optimistic faith in the progress of mankind which suggest that Arcos, like so many of the French writers who gave literary accounts of their war experiences, found inspiration in Whitman's *Drum-Taps* poems.

C. Charles Vildrac

In the poetry that Vildrac was writing during his years of association with the Abbaye, the human and social atmosphere is frequently reminiscent of Whitman. In *Les Poèmes de l'Abbaye*, for example, Vildrac defines the social role of the poet in language and imagery that recall Whitman:

> Et nous essaierons d'ouvrir tous les yeux,
> Et de greffer l'amour au coeur des hommes;

Qui . . . l'art: He who cannot restrain himself cannot write. . . . It seems to me that Whitman had too much contempt for art.

Dans . . . d'eau: In the endless rocking of the waves, the isles at water level . . . ("In the Endless Rocking of the Waves")

Et nous . . . prêtres: And we will try to open all eyes,/ And to graft love to the hearts of men;/ And we will try to build the Best,/ And we will give joy to the eyes./ We will point out the bad priests/ Bad temples and bad gods;/ And who knows if we might not be/ For better temples, better priests. ("The Abbey")

Et nous essaierons de bâtir du Mieux,
Et nous donnerons de la joie aux yeux.

Nous montrerons du doigt les mauvais prêtres
Des temples mauvais et des mauvais dieux;
Et qui sait si nous ne pourrions être
Pour de meilleurs temples, de meilleurs
prêtres.

("L'Abbaye," p. 44)[73]

In his initial repetitions, parallelisms, and reiterations, Vildrac reveals a stylistic debt to Whitman. His concept of the religious role of the poet recalls Whitman's idea of the poet as the new priest of man; and his description of the poet as an initiator into new vision is reminiscent of the Adamic mode, the attitude of "consentement" and "ferveur" that Vildrac associated with Whitman.

In *Les Poèmes de l'Abbaye*, Vildrac also uses themes of fraternity and the open road that are reminiscent of Whitman. For example, after developing the theme of the poet as the celebrator of the future in his poem "Mais non, tout nous étouffe," Vildrac ends with an exhortation to his readers to depart "en route"; this exhortation clearly echoes the road and companionship themes of such poems as "Song of the Open Road":

Tenons-nous par la main, et allons seuls,
mes frères;
Les bouviers sauront bien où nous serons
passés.
Allons seuls dans l'exaltation et dans la
joie.
De chercher un peu de neuve lumière.

(p. 42)

In the poem "Les Idées," Vildrac makes a similar use of such Whitmanian images as the processional, the march, and the open road:

Tenons . . . lumière: Let us join hands, and go alone, my brothers;/ The herdsmen will certainly know where we have gone./ Let us go alone in exaltation and in joy./ To look for a little new light. ("Everything Stifles Us")

Les Idées sont en route
   Depuis longtemps.
....
Elles s'en vont, épiques, vers demain,
Et nous tendent leurs mains.
(p. 59; p. 62)

And the poem ends with a vision of love and hope,

Nous les prendrons, ces mains, et nous
   ferons la chaîne
Immense et palpitante d'amour et d'espoir
(p. 62),

which is reminiscent of Whitman's vision of the sleepers flowing "hand in hand over the whole earth" ("The Sleepers," 162).

Vildrac reveals further Whitmanian roots in the theme of continual rediscovery and renewal that animates his series of prose sketches *Découvertes* (1912). Like Whitman, Vildrac discovers in the Adamic vision of the child the perpetual renewal of himself and the world. In the title piece, "Découvertes," for example, Vildrac presents the world through the eyes of a seven-year-old child: "Son corps savait les contacts avec l'herbe, le sable, la terre labourée, la pierre, la paille, les genoux d'hommes."[74] In these lines, as throughout the volume, Vildrac may have remembered the Adamic mode of such poems as "'There Was a Child Went Forth" and "Out of the Cradle Endlessly Rocking."

Although Vildrac's debt to Whitman is most evident in such early volumes as *Poèmes de l'Abbaye* and *Découvertes*, in the hopeful and fraternal vision that runs through such later works as *Le Livre d'amour* (1920) and the play *Le Pâquebot Tenacity* (1920), Vildrac continues to reveal his Whitmanian antecedents. Ultimately, in the children's

---

Les idées . . . mains: Ideas have been on the road/ For a long time./ . . . They go forth, epic, toward tomorrow,/ And hold out their hands to us. ("Ideas")

Nous . . . d'espoir: We will take hold of these hands, and we will make a chain/ Of love and hope, immense and palpitating.

Son corps . . . d'hommes: His body had been in contact with the grass, the sand, the tilled soil, stone, straw, and the knees of men. (*Discoveries*)

stories *L'Ile rose* and *Les Lunettes du lion*, Vildrac turned his talents to writing not only as the child but for the child.

It was Vildrac's Abbaye associate, Georges Duhamel, who first pointed up Vildrac's debt to Whitman. In the humanitarian impulse, the theme of love and companionship, that animates all of Vildrac's works, Duhamel found evidence that "le souffle dont s'est enivré le grand Whitman a franchi l'Océan."[75] In remarking the Whitmanian antecedents of his compatriot, Duhamel might very well have mentioned himself, for of all the Abbaye associates, it is Duhamel who presents the clearest indication that Whitman's spirit had indeed crossed the ocean.

D. *Georges Duhamel*

In *Propos critiques*, Duhamel describes the two primary impulses that motivated himself and the other Abbaye writers: "Etre un homme dans toute la force du terme, et connaître le monde. Plus simplement: être et connaître."[76] Discovering and possessing the resources of joy in oneself and the world: this is the constant theme of Duhamel's life as well as his writing. In Whitman, Duhamel found not only a "grand introducteur à la vie poétique," but also a valuable model in his own attempt to give in his writings a simple, direct, and human account of man and the world.

It is Whitman's lesson of joy and faith, acceptance and optimism, companionship and community, that is the controlling theme of the poetry that Duhamel wrote during his Abbaye years. The poems in such volumes as *Des Légendes, des batailles* (1907), *L'Homme en tête* (1909), and *Selon ma loi* (1910) all reflect a Whitmanian impulse. But it is the poems of *Compagnons* (1912) that most clearly reveal the "Whitmanism" of Duhamel's early years.

As the title might suggest, *Compagnons* is animated by a humanitarian and fraternal impulse that is reminiscent of Whitman in word, tone, and image. In the opening section, "Visages," Duhamel probably recalled the title and theme of Whitman's "Faces." In this section, Duhamel moves from a retreat into nature back into an urban

---

Le souffle . . . l'Océan: The breath that intoxicated the great Whitman has crossed the Ocean.

Etre . . . connaître: To be a man in the full sense of the word, and to know the world. More simply: to be and to know.

setting and the company of men. He begins with a Whitmanian exhortation to the reader:

> A vous donc! Acceptez l'homme qui se
> présente
> Avec cette figure anxieuse et troublée.
> Acceptez l'homme qui peut mesurer votre âme,
> Et qui sait ce que vaut le toucher d'une
> main.
> Acceptez-moi, compagnons aux mille visages!
> Car j'ai quitté de grands et d'émouvants
> spectacles
> Pour ce spectacle que vous êtes.
> ("Ode à quelques hommes," p. 13)[77]

Throughout *Compagnons* there is the same tone of urgency and excitement, the same drive toward companionship and contact that propel the poet in *Leaves of Grass*. "La Dette," for example, contains these Whitmanian lines:

> Vous, mes compagnons! O vous, tous les
> hommes!
> Laissez-moi saisir ce bonheur perdu,
> Laissez, et si mes mains tendues ne me
> suffisent,
> Aidez-moi donc pour l'atteindre et le
> posséder.
> (p. 83)

And in "L'Heure désirable," Duhamel urges his readers to depart "en route" in words that again echo Whitman: "Allons! venez, venez avec moi. . . . Suivez-moi, suivez-moi!" (pp. 97-98).

A vous . . . êtes: To you then! Accept the man who presents himself/ With this anxious and troubled face./ Accept the man who can measure your soul,/ And who knows the value of a touch of the hand./ Accept me, companions of a thousand faces!/ Because I have left grand and moving spectacles/ For this spectacle that is you. ("Ode to Some Men")

Vous . . . posséder: You, my companions! O you, all men!/ Allow me to seize this lost happiness,/ Allow, and if my outstretched hands are not sufficient,/ Help me, then, to attain and possess it. ("The Debt")

Allons . . . suivez-moi: Let's go! Come, come with me. . . . Follow me, follow me. ("The Desired Hour")

Despite these rather public exhortations to the "en masse," Duhamel's aspiration toward fraternal communion tended to be exclusive rather than inclusive, individual rather than epic. "A Un Pauvre Homme," for example, is addressed to *a* man rather than to men in general. Duhamel expresses an intimacy and proximity with the individual that is clearly reminiscent of Whitman:

> Je te donne donc de parler,
> Je te donne d'être toi-même
> Et de savoir ce que tu sais.
>
> ....
>
> Et tes actes et tes paroles
>
> ....
>
> Je les surveille de si près,
> Avec tant de sollicitude.
>
> (pp. 22-23)

Like other writers of the Abbaye, Duhamel was most moved by the private, individual rapports between man and man, and consequently the tone of his poems comes closer to the personal and confessional mood of Whitman's *Calamus* poems than to the public and cosmic sentiment of "Salut Au Monde" and "Song of the Open Road." In "Le Royaume intermédiare," for example,

> Ce silence est mieux que nous-mêmes
> La règne de notre bonheur.
>
> Nos regards ne se cherchent pas:
> Deux soucis différents, sans doute,
> Attachent nos yeux et nos mains
>
> (p. 68),

Duhamel's private and even secretive mood is reminiscent of such Calamus poems as "A Glimpse":

Je te . . . sollicitude: I let you speak, then,/ I let you be yourself/ and know what you know./ . . . . And your acts and your words/ . . . I watch over them so closely,/ With so much solicitude. ("To a Poor Man")

Ce silence . . . mains: This silence is better than ourselves/ The reign of our happiness./ Our looks do not seek each other out: Two different worries, no doubt,/ Attach our eyes and our hands. ("Middle Kingdom")

A glimpse through an interstice caught,

. . . .

Of a youth who loves me and whom I love,
silently approaching and seating himself
near, that he may hold me by the hand,
A long while amid the noises of coming and
going, of drinking and oath and smutty
jest,
There we two, content, happy in being
together, speaking little, perhaps not
a word.

(1; 3-5)

We find a similarly Whitmanian voice in "Voyages":

Homme, te voici, pour une heure,
Pour cette heure que nous vivons,
Le député du vaste monde;
Et je ne te connaissais pas.

. . . .

Et pourtant, l'hiver à venir,
Quand tu seras seul en voiture
Avec deux cris de bise aux joues,
Je sais qu'il y aura quelqu'un
Tout près de toi, dans ta voiture.

(p. 57; p. 59)

In this poem as throughout *Compagnons*, Duhamel expresses a sense of phantom presence and the mysterious rapports between individuals, even strangers, which is very close to Whitman.

Duhamel seeks to achieve a similarly intimate and mysterious rapport with his readers. Again, Whitman provided an important analogue. For example, in the poem "Ceux que je connais," Duhamel makes this Whitmanian address to the reader:

Homme . . . voiture: Man, here you are, for an hour,/ For this hour that we live,/ The deputy of a vast world;/ And I do not know you./ . . . And yet, next winter,/ When you are alone in a car/ With two blasts of wind on your cheeks,/ I know that there will be someone/ Very close to you, in your car. ("Voyages")

Vous qui êtes mes compagnons,
Les figures que j'aperçois parmi la foule,
Sachez qu'en vous je me salue,
En vous qui me portez toujours.

Depuis le jour qui nous mit en présence,
J'ai pris place dans votre esprit ou votre
coeur,
Et chacun de vous a reçu
Le même homme, différemment.
(p. 103)

Although the poem begins in the more public mood of Whitman's "Salut Au Monde," it ends with a focus on the individual reader that is reminiscent of the *Calamus* poem "Whoever You Are Holding Me Now in Hand," in which Whitman addresses the reader in a similar tone:

Or if you will, thrusting me beneath your
clothing,
Where I may feel the throbs of your heart or
rest upon your hip,
Carry me when you go forth over land or sea;
For thus merely touching you is enough,
is best,
And thus touching you would I silently
sleep and be carried eternally.
(22-26)

Like Whitman, Duhamel also rejects the merge with the "en masse" to thrust himself into the heart of the individual reader.

In his concept of literature as a personal and vital communion between reader and writer, Duhamel found an inspirational model in Whitman's "Whoever You Are Holding Me Now in Hand." In *Propos critiques*, Duhamel urges his readers to spread the "poetic life" among

---

Vous qui . . . différemment: You who are my companions,/ The faces that I perceive among the crowd,/ Know that in you I salut myself,/ In you who carry me always./ Since the day that brought us together,/ I have taken a place in your mind or your heart,/ And each of you has received/ The same man, differently. ("Those Whom I Know") their friends: "Si tu les crois découragés, diminués, honteux, lève-toi et lis-leur ces strophes de Walt Whitman. . . . 'Oh! qui que vous soyez.' "[78] After citing the poem in its entirety, Duhamel remarks: "Citer, c'est faire en quelque sorte un acte de reconnaissance. Et quelle reconnaissance n'aurais-je pas pour ce poète qui exprime si complètement, si fortement tout ce qu'il est urgent de dire à cette minute même."[79] For Duhamel, as for Gide and his group, the poem "Whoever You Are Holding Me Now in Hand" was a consummate expression of the extra-literary, life-giving function of art.

In his attempt to make literature both an introduction to the poetic life and a fraternal communion between man and man, Duhamel strove to keep his writing close to the rhythms of the voice and breath. Here again, Whitman provided a model. In his article on Mallarmé and Whitman, Duhamel called attention to Whitman's attempt to duplicate in his writing the rhythms of the speech and the breath. He referred to Whitman as the "puissant introducteur à la vie poétique" who left "une oeuvre imparfaite et confuse qui est comme le procès-verbal fidèle d'une vie de cordialité, de dévouement, d'entreprise."[80] In his own writing, Duhamel attempted to capture the rhythms of Whitman's effusive spoken style.

The example of Whitman's rhythmic verse also provided an instructive model for *Notes sur la technique poétique*, which Duhamel wrote in collaboration with Charles Vildrac in 1910. Although Duhamel and Vildrac set out to explain vers-libre to the public, they define, through their reliance on syllabic count and the caesura, a theory of vers-libre that is in fact more conservative and "Latin" than the freer and more Whitmanian procedures of the verse they were writing at the time. However, their insistence on the idea that form must follow content and their definition of the rhythmic and musical base of poetry indicate the extent to which Whitman's organic and rhythmic theory of verse had been absorbed into the French literary tradition.

Si . . . soyez: If you believe them discouraged, diminished, ashamed, rise up and read them these stanzas from Walt Whitman. . . . "Whoever You Are."

Citer . . . même: To cite, is in some ways to acknowledge. And what acknowledgement would I not have for this poet who expresses so completely, so strongly, all that it is urgent to say at this very time.

Although Duhamel is most Whitmanian in the works that he wrote during his Abbaye years, his later works continue to reveal his antecedents in Whitman. For example, Duhamel may have had Whitman's "wound-dresser" in mind when, in the collection of poems entitled *Vie des martyrs* (1917), he recorded his own experiences as a doctor on the front during World War I. In the poems of *Vie des martyrs*, Duhamel expresses a sympathy, a compassion, and an acceptance of human suffering that clearly recall the voice of Whitman in his war diaries and in the poetry of *Drum-Taps*.

When Léon Bazalgette died in 1929, Duhamel commented on the continued presence of Bazalgette and Whitman in his life. He says of Bazalgette: "Il me semble qu'il a toujours été là. Son image dans ma pensée est mariée à celle du grand Whitman; les deux hommes comparaissent, bras dessus, bras dessous, quand j'appelle les plus émouvants souvenirs de ma jeunesse."[81] Although Duhamel turned to novel writing in his later years, his work continues to reveal Whitman's presence. It is Whitman's lesson of acceptance, love, and human community that is the recurrent theme of the two cycles of novels, *Vie et aventures de Salavin* and *Chronique des Pasquier*, which Duhamel wrote in his later years.

E. *Jules Romains and Unanimism*

Jules Romains was a frequent visitor of the Abbaye group, and in 1908 the Abbaye published his first book of poems, *La Vie unanime*. Because of this early connection between the Abbaye and Romains, the Abbaye writers have frequently been associated with Romains and his philosophy of unanimism. It was through the Abbaye group that Romains gained his first acquaintance with Bazalgette's translation of *Leaves of Grass*. In a recent tribute to Whitman, Romains recalls the early enthusiasm that he and his Abbaye friends had for the work of the American poet:

"I remember the time when my friends and I—we were still very young—discovered *Leaves of Grass* in Bazalgette's translation. (I was not to read the original text until much later.) I must add that we were quite prepared to welcome this book, for we had read some time before

---

Il me . . . jeunesse: It seems to me that he was always there. His image in my thoughts is linked with that of the great Whitman; the two men appear, arm in arm, when I recall the most moving memories of my youth.

the substantial study which Bazalgette had devoted to Whitman. Our enthusiasm was aroused by the fact that the American poet renewed the relationship between poetry and man, a relationship which so many poets in recent times had done their best to break."[82]

Unlike his Abbaye friends, however, who were most inspired by Whitman's expression of the "simple separate person," it was in Whitman's vision of the ensemble, the "en masse," that Jules Romains found an important analogue for the philosophy of unanimism which underlies all of his work.

Romains and his disciple Georges Chennevière first used the word *unanimisme* in 1905 to express a basically mystic and poetic vision of men in groups. For Romains and Chennevière, an *unanime* was the collective spirit, or soul, which animates and unifies any human group: a couple, a city, the cosmos. In shifting the focus from the individual to the collectivity, from a natural to a social and urban setting, unanimism was preeminently a philosophy of the modern world. Quite appropriately, it was among those writers who gave an artistic voice to the predominantly human milieu of the city that Romains found his models: he saluted Whitman, Zola, Baudelaire, and Hugo as precursors of unanimism.[83]

In his attempt to formulate and express his unanimist philosophy, Romains may have remembered the images of human community, the ensemble, and the "en masse" which animate all of Whitman's work. Although the "en masse" was an early and constant theme of Whitman's work, in his later years he turned toward a more concentrated focus on the human aggregate that truly anticipated the work of Jules Romains. In the 1872 Preface to his new volume of poems, Whitman avows his intent to replace the voice of the democratic individual with "the thread-voice, more or less audible, of an aggregated, inseparable, unprecedented, vast, composite, electric *Democratic Nationality*" (*LG*, p. 744). If Whitman never realized this new departure in his own work, Jules Romains did. Whitman knew and acknowledged the French love for solidarity and the ensemble; and it would not have surprised him to know that his "composite, electric" human aggregates would await the hands of a Frenchman to be philosophically defined and artistically realized.

Romains reiterates Whitman's desire to shift the center of attention from the individual to the collectivity: "Un de mes soucis les plus anciens et les plus constants a été justement de chercher *un mode de composition* qui nous permît d'échapper à nos habitudes de vision centrée sur l'individu."[84] It was in *Le Bourg régénéré conte de la vie unanime* (1906) that Romains first attempted a mode of composition in which the central focus was shifted from the individual characters to the collective life and soul of a small town. But, according to Romains, it was *La Vie unanime,* published two years later, that provided the true "émoi initial" for most of his later work.[85]

Although *La Vie unanime* was published by the Abbaye in 1908, one year before the appearance of Bazalgette's translation of Whitman in 1909, the similarities between *La Vie unanime* and *Leaves of Grass* suggest that through his friends, through Bazalgette's 1908 biography of Whitman, and through the translations of Whitman that were regularly appearing in the French reviews, Romains had acquired some general acquaintance with Whitman before he composed his volume of unanimist poems. In fact, as several critics have suggested, it is in the lyric poetry of *La Vie unamine* that Romains reveals his fullest debt to Whitman.[86]

In the poems of *La Vie unanime,* Romains, like Whitman, attempts to change the center of attention from a static, one-dimensional view of the world to the ever-shifting faces of the ensemble. Throughout *La Vie unanime,* Romains expresses, as he ambles in Whitmanian fashion through a modern urban landscape, the multiple impressions of the ensemble in its immediacy, detail, and constant becoming. "Je marche sans passé, sans aieux et sans moi," Romains declares in the poem "Quelqu'un qui n'est pas moi," as he loses his individual self in the collective soul of the world.[87]

Again like Whitman, Romains attempts to shift the focus from the individual to the collectivity by exploring the mystic ties that unite various concentrations of men in an urban setting. The collective soul, or unanime, created by groups of men in the street, in church, in the railroad station, or in the city as a whole, is the constant theme of Romains' poems. For example, in a section entitled "Les Unanimes,"

Un . . . l'individu: One of my oldest and most constant worries was, in fact, to search for *a mode of composition* that permitted us to escape from our habits of vision that are centered on the individual.

Je marche . . . moi: I walk without past, without ancestors, and without myself. ("Someone Who Is Not Me")

Romains says of the shopkeepers lounging on the doorsteps of a Parisian street: "Quelque chose s'est mis à exister soudain" (p. 20). Forgetting their desire to make money in the common desire to get fresh air, the shopkeepers lose their individual selves in the soul of the ensemble. Similarly, in "Une Autre Âme s'avance," Romains describes the unanime that unites a crowded city boulevard:

> Qu'est ce qui transfigure ainsi le boulevard?
> L'allure des passants n'est presque pas
> physique;
> Ce sont plus des mouvements, ce sont des
> rythmes,
> Et je n'ai plus besoin de mes yeux pour les
> voir.
>
> (p. 21)

The mystic ties that unite the shopkeepers and passers-by in Romains' poetry are reminiscent of the "efflux of the soul" in Whitman's "Song of the Open Road":

> What is it I interchange so suddenly with
> strangers?
> What with some driver as I ride on the seat
> by his side?
> What with some fisherman drawing his seine by
> the shore as I walk by and pause?
> What gives me to be free to a woman's and a
> man's good-will? what gives them to be free
> to mine?
>
> The efflux of the soul is happiness, here is
> happiness,
> I think it pervades the open air, waiting at
> all times,
> Now it flows unto us, we are rightly charged.
>
> (101-107)

Quelque . . . soudain: Suddenly, something came into existence. ("The Unanimes")

Qu'est ce qui . . . voir: What is it that so transfigures the boulevard?/ The gait of the passers-by is almost not physical;/ There are no longer movements, there are rhythms,/ And I no longer need my eyes to see them. ("Another Soul Advances")

Although Romains' unanimist vision is more structured and determined than anything in Whitman, his "unanimes" are not much different from Whitman's "ensembles"; and the mystic ties that unite the unanimes are not much different from "the subtle electric fire" that passes between man and man, artist and reader, not only in the *Calamus* poems, but throughout *Leaves of Grass*.

Romains' unanimist impulse has none of the homosexual implications of Whitman's Calamus motif, but his philosophy is in many ways an elaboration of the more public, fraternal dimension of adhesive love that Whitman stressed in his later years. In the 1876 Preface, Whitman defines adhesiveness in words that directly anticipate the unanimist philosophy of Romains:

> I also sent out LEAVES OF GRASS to arouse and set flowing in men's and women's hearts, young and old . . . endless streams of living, pulsating love and friendship, directly from them to myself, now and ever. To this terrible, irrepressible yearning (surely more or less down underneath in most human souls,)—this never-satisfied appetite for sympathy—this universal democratic comradeship—this old, eternal, yet ever-new interchange of adhesiveness, so fitly emblematic of America—I have given in that book, undisguisedly, declaredly, the openest expression.
>
> (*LG*, p. 751)

As one of the few nineteenth-century artists who gave a poetic voice to the mystic and quasi-religious feelings that pass between man and man in a social context, Whitman provides a suggestive analogue for the similarly mystic sense of human community in the work of Jules Romains. In his study *Jules Romains et unanimisme*, André Cuisenier points up the importance of Whitman's precedent for the unanimist writers. Speaking of the unanimist spirit that characterizes the work of Jules Romains and such other poets of the new generation as Charles Vildrac, Georges Duhamel, Georges Chennevière, and Henri Franck, Cuisenier says: "Nulle part encore, au cours du siècle

---

Nulle . . . présence: Nowhere as yet, in the course of the last century, except perhaps in the verse of Whitman, did the song of recognition of man for men break forth, free and spontaneous, expressing the thrill that man feels, no matter where, in the presence of men. (*Jules Romains and Unanimism*) dernier, sauf peut-être dans le vers de Whitman, n'a jaillis, libre et spontané, le chant de reconnaissance de l'homme aux hommes, exprimant le frisson qu'il éprouve, où qu'il soit, en leur présence."[88]

Jules Romains also acknowledged Whitman's importance for the new generation of French writers. In an article on "La Poésie immédiate," Romains says of Georges Duhamel: "Ses vers célèbrent une joie où tout le corps est convié. J'admire en lui un des lyriques de l'organisme, dont le premier fut Whitman, dont les plus puissants se nomment Paul Claudel, Emile Verhaeren, Charles-Louis Philippe, et, déjà, Luc Durtain."[89] In listing the "lyricists of the body" of whom Whitman was the precursor, Romains might well have included himself. Throughout *La Vie unanime* Romains celebrates in lyrics that are frequently reminiscent of Whitman a mystic dimension of physicality and the body. For example, in the following lines from "Dormir sous les feuilles,"

Dormir sous les feuilles,
Le bras replié
Pour poser ma joue

Etre un corps défait
Et presque dissous

. . . .

Et semer à terre
Toutes mes pensées
(p. 185),

Romains not only recalls Whitman's classic posture of loafing on the grass, but also echoes the end of "Song of Myself," in which Whitman joyously describes a similar process of bodily dissolution:

I depart as air, I shake my white locks
at the runaway sun,

Ses vers . . . Durtain: His verse celebrates a joy in which the whole body takes part. I admire in him one of the lyricists of the organism, the first of whom was Whitman, and the strongest of whom are Paul Claudel, Emile Verhaeren, Charles-Louis Philippe, and, already, Luc Durtain. ("Immediate Poetry")

Dormir . . . pensées: To sleep under the leaves,/ Arm bent/ To rest my cheek/ To be a decomposed body/ And almost dissolved/ . . . And to sow the earth with/ All my thoughts. ("To Sleep Under the Leaves")

I effuse my flesh in eddies, and drift it
in lacy jags.

I bequeath myself to the dirt to grow from
the grass I love,
If you want me again look for me under your
boot-soles.
(1337-1340)

At times Romains expresses in words that directly recall Whitman a sense of the spiritual or electric currents that surge through the body. In "Mais, au fond des corps, les cellules," for example, Romains celebrates the physiology of the body and equates physical impulse with the "electricity" of the soul in words reminiscent of Whitman's "I Sing the Body Electric":

Je vous vénère, cellules de mon cerveau.
. . . .
Vous avez fait le flamboiement de mon
cerveau.
C'est votre bourg; je le sens vivre dans
ma tête
En rumeurs, en tournoiements, en feux
électriques,
Comme un tas de fêtes foraines et d'usines.
(pp. 219-220)

In the same poem, Romains echoes Whitman's

Mine is no callous shell,
I have instant conductors all over me
whether I pass or stop,
They seize every object and lead it
harmlessly through me
("Song of Myself," 614-616),

when he describes himself as a "condenseur" of universal energy:

Je vous . . . d'usines: I revere you, cells of my brain./ . . . You have made a blaze in my brain./ It is your borough; I feel it alive in my head/ In clamor, tumult, electric fires,/ Like a group of travelling shows or factories. ("But, Deep in the Body, the Cells")

Je vous imiterai, neurones, je serai
. . . .
Un carrefour joyeux des rythmes unanimes,
Un condenseur de l'énergie universelle;
A mon approche, il jaillira des étincelles.
(p. 220)

In giving a mystic and poetic voice to the energy that vibrates through man and the cosmos, Romains probably found a suggestive model in the poems of Whitman. Both Whitman and Romains anticipate the similar efforts of the Cubists, Futurists, and Surrealists to express artistically the dynamic energy and flow of the universe.

After *La Vie unanime*, Romains' creative output consisted largely of prose. But even in his prose works, he continued to exhibit his Whitmanian antecedents. In the novel *Les Copains* (1913), Romains expresses the comradeship theme of Whitman's verse. Whitmanian sentiments are also evident in the long series of novels entitled *Les Hommes de bonne volonté*, which occupied the final years of Romains' life. In centering his vision upon the group rather than upon the individual, in his mystic sense of the ensemble, in his desire to render the dynamism and flux of life, and in his constant effort to build a relationship of confidence and intimacy with the reader, Romains continued to elaborate and develop in the novels of *Les Hommes de bonne volonté* the Whitmanian strains of *La Vie unanime*.

Through the apparent disorder of *Les Hommes de bonne volonté*, a disorder which is an attempt to duplicate the apparent disorder of life itself, Romains, like Whitman, tries to suggest the "form, union, plan" that animates the whole. Like Whitman, and like Romains' compatriot Laforgue in *Les Fleurs de bonne volonté*, Romains expresses his own faith and the faith of his age in the ultimate triumph of good will: "Les Hommes de Bonne Volonté! Une antique

---

Je vous . . . étincelles: I will imitate you, neurons, I will be/ . . . A joyous crossroads of unanime rhythms,/ A condenser of universal energy;/ At my approach, sparks will fly forth.

Les Hommes . . . pas: Men of Good Will! An ancient blessing is going to seek them out in the crowd and retrieve them . . . so that this world, in which they are the merit and the salt, will not perish. *(Men of Good Will)*

bénédiction va les chercher dans la foule et les recouvre . . . afin que ce monde, dont ils sont la mérite et le sel, ne périsse pas."[90]

In the course of several visits to the United States during the time that he was writing the *Les Hommes de bonne volonté* series, Romains frequently thought and spoke of Whitman. In a recent article, he says: "I discovered with pleasure, thanks to the many conversations I had there at quite different times, that for most American intellectuals, even those who represented entirely different tendencies, Walt Whitman remained specifically the greatest American poet." He expresses disappointment, however, that Whitman is neglected by the American public. At one point, Romains finds himself the single visitor at a Whitman exhibition in New York: "Maybe I had chosen the wrong moment," he says, "and, if I had gone at a different time, I would have had the joy of seeing American crowds pressing in front of all those mementoes of the poet who knew so well how to sing of them."[91] But Romains had not gone to the Whitman exhibition at the wrong moment. At the time of the Whitman centennial in 1955, "America's greatest poet" had still not found the critical, artistic, and popular following that he had found in France even before his death.

IV. Whitmanism in France

The focus of this study has been the major French writers on whom Whitman had impact; but it is essential to bear in mind that during the post-Symbolist period, *whitmanisme* had become a pervasive force in French literature and life. Although it would be difficult to discuss all of the French writers who participated in the wave of *whitmanisme*, a brief look at a few minor figures might suggest some of the dimensions of the Whitman cult in France.

A. *Georges Chennevière*

At times the minor French writers are the best measure of the extent to which Whitman had entered into the very breath and spirit of post-Symbolist French literature. Georges Chennevière, for example, is one of the most Whitmanian of the French writers. A disciple of Jules Romains, Chennevière, in his early years, helped Romains to formulate the doctrine of unanimism. In 1923, Chennevière collaborated with Romains in composing *Le Petit Traité de versification*, in which both poets turn away from the license of vers-librism to define a more rigid theory of versification that adheres to the traditional formalism and classicism of French poetry.

Although Chennevière rejects in theory many of the innovations in the language and form of French poetry—innovations in part inspired by Whitman—in actual practice he is very close to Whitman in the content and in the technique of his verse. In *Poèmes 1911-1918*, Chennevière, like several of the Whitmanian poets of the post-Symbolist period, sets his poetry in an urban and cosmopolitan milieu, where he explores the fraternal and sympathetic bonds between man and man in a modern industrial world. In "Fenêtre," Chennevière joins such other Whitmanian writers as Duhamel, Vildrac, and Romains in exploring that "electric" fellow feeling which passes between strangers in an urban setting:

> Sais-tu, sauras-tu un jour,
> Mon nocturne compagnon,
> Ce que te doit pour ta lampe
> Un passant silencieux
> Dont tu ignores le nom?[92]

In "En Route," Chennevière uses a road image to express Whitman's comradeship theme:

> En route! Le jour va plus vite que nous!
> En route! La joie est pendue à ton cou!
> En route! La vie est si jeune et si belle.
> On chante un air pour tout ce qui n'a pas
> de voix.
> ....
> Ah! si vous pouviez me suivre,
> Voici que j'ai milles vies!

Sais-tu . . . nom: Do you know, will you know one day,/ My nocturnal companion,/ What he owes you for your light/ A silent passer-by/ Whose name you do not know? ("Window")

En route! . . . vies: Let's go! The day is going faster than us!/ Let's go! Joy is hanging around your neck!/ Let's go! Life is so young and so beautiful./ One sings a tune for all who do not have a voice./ . . . Ah! If you could follow me,/ Here I have a million lives! ("Let's Go")

The effusive style of this passage, the exclamations and exhortations that recall Whitman, belie the more conservative principles of versification that Chennevière sets forth in *Le Petit Traité de versification*. Similarly, in the following vision of men in a French café, he uses a participal technique that is reminiscent of Whitman:

> Parlant comme il y a mille ans, et
> comme on parlera plus tard,
> Entrant et sortant, les mêmes toujours,
> cinq ou six ensemble,
> Criant et buvant, les verres passant d'une
> bouche à l'autre.
>
> ("En Route")

In his attempt to find an immediate language that directly expresses the flux of modern life—a language that simultaneously records duration and change, continuity and incessant becoming—Chennevière, like many of the new generation of French writers, found an instructive model in the verse technique of Whitman.

In his biographical introduction to the works of Chennevière, André Cuisenier speaks of "ce sentiment, presque organique, de fraternité, qui animait déjà les vers de Whitman, et qui anime ceux de Chennevière et ses amis."[93] Faced with the growing tendency toward fragmentation and automation in the modern urban world, the new generation of French writers found a heightened relevance in Whitman's message of comradeship and fraternal love. After the terror and destruction of World War I, the modern French writers looked with an even greater intentness to Whitman's message of fraternity and international good feeling. Chennevière's post-war volume of poems, *Appel au monde* (1919), evokes the cosmopolitan spirit of Whitman's "Salut Au Monde!" Throughout the volume, in a Whitmanian tone of intimacy and confidentiality, he attempts to recreate the bonds of fraternal love after the shattering experience of the war:

Parlant . . . l'autre: Speaking like a thousand years ago, and like one will speak in the future,/ Coming and going, always the same ones, five or six together,/ Shouting and drinking, glasses passing from mouth to mouth.

Ce sentiment . . . amis: This almost organic feeling of fraternity that already animated the verse of Whitman and that animates the verse of Chennevière and his friends.

Homme, mon frère, écoute-moi bien:

....

Qui que tu sois, je te connais: tu es mon
frère.

....

Alors, approche-toi, crois-moi, rejouis-toi,
Et lorsque tu seras las ou découragé
Frappe à ma porte, viens auprès de moi
t'asseoir.

("De Profundis")

A few years later, in a poem entitled "Réponse à Whitman," Chennevière laments the dissolution of international brotherhood amid the chaos of the peace negotiations of 1919:

Des trafiquants, vautrés sur la carte du
monde,
Rayent les peuples à coups d'ongle
Et marquent les hommes au fer.[94]

Chennevière's outlook is gloomy; but the title of the poem reveals the extent to which Whitman's fraternal vision affected the ideals and aspirations of the new generation of French writers both before and after the war.

B. *Philéas Lebesgue*

Philéas Lebesgue was one of the writers of the Normand revival which took place in the late nineteenth and early twentieth centuries. Insisting, like his fellow Normand artists, that the roots of Normand art were Celtique and Nordic rather than Latin, Lebesgue found support in Whitman for his theories of racial development and Normand art. As early as 1906, in a discussion of the racial origins of the French nation in *Aux Fenêtres de France*, Lebesgue speaks of the

---

Homme . . . t'asseoir: Man, my brother, listen closely to me:/ . . . Whoever you are, I know you: you are my brother./ . . . So, come closer, believe me, rejoice,/ And when you are weary or discouraged/ Knock at my door, come in, and sit yourself down by my side. ("From the Depths")

Des trafiquants . . . fer: Traffickers, sprawled across the map of the world,/ Scratch people with their nails/ And brand men with iron. ("Response to Walt Whitman")

development of "son *awen*, comme disaient les vieux Gallois, de leur *identity* comme a dit Walt Whitman."[95] And in singing the praises of Whitman a few years later, in a review of Bazalgette's Whitman biography, he attributes part of Whitman's glory to his "ancestralité celtique."[96]

Lebesgue's Normand patriotism did not prevent him from seeing Whitman's seminal role in the development of French literature. "Si le symbolisme avait compris dès le début sa propre grandeur," he asserts in the same review of Bazalgette, "il y a beau temps que le Bard du Manhattan aurait dû être revendiqué comme précurseur."[97] It was particularly in Whitman's hymn to energy and progress, his celebration of humanitarian and technological advance, that Lebesgue found Whitman's importance for the new generation of French writers. He says in a lecture entitled "Walt Whitman et la poésie contemporaine," which he gave at Rouen in 1910: "Cette appropriation par l'intelligence et par le peuplement, par l'exploitation industrielle et commerciale, par le fer et par l'or, est le grand fait épique de notre ère. Il lui faut ses aides, ses bardes. Un Américain, le premier, un Yankee sorti du peuple, l'a compris. C'est Walt Whitman."[98] In his own work, Lebesgue profited by the example of Whitman, for it is precisely in the humanitarian and technological themes of such volumes of poetry as *Les Servitudes* (1913) and *La Grande Pitié* (1920) that Whitman's voice is most clearly audible.

Just as Whitman in "Bravo, Paris Exposition" calls attention to America's French ancestry, so Lebesgue, in his discussion of Whitman and contemporary French poetry, recognizes Whitman as a kind of grandfather of the French: "Ah! ne croyez point que je veuille ici vous entretenir d'un lointain étranger," he exclaims; "plus que

---

Son awen . . . Whitman: His *awen*, as the old Gauls used to say, or their identity as Whitman said. (*Through the Windows of France*)

Si . . . précurseur: If Symbolism had understood its own magnitude from the beginning . . . the Bard of Manhattan should have been claimed as a precursor a long time ago.

Cette . . . Whitman: This appropriation, by intelligence and settlement, by industrial and commercial exploitation, by iron and by gold, is the great epic feat of our era. It needs its aids, its bards. An American, a Yankee born of the people, was the first to understand this. It is Walt Whitman. ("Walt Whitman and Contemporary Poetry") nous pensons, Whitman nous est parent. Il nous résume et nous complète. Il est tout notre passé et déjà il incarne notre avenir."[99] And in his attempt to prove Whitman's French paternity, Lebesgue refers to Whitman's "O Star of France": "Et ne peut-on être français par libre choix. Une pièce, 'O Etoile de France,' écrite à propos de nos désastres de l'Année terrible, suffirait à nous faire considerer comme un concitoyen le grand barde de Manhattan."[100] Whitman as a citizen of France! Again we see how Whitman's sympathy for France, the "pale symbol" of his soul, prepared the way for his later reception among the French people.

During and after World War I, Lebesgue, like such other French writers as Duhamel and Chennevière, was particularly attracted to the themes of suffering and endurance, sympathy and reconciliation, that he found in Whitman's *Drum-Taps* poems. The effect that these poems had on the French writers was enhanced by Bazalgette's publication in 1917 of a volume of Whitman's war poetry entitled *Le Panseur de plaies, poèmes, lettres et fragments de Walt Whitman sur la guerre.* Lebesgue remembered Whitman's "wound-dresser" when he composed his own volume of war poetry entitled *La Grande Pitié* (1920). The volume opens with an epigraph from Whitman: "Over the carnage rose prophetic a voice."[101] The brotherhood and reconciliation themes of Whitman's poem of the same title, "Over the Carnage Rose Prophetic a Voice," are the controlling themes of Lebesgue's poem "Sois mon camarade":

> Sois mon camarade,
> Loyalement!
> Tends-moi la main, comme on la tend

Ah! . . . avenir: Ah! Do not think that I want to speak, here, of a distant foreigner. . . . To a greater extent than we think, Whitman is our parent. He contains and completes us. He is all our past, and he already embodies our future.

Et . . . Manhattan: And can't one be French by free choice. A piece, "O Star of France," written about the calamities of the year 1871, should suffice to make us consider the great bard of Manhattan a fellow citizen.

Sois . . . homme: Be my comrade,/ Loyally!/ Hold out your hand to me, like one holds one's hand/ To the flame when it is cold and one is escaping/ From some difficult task in the fields. . . ./ Let's chat!/ I do not want to know/ If you are from France/ From Italy or from Germany/ I do not want to see you as anything but a man. ("Be My Comrade")

Vers la flamme quand on a froid et que l'on
 s'évade
De quelque travail dur aux champs . . . .

Causons!
Je ne veux pas savoir
Si tu es de France
D'Italie ou d'Allemagne
. . . .
Je ne veux voir en toi qu'un homme.
(pp. 7-8)

Throughout the volume we hear the prophetic voice of Whitman's wound-dresser as Lebesgue describes with realism and compassion the scenes of individual suffering and heroism that are part of trench warfare.

C. *Henri Franck and Luc Durtain*

Henri Franck and Luc Durtain, two of the minor voices among the Whitmanian singers of life, joy, and comradeship in France, both gained their first acquaintance with Whitman through Bazalgette's translation. According to André Spire, Henri Franck met around 1909 with a group of writers associated with *La Phalange*: "Avec eux, il se passionnait pour le rythme libre et puissant des versets de Whitman que Léon Bazalgette venait de révéler aux lecteurs du *Mercure de France*."[102]

Franck absorbed something of Whitman's style and vision into his own work.[103] Whitman's voice is particularly audible in the Adamic and fraternal themes of *La Danse devant l'arche* (1921). In the poems of this volume, Franck, like Whitman, makes use of the voyage motif to organize his enumerations of the joys of life and comradeship on the open road. At times the Whitmanian echoes are direct, as in the lines:

Tendresse humaine, adhésion de l'homme
 à l'homme,

Avec . . . France: Along with them, he became impassioned with the free and powerful rhythm of Whitman's verse, which Léon Bazalgette had just revealed to the readers of the *Mercure de France*.

O joie de nous sentir des coeurs contemporains
Et de multiplier nos esprits l'un par
l'autre.[104]

(p. 59)

Franck must have remembered Whitman's similar celebration of "manly affection" or "adhesiveness" in the *Calamus* poems.

We hear the same Whitmanian overtones in the poetry of Luc Durtain, who was an early associate of the Abbaye group. In *Pégase* (1908), Durtain expresses an infatuation with the physical world that is sometimes reminiscent of Whitman's Adamic mood. Durtain's Whitmanian antecedents are particularly evident in such post-war volumes as *Le Retour des hommes* (1920), in which he recounts his experiences as a doctor on the war front, and in *Perspectives* (1924), where he celebrates "mon vif amour pour vous ô mes frères."[105]

D. *Whitmanisme*

The presence of Whitman in the mainstream of French literature in the early twentieth century is nowhere better indicated than in the anthology of new poetry published in 1912 by Jean-Richard Bloch, the editor of *Effort Libre*. This collection of contemporary French poetry, entitled *L'Anthologie de l'Effort*, ends with a lengthy section of translations from Whitman, the only foreign poet to appear in the volume.[106] In previous years, the *Effort Libre* had carried several articles on Whitman; and in 1912 Bloch himself published a book of stories entitled *Lévy*, which opens with lines from Whitman's "One's-Self I Sing":

La vie immense en passion, en pulsion et
en puissance,

Tendresse . . . l'autre: Human tenderness, adhesion of man to man,/ O joy of feeling ourselves contemporary hearts/ And of multiplying our spirits one by one. (*Dance Before the Arch*)

Mon . . . frères: My intense love for you O my brothers. (*Perspectives*)

La vie . . . chante: Of life immense in passion, pulse, and power,/ Cheerful, for freest action form'd under the laws divine,/ The Modern Man I sing. ("One's-Self I Sing," 6-8)

La vie heureuse, formée pour la plus libre
  action sous l'empire des lois divines,
L'homme moderne, voilà ce que je chante.[107]

In his own work, as well as in the pages of the *Effort Libre*, Bloch attempted to define a social and proletarian art for which he found an inspirational precedent in the work of Whitman.

The *Anthologie de l'Effort* includes selections from such poets as André Spire, Paul Fort, Georges Duhamel, Charles Vildrac, René Arcos, Jules Romains, Georges Chennevière, Henri Franck, Marcel Martinet, Henri Ghéon, Georges Perin, and Henri Aliès. Despite the apparent diversity of the poets who appear in this collection, they are united by one thing: their common relation to Walt Whitman. The Whitmanian impulse that unites this group of writers was pointed up by Henri Ghéon in an article entitled "Le Whitmanisme," which appeared in the *Nouvelle Revue Française* in 1912. Ghéon praises Bloch's anthology as "la plus significative manifestation du jeune lyrisme de ce temps."[108] He goes on to describe *le whitmanisme* that unites the poets of this volume: "Dans cette anthologie c'est leur ressemblance qui m'intéresse, c'est la source commune de leur émotion. Ne disons pas 'unanimisme'; le mot, en toute rigueur, ne saurait désigner que l'esthétique de Romains; adoptons le mot 'whitmanisme'; il offre l'avantage de préciser l'esprit de l'origine de cet idéal lyrique nouveau: et en partant des *Feuilles d'Herbes* nous ne risquons pas de nous égarer."[109]

Although Ghéon expresses a certain fear that the young poets in their enthusiasm for Whitman might lose the concern with formal perfection that is the heritage of the French, he applauds the vital renewal that *le whitmanisme* brought to French literature at the turn of the century. "Il a nourri notre jeunesse," he says of Whitman. "Nul

---

Dans . . . égarer: In this anthology, it is their resemblance that interests me, and the common source of their emotion. Do not say "unanimism"; the word, strictly speaking, only refers to the aesthetic of Romains; let us adopt the word "whitmanism"; it has the advantage of specifying the original spirit of this new lyric ideal; and in starting with *Leaves of Grass*, we do not risk being led astray. ("Whitmanism")

Il a . . . humaine: He nourished our youth. . . . No one was more delighted than I to see the young people come to drink at this source; from it, they drew vigor, courage, hope, and the most noble vision, and the most abundant human sympathy.

plus que moi ne se rejouit de voir les jeunes gens s'en venir boire à cette source: ils y puiseront la vigueur, le courage, l'espoir, et la plus noble vision, et la plus ample sympathie humaine."[110]

The spirit of "Whitmanism" in France had a social and political as well as a literary dimension. As always, Whitman's literary reputation tended to correspond to the political atmosphere of the time. At the beginning of the twentieth century, as the French writers who were involved in the Dreyfus Affair turned away from Mallarméan seclusion to the aesthetics of "engagement," the example of Whitman's social art once again provided a valuable precedent to the French, who were among the first to recognize the socio-political origins and end of Whitman's work. Borrowing the French rubric that Whitman gave his collection of democratic verse in the 1860 edition of *Leaves of Grass*, the Socialist critic Daniel Halévy published in 1901 a series of Whitman translations entitled "Chants démocratiques" in *Pages Libres*, a journal sympathetic to the Socialist cause in France.[111] In his translations, Halévy stressed Whitman's revolutionary attitude. Citing Whitman's "Europe, The 72d and 73d Years of These States," Halévy applauds Whitman's sympathy with the 1848 revolutions in Europe: "Walt Whitman suivit avec passion les phases de la révolution de 1848. Le triomphe de la réaction europèene l'attriste sans le désespérer."[112] In his selection of translations, which includes "Aux Ouvriers" ("A Song for Occupations") and "A Un Révolté ou à une révoltée vaincue" ("To a Foil'd Revolutionaire"), Halévy further attempted to accentuate the Socialist and revolutionary implications of Whitman's verse. His lead was followed in the proceeding years by a number of critics, who attempted to place Whitman in the vanguard of French Socialism and political activism.[113]

At the same time that Whitman was being billed as a revolutionary Socialist and example *par excellence* of the *poète engagé*, the editors of *Pages Libres* organized the *Universités Populaires*; through a series of lectures in Paris and the provinces, these *Universités Populaires* were intended to acquaint the French workers with revolutionary writers. Several lectures on Whitman were part of the program. The

---

Walt . . . désespérer: Walt Whitman passionately followed the phases of the 1848 revolution. The triumph of the European reaction saddened him without causing him to despair.

atmosphere of "Whitmania" that prevailed in French literary and social circles in the early twentieth century is described by the *avant-garde* writer and critic Valery Larbaud in an article on Whitman, written for *La Phalange* in 1909. Commenting on his own intention of giving a lecture on Whitman through the *Universités Populaires*, Larbaud says: "Dès 1901-1902 dans une chambre d'étudiant, rue de la Sorbonne, quelques amis commémoraient, simplement mais avec dignité, la naissance et la mort du Poète de la Démocratie. Quels projets notre enthousiasme nous faisait faire alors! Je devais parler sur 'Walt Whitman et la guerre de Sécession' dans une sorte de cercle populaire, à Grenelle (j'ai encore mes notes). Nous voulions proposer la vie de notre poète en exemple aux ouvriers. De tout cela rien ne sortit . . . . Je crois bien que plusieurs articles et des traductions de nombreuses pièces de 'Feuilles d'herbe' furent ainsi préparés et ne virent jamais le jour."[114]

The "presence" of Whitman among the small gatherings of *avant-garde* writers, the popular lectures, the unpublished translations and articles are ample testimony that, by the turn of the century in France, Whitman had truly become *notre poète*.

Dès . . . jour: From 1901-1902 in a student's room on Sorbonne Street, some friends used to commemorate, simply but with dignity, the birth and death of the Poet of Democracy. What projects our enthusiasm caused us to conceive for ourselves then! I was supposed to speak about "Walt Whitman and the War of the Secession" in a kind of popular circle, at Grenelle (I still have my notes). We wanted to set forth the life of our poet as an example to the workers. Nothing came from all this. . . . I do believe that several articles and translations of numerous selections from "Leaves of Grass" were prepared in this manner, and they never saw the light of day.

CHAPTER IV

WHITMAN AND *L'ESPRIT NOUVEAU*

Of Life immense in passion, pulse, and power,
Cheerful, for freest action form'd under the
laws divine,
The Modern Man I sing.
"One's-Self I Sing"

IN THE YEARS immediately before and after World War I in France, Walt Whitman became associated with *l'esprit nouveau*, which was to give rise to such important artistic movements as Dynamism, Paroxysm, Futurism, Cubism, Dadaism, and Surrealism. Despite their individual differences, all of these movements had one thing in common: a desire to break through the static structures of the past in order to open new vistas in man and in the world.

In his article on "L'Esprit nouveau et les poètes," Guillaume Apollinaire described the new spirit among the poets as a struggle for "le rétablissement de l'esprit d'initiative, pour la claire compréhension de son temps et pour ouvrir des vues nouvelles sur l'univers extérieur et intérieur qui ne soient point inférieures à celles que les savants de toutes catégories découvrent chaque jour et dont ils tirent des merveilles."[1] Initiative, invention, discovery became the words of the day. And among the more innovative writers of *l'esprit nouveau*, Walt Whitman was hailed as a master and prophet.

Le rétablissement . . . merveilles: The restoration of the spirit of initiative, in order to clearly understand one's time, and in order to open new vistas upon the exterior and interior universe, vistas not at all inferior to those that scholars of all kinds discover each day and from which they derive miracles. ("The New Spirit and the Poets")

"Walt Whitman est essentiellement moderne . . . sa poésie enregistre vastement l'émotion des machines," wrote Henri Guilbeaux, the spokesman for the Dynamist group of French writers.[2] Guilbeaux advocated a literature that would register in both its form and content the variety, energy, and dynamism of the modern world. In formulating his aesthetic, Guilbeaux, along with such Dynamist writers as A. M. Gossez and Philéas Lebesgue, recognized an important precursor in Whitman.[3]

In the attempt to give a literary voice to the urban and industrial landscape, the Dynamist aesthetic is closely related to the Futurist ideas that Filippo Marinetti outlined in his "Manifeste du futurisme" in 1909. Marinetti demanded a literature of total subjectivism that would record in both its form and its content the energy, noise, and tumult of the machine age. Like the Dynamists, Marinetti found an important precedent for his Futurist aesthetic in the work of Whitman. As he says in his book *Le Futurisme:* "Nous acceptons seulement l'oeuvre illuminante des cinq ou six grands précurseurs du futurisme. Je fais allusion à Emile Zola, Walt Whitman; Rosny aîné . . . Paul Adam . . . Octave Mirbeau . . . Gustave Kahn . . . et Verhaeren."[4] Among the French writers, Whitman is once again the only foreign voice.

The Whitmanian craze of the pre-war years corresponded to an era of good feeling between France and America. For the *avant-garde* artist, the variety, energy, and apparent disorder of the United States was a kind of metaphor for the new spirit; and Walt Whitman, the poet of this *nouveau monde*, was a vital embodiment of this new spirit in literature. Not only were the French writers sympathetic in their response to Whitman; in such works as Larbaud's *Barnabooth*, Cendrars' "Les Pâcques à New York," Apollinaire's "L'Immigrant de Landor Road," and Perse's *Vents*, the myth of America itself became part of the subject matter of the new literature.

Walt . . . machines: Walt Whitman is essentially modern . . . his poetry records extensively the emotion of machines.

Nous . . . Verhaeren: We accept only the illuminating work of five or six great precursors of Futurism. I allude to Emile Zola, Walt Whitman; Rosny the elder...Paul Adam...Octave Mirbeau...Gustave Kahn...and Verhaeren. (*Futurism*)

With the rapprochement between America and France during the war years and after, the French interest in Whitman became as much political as literary. Translations of Whitman's poetry, ranging from special editions of *Calamus*, *The Wound-Dresser*, and *The Sleepers* to Gide's *Walt Whitman: oeuvres choisies*, and a re-edition of Bazalgette's *Feuilles d'herbe*, appeared regularly in the period from 1914 to 1922.[5] In the post-war period, the French writers and critics hailed Whitman as a social and literary prophet. For example, in his book *L'Ame américaine*, Jean Richepin says of Whitman: "Pour nous, hommes de l'Europe, qui l'avons découvert presque avant ses compatriotes, il est, en réalité ce qu'il a voulu être: le prophète de la démocratie."[6] Similarly, in an article entitled "Whitman, Wilson et l'esprit moderne," Jean Guehenno notes that "un rapport spirituel unit la France et l'Amérique,"[7] and he recommends Whitman as a guide for the social and cultural renewal of France. Speaking of the origins, in America, of the modern spirit, he says:

"Cette terre neuve devait produire l'évangile des temps modernes. Toute l'âme de notre temps était déjà dans les poèmes écrits par Walt Whitman, il y a plus de cinquante ans. Puissions-nous, pour le renouvellement de la France, pour la grande carrière qu'elle a encore à courir, nous laisser guider par cet esprit vivant et conduire le présent d'une main amicale vers l'avenir."[8]

Guehenno's evangelical note is characteristic of the response to Whitman in the years following the First World War in France. Whitman was commemorated, translated, imitated, and quite generally saluted as the poet of America and the prophet of a new age by writers and politicians alike.[9]

Pour . . . démocratie: For us, men of Europe, who discovered him almost before his compatriots, he is, in reality, what he wanted to be: the prophet of democracy. (*The American Soul*)

Un rapport . . . l'Amérique: A spiritual rapport unites France and America. ("Whitman, Wilson, and the Modern Spirit")

Cette . . . l'avenir: This new land was supposed to produce the gospel of modern times. The entire soul of our times was already in the poems written by Walt Whitman more than fifty years ago. Could we, for the renewal of France, for the great course that she has yet to run, let ourselves be guided by this living spirit, and conduct the present, with a friendly hand, toward the future.

I. Valery Larbaud

As both writer and critic, Valery Larbaud was instrumental in making Whitman known to the literary *avant-garde* in France at the beginning of the twentieth century. When in 1899, at the age of eighteen, Larbaud discovered Whitman, he at once began translating some of his poems.[10] Speaking of the Whitmanism of his early years, Larbaud recalls: "On nous interrogeait nous autres Whitmaniens; on nous demandait quel homme avait été ce Whitman, et on écoutait attentivement nos traductions orales."[11] Larbaud was among the French Whitmanians who gathered to recite and discuss the poems of Whitman in the early 1900's,[12] and in the year 1901, at the request of Karl Boés, he began a study of Whitman that was to appear in *La Plume.* A few years later, in 1904, he translated Whitman's "Tears" and a passage from "The Sleepers"· entitled "Squaw Rouge" for Apollinaire's *Festin d'Esope.*[13] Although neither Larbaud's study nor his translations appeared as scheduled, his enthusiastic interest in Whitman continued.

In 1909, Larbaud began his review of Bazalgette's Whitman translation with the following salute: "Enfin le grand Camarade nous parle en français."[14] Although, like Gide, he is critical of Bazalgette for translating the word *love* as *affection*, his review is full of high praise for both the American poet and the French translator. Because of Whitman's technical innovations, however, Larbaud doubts whether Bazalgette's translation will be accessible to the majority of French readers. Ending his article with a comparison between Whitman and that other technical innovator, Paul Claudel, he observes: "Les versets des 'Feuilles d'herbe' auront à attendre comme les versets de Paul Claudel, que l'éducation de l'oreille populaire soit faite. Mais dès à présent la divine musique de l'original vibre, pour les initiés, dans maintes pages de cette traduction."[15]

It was as one of the "initiated" Whitmanians that Larbaud was chosen to do the Preface and several translations for Gide's edition of

---

Enfin . . . français: At last the great Comrade speaks to us in French.

Les versets . . . traduction: The *versets* of "Leaves of Grass," like the *versets* of Paul Claudel, will have to wait until the ear of the people is educated. But from the present time, the divine music of the original vibrates, for initiates, through many pages of this translation.

Whitman's poetry, *Oeuvres choisies*, which appeared in 1918. In his Preface, Larbaud finally completed the study of Whitman that he had begun in 1901. For the same volume he completed the translation of "The Sleepers" that he had begun for Apollinaire in 1904, and he also translated several sections of *Specimen Days* and *Democratic Vistas*. Larbaud's Preface, which includes a review of Whitman scholarship and a discussion of his poetic development, is still one of the most thoughtful and balanced responses to Whitman's work. Although Larbaud recognizes the vital relationship between Whitman's ethics and aesthetics, between the preacher-philosopher and the poet-lyricist, it is in his "grande source lyrique" and its expression in a "ton de conversation" or "effusion" that he finds the essential Whitman.[16]

The effects of Larbaud's sympathetic critical response to Whitman are discernible in his major work, A. O. *Barnabooth, Ses Oeuvres complètes*. At the same time that Larbaud began studying and translating Whitman, he conceived of the character of A. O. Barnabooth, the "richissime" South American and naturalized citizen of the United States, who as "un grand patriote cosmopolite" spends his life voyaging from continent to continent in search of pleasure and sensation. As Georges Jean-Aubry says in *Valery Larbaud: sa vie, son oeuvre:* "Le contact quotidien de la poésie whitmanienne imprégnait l'inspiration des poèmes qu'il écrivait et qu'il attribuait à son personnage A. O. Barnabooth."[17]

In a conversation with the poet Léon-Paul Fargue, Larbaud describes an ideal poet who might have sat for the portrait of Barnabooth. He speaks of his desire to find a poet: ". . . fantaisiste, sensible à la diversité des races, des peuples, des pays; pour qui tout serait exotique . . . très 'internationale,' humoriste, c'est-à-dire

---

Le contact . . . Barnabooth: His daily contact with Whitmanian poetry impregnated the inspiration of the poems that he wrote and that he attributed to his persona A. O. Barnabooth. (*Valery Larbaud: His Life and Work*)

Fantaisiste . . . Whitman: Whimsical, sensitive to the diversity of races, peoples, countries; for whom everything would be exotic . . . very "international," a humorist, that is to say, capable of doing Walt Whitman humorously, of giving a comic note of joyous irresponsibility that is lacking in Whitman. In essence, what I was looking for, on the tables, the racks and the shelves of the lovely revolving bookcases at Brentano's was the poet who was, at one and the same time, the successor of Laforgue, of Rimbaud, and of Whitman.

capable de faire du Walt Whitman à la blague, de donner une note de comique, de joyeuse irresponsabilité, qui manque dans Whitman. Au fond, ce que je cherchais sur les tables, les casiers et les rayons des jolies bibliotèques tournants de chez Brentano, c'était le poète qui eût été le successeur à la fois de Laforgue, de Rimbaud et de Whitman."[18] In creating the Barnabooth persona, Larbaud realized his dream of a poet who would combine the ironic humor of Laforgue, the exotic fantasy of Rimbaud, and the lyrical power of Whitman.

Like *Leaves of Grass*, which appeared anonymously on the Fourth of July in 1855, the first edition of the Barnabooth poems was published anonymously on the Fourth of July in 1908. The poems were preceded by a "Biographie de M. Barnabooth" signed by another fictional personage, X. M. Tournier de Zamble. In this biography, which bears a striking resemblance to Larbaud's own life, we find some of the more explicit Whitmanian antecedents of the Barnabooth persona. M. Zamble tells us that it was in reading Whitman at the age of thirteen that Barnabooth discovered his vocation as a poet:

"Il lut un poème de l'Américain Walt Whitman, qui le plongea dans une rêverie si grande qu'il oubliait de se rendre aux repas de son collège, et s'enfermait dans sa chambre de pensionnaire pour déclamer ce poème. Il ecrivit alors un volume entier de vers anglais, qu'il brûla depuis, sans l'avoir publié. . . . Dès ce moment, il écrivait la plupart de ces poèmes en vers libres, n'employant le vers régulier que dans les pièces légères et humoristiques" (*Oeuvres*, p. 1150). Beneath the "Walt Whitman à la blague" that we find in this passage, Larbaud seems to be acknowledging his own very real debt to the form and content of Whitman's verse.

The section on Barnabooth's birth place, his family background, and his early education, with which the biography begins, closely parallels the format of Whitman's description of his origins in the opening pages of *Specimen Days*. In both background and temperament Barnabooth resembles the Whitmanian persona. According to

---

Il lut . . . humoristiques: He read a poem by the American Walt Whitman, which plunged him into a reverie so great that he forgot to show up for his meals at his college, and he shut himself up in his room to recite this poem. Then he wrote an entire volume of English verse, which he has since burned, without having published it. . . . From this time, he began writing most of his poems in *vers libres;* he only used regular verse in light or humorous pieces. ("Biography of Mr. Barnabooth")

Larbaud, Whitman's primary matter is a man, an uprooted European: "Nous avons la matière première, l'homme, l'Européen dépaysé," he says in his preface to Whitman's works (*Poèmes*, p. 29). Similarly, Larbaud's primary matter in A. O. *Barnabooth* is an uprooted man: in his biography Barnabooth is described as "un sans-patrie" (*Oeuvres*, p. 1136). In his Preface to Whitman, Larbaud also stresses the major role that "le spectacle des Etats-Unis, en pleine formation" played in Whitman's poetic development. "Vivre à New York suffisait," he says, "c'était toucher le pouls du pays" (*Poèmes*, p. 36). Likewise, Barnabooth touched the pulse of modern life in spending his youth in New York.

At times Larbaud's Barnabooth parodies the Whitmanian persona. For example, in describing Barnabooth as both cynical and sentimental, Larbaud plays on Whitman's multitude of contradictions. He says of Barnabooth: "Dirai-je qu'il est cynique? Donnerai-je à entendre qu'il est, en même temps, sentimental? Que de contradictions dans la psychologie d'un même individu" (*Oeuvres*, p. 1144). Similarly, in Barnabooth's desire to write a poem enumerating his possessions, Larbaud pokes fun at Whitman's catalog technique: "Ce style impassible, énumérant des choses possédées, me ravit," exclaims Barnabooth. "Quand j'écrirai mon poème des poèmes, ce sera aussi une espèce de catalogue de tout ce qu'on peut avoir pour de l'argent" (*Oeuvres*, p. 1150).

Although Larbaud eliminated the biography of Barnabooth from the final edition of *A. O. Barnabooth, Ses Oeuvres complètes* (1913), we continue to hear Whitman's voice in the poems of this volume. Throughout the *Poésies* of Barnabooth, Larbaud employs a rhythmic, long-lined *verset* that, in its effusive style, its catalogs and repetitions, exclamations and parentheses, closely resembles the technique of Whitman's free verse. Throughout the poems we also hear the

Vivre . . . pays: To live in New York was enough. . . . It was to touch the pulse of the country.

Dirai-je . . . individu: Shall I say that he is cynical? Shall I give you to understand that he is, at the same time, sentimental? How many contradictions there are in the psychology of the same individual.

Ce style . . . l'argent: This impassive style, enumerating the things one possesses, delighted me. . . . When I write my poem of poems, it will also be a kind of catalog of all that money can buy.

voice of Larbaud's "Whitman à la blague." For example, in the first poem "Les Borborygmes," Barnabooth appears as a humorous and vulgarized version of Whitman's American rough as he celebrates "les borborygmes," or the noisy rumblings of the stomach and bowels. It is in the borborygmes that Barnabooth finds the true song of himself:

> Amie, bien souvent nous nous sommes
> interrompus dans nos caresses
> Pour écouter cette chanson de nous mêmes.
> (*Oeuvres*, p. 43)

But beneath the humor is a more serious intent. Like Whitman's

> I do not press my fingers across my mouth,
> I keep as delicate around the bowels as
> around the head and heart,
> Copulation is no more rank to me than death
> is
> ("Song of Myself," 519-521),

Larbaud's borborygmes are intended to shock Philistine sensibility into a more liberated attitude about physiology and the body. But more important, like Whitman's barbaric yawp, Larbaud's borborygmes are the metaphor for his poetic voice:

> Borborygmes! borborygmes!...
> Y'en a-t-il aussi dans les organes de la
> pensée,
> Qu'on n'entend pas, à travers l'épaisseur
> de la boîte crânienne?
> Du moins, voici des poèmes à leur image.
> (*Oeuvres*, p. 44)

In making his poems the "borborygmes" of thought, Larbaud, like Whitman, is trying to get in touch with what he calls "la bête lyrique"

Amie . . . mêmes: My love, how often we interrupted our caresses,/ To listen to this song of ourselves.

Borborygmes! . . . image: Borborygms! Borborygms!/ Are there also some in the organs of thought,/ That one does not hear, through the thickness of the cranium?/ In any case, here are some poems in their image. ("Borborygms") in man. It is this same primitive, buried voice of man, this barbaric yawp, that Dadaist, Futurist, and Surrealist alike wanted to tap in all of their essential writings.

Again like Whitman, Barnabooth is both mystic and materialist. For example, in the poem "Ode," Barnabooth identifies the inner pulse of himself and his poem with the fierce energy and movement of the locomotive:

> Ah! il faut que ces bruits et que ce
> mouvement
> Entrent dans mes poèmes et disent
> Pour moi ma vie indicible. . . .
> (*Oeuvres*, p. 45)

Larbaud directly echoes Whitman's celebration of the locomotive in "To a Locomotive in Winter":

> Type of the modern—emblem of motion and
> power—pulse of the continent,
> For once come serve the Muse and merge in
> verse, even as here I see thee.
> (13-14)

In his effort to capture in verse the lyricism of the modern technological world, Larbaud seems to have found an apt example in the "lawless music" of Whitman's locomotive.

For Larbaud as for many of the writers of the new spirit, Whitman's locomotive became a symbol for the hidden resources of energy, "la bête lyrique," in man and the world. Unlike Whitman, however, Larbaud makes Barnabooth's romance with the modern world both lyric and comic. The comedy comes from the clash between the old world and the new. Barnabooth sees Europe through the eyes of Whitman's American rough:

> Je chante l'Europe, ses chemins de fer et
> ses théâtres
> Et ses constellations de cités, et cependant

Ah! . . . indicible: Ah! It is necessary that these sounds and this movement/ Enter into my poems and express/ For me, my inexpressible life. ("Ode")

J'apporte dans mes vers les dépouilles d'un
nouveau monde:
Des boucliers de peaux peints de couleurs
violentes,
Des filles rouges, des canots de bois
parfumés, des perroquets.
("Ma Muse," *Oeuvres*, p. 60)

But A. O. Barnabooth is also Whitman seen through the eyes of a "civilized" European. To express Barnabooth's naive infatuation with the speed, movement, and pulse of modern life, Larbaud consistently makes use of such Whitmanian motifs as the voyage, the vagabond, and the road. In "L'Europe," for example, we find direct echoes of Whitman's theme of the open road:

Je partirais,
Un bâton à la main, et j'irais, et j'irais,
Je marcherais sans m'arrêter vers l'Equateur!
(*Oeuvres*, p. 72)

We find Whitman's geographical catalogs:

Le Nil blanc, Téhéran, Timor, les Mers du Sud,
Et toute la surface planétaire sont à nous,
quand nous voudrons!
(*Oeuvres*, p. 71);

and Whitman's urban catalogs:

Kherso, Abbazzia, Fiume, Veglia, villes
neuves,

Je chante . . . perroquets: I sing of Europe, its railroads and its theatres/ And its constellations of cities, and yet/ I bring to my verse the spoils of a new world:/ Rawhide bucklers painted loud colors,/ Red-skinned girls, canoes of scented wood, parrots. ("My Muse")

Je partirais . . . l'Equateur: I would depart,/ Staff in hand, and I would go, and I would go,/ I would walk without stopping toward the Equator! ("Europe")

Le Nil . . . voudrons: The White Nile, Tehran, Timor, the South Seas,/ And all the planetary surface is ours when we want it!

Kherso . . . flots: Cherso, Abbazia, Fiume, Veglia, new cities,/ Or at least they appear new, without our knowing/ Why; Zara, Sebenico, Spalato, and Ragusa/ Like a basket of flowers tipped toward the waves.

Ou du moins qui paraissaient neuves, sans
qu'on sache
Pourquoi; Zara, Sebenico, Spalato, et Raguse
Comme un panier de fleurs incliné près des
flots.
(Oeuvres, p. 73)

But Larbaud's self-consciously humorous and ironic perspective is lacking in such similarly cosmopolitan poems as Whitman's "Salut Au Monde!"

Larbaud was one of the first critics to recognize the discrepancy between Whitman's public image and his private life. He says in his Preface to the works of Whitman: "Attention: peut être que le grand 'vivant' a surtout vécu avec et dans son livre; peut-être que le 'grand-camarade' a été un grand solitaire" (p. 39). Larbaud makes use of the theme of the divided self in several of the Barnabooth poems, and at times he directly echoes Whitman. For example, in "Le Masque" he uses the motif of a mirror, a motif he may have remembered from Whitman's "A Hand-Mirror." As in Whitman's poem, Larbaud contemplates his real self beneath the public mask:

Je me contemple dans le miroir, en face
Et tourné de trois quarts, je m'y vois
Ce profil enfantin et bestial que j'aime.
(*Oeuvres*, p. 47)

Like Whitman in such poems as "So Long," Barnabooth also wants to exchange a kiss with the reader:

Oh, qu'un lecteur, mon frère, à qui je parle
A travers ce masque pâle et brillant,
Y vienne déposer un baiser lourd et lent.
(*Oeuvres*, p. 47)

Attention . . . solitaire: Watch out: perhaps the great "lover of life" lived mostly with and in his book; perhaps the "great comrade" was a great loner.

Je me . . . j'aime: I contemplate myself in the mirror, face to face/ And at three quarters of a turn, I see myself there/ This childish and bestial profile that I love. ("The Mask")

Oh . . . lent: Oh, if only a reader, my brother, to whom I speak/ Through this pale and brilliant mask,/ Would come and plant a heavy and slow kiss upon it.

In such lines as these, we hear the confidential tones of Whitman's "grand solitaire."

In Barnabooth's *Journal intime*, which follows the poems, Larbaud again alludes to the conflict between vision and reality in Whitman's verse. As Barnabooth dreams of a new life of simplicity and comradeship in South America, he thinks of Whitman: "J'avais essayé d'imaginer cette existence, aussi: les courses à cheval, le ranch, des amitiés avec des hommes rudes, le contact quotidien avec des grandes âmes plébéiennes. 'O camerado close!...' Eh oui, c'était de la poésie de Walt Whitman, quelque chose de très beau; mais la vie ne se conforme pas souvent aux oeuvres des grands classiques" (*Oeuvres*, p. 302). In this passage Larbaud breaks through the persona of Barnabooth to make an important statement about the relationship between art and life in the poetry of Whitman.

Throughout the *Journal intime*, Larbaud stresses the Whitmanian underpinnings of his hero. For example, at one point, Barnabooth, in order to advance one of his love affairs, alludes to Whitman's "A Woman Waits for Me": "Vous savez, Gertie, comme dit le vieux Whitman: 'Ce qui s'est si longtemps accumulé en moi . . .' " (*Oeuvres*, p. 232). Similarly, in the first edition of Barnabooth's poems, Larbaud includes in a section entitled "Opinion de la Presse," this fictional note on the relationship between Whitman and Barnabooth: "Nous nous sommes laissés dire que M. Barnabooth avait l'intention de poursuivre devant les tribunaux ceux de nos confrères qui prétendaient qu'il imite Walt Whitman. Mais il n'aura pas à le faire . . . il faut être dément pour ne pas voir quel abîme sépare les deux poètes, fils, tous deux de l'Amérique, et que les vers de

---

J'avais . . . classiques: I had tried to imagine this existence too: horse races, the ranch, friendships with rugged men, daily contact with great plebeian souls: "O camerado close! ..." Yes, it's a line from Walt Whitman's poetry, something very beautiful; but life seldom conforms to the great classic works. (*Intimate Journal*)

Vous . . . moi: You know, Gertie, as old Whitman said: 'What has so long accumulated in me . . . '

Nous . . . l'autre: We permitted ourselves to say that Mr. Barnabooth had intended to pursue, before the tribunal, those of our confreres who claimed that he imitates Walt Whitman. But he will not have to do it. . . . One must be crazy not to see what an abyss separates the two poets, both sons of America; the verse of the one seems to be a crude parody of the poems of the other.

l'un semblent être une grossière parodie des poèmes de l'autre" (*Oeuvres*, p. 1186). In the character of Barnabooth, Larbaud succeeded in creating his Walt Whitman "à la blague," and his rich South American is in many ways a "grossière parodie" of the American poet. But, beneath the joking, we hear the voice of the lyricist and idealist that, according to Larbaud, was the essential Whitman.

Larbaud is a central figure in the study of Whitman's influence on the modern French writers. Through his translations and criticism as well as through the *Oeuvres* of A. O. Barnabooth, he helped to make Whitman known to the writers of the French *avant-garde*. The first to incorporate the Whitmanism of the new spirit in a poetic persona, Larbaud also provided the link between the Symbolist and humanitarian vision of Gide and Romains and the Cubist and Modernist mode of Cendrars and Apollinaire. The Whitmanian Barnabooth is the heir of Gide's *Les Nourritures terrestres* and Romains' *La Vie unanime*, but he is also the ancestor of Cendrars' *Au Coeur du monde entier* and Apollinaire's *Alcools*.

II. Blaise Cendrars

For the group of *avant-garde* writers, painters, and musicians in which he circulated in the pre-war years, Blaise Cendrars became a living embodiment of the Whitman legend. Cendrars actually lived the life of comradeship and adventure that Whitman described in such poems as "Salut Au Monde!" He literally "pass'd in compassion and determination around the earth" and mixed indiscriminately with different "ranks, colors, barbarisms, civilizations" throughout the world (161; 212). As Cendrars himself declared: "En somme je puis aussi bien vivre à San Francisco ou à New York qu'au Tremblay-sur-Mealdre. J'aurai été un des premiers poètes du temps à vouloir mener ma vie sur un plan mondiale."[19] It is this life of vagabonding on the open road that impels the form and content not only of his collected poems *Du Monde entier au coeur du monde*, but of all his work in journalism and fiction, painting and the cinema. In proving and

En somme . . . mondiale: In short, I can just as well live in San Francisco or New York as in *Tremblay-sur-Mealdre.* I will have been one of the first poets of the time to want to lead my life on a worldly basis.

defining those "one or two indicative words for the future" that Whitman had bequeathed to the "new brood" of writers in "Poets to Come," Cendrars went farther than any other artist of the time.[20]

Although there are few instances in which Cendrars reveals a direct debt to the American poet, Whitman's style and vision inform the entire volume of his collected poetry in *Du Monde entier au coeur du monde*.[21] Whitman's passage from the circumnavigation of the globe to the spiritual center of the universe in "Passage to India" is the controlling metaphor of *Du Monde entier au coeur du monde*, in which Cendrars similarly voyages from the material to the spiritual, from the entire world to the heart of the world.

Cendrars was particularly interested in *Leaves of Grass* as a language experiment. Just as Whitman sang "the strong light works of engineers" in such poems as "Passage to India," so Cendrars announced his desire to "créer un style nouveau en collaboration avec les ingénieurs" in an article entitled "Les Poètes modernes dans l'ensemble de la vie contemporaine."[22] In his call for a renewal of modern French poetry by incorporating in writing the immense number of popular and technological terms that had hitherto been excluded from the written language, Cendrars cites Whitman as the pioneer who had already discovered the voice of modern poetry in the "Intercommunication du monde." Cendrars quotes the following Whitman catalog of technological achievements in communication and industry:

> La force de la vapeur, les grandes lignes
> express, le gaz, le pétrole,
> Ce triomphe de notre époque, le fin câble
> de l'Atlantique.

Créer . . . ingénieurs: To create a new style in collaboration with the engineers. ("Modern Poets in the Ensemble of Contemporary Life")

La force . . . fer: Steam-power, the great express lines, gas, petroleum,/ These triumphs of our time, the Atlantic's delicate cable,/ The Pacific railroad, the Suez canal, the Mont Cenis and Gothard and Hoosac tunnels, the Brooklyn bridge,/ This earth all spann'd with iron rails, with lines of steamships threading every sea ("Song of the Exposition." 161-164) Iron-works, forge-fires in the mountains or by river-banks, men around feeling the melt with huge crowbars, lumps of ore, the due combining of ore, limestone, coal,/ The blast-furnace and the puddling-furnace, the loup-lump at the bottom of the melt at last, the rolling-mill, the stumpy bars of pig-iron, the strong clean-shaped T-rail for railroads. ("A Song for Occupations," 108-109)

Le chemin de fer du Pacifique, le canal de Suez, les tunnels du mont Cenis, du Saint-Gothard et de Hoosac, le pont de Brooklyn.
Cette terre toute bridée de rails de fer, de lignes de bateaux à vapeur qui parcourent toutes les mers.
Les forges, les feux de forge dans les montagnes ou au bord des rivières, les hommes alentour qui tâtent la fonte à l'aide d'énormes pinces, les blocs de minerais, la dure combinaison du minerai, de la castine, de la houille,
Le haut-fourneau et le fourneau à puddler, le culot qui pour finir est à la base de la fonte, le laminoir, les barres trapues de fer en saumon, les solides rails en T de belle venue pour les chemins de fer.[23]

By including this melange of passages from "Song of the Exposition" and "A Song for Occupations" in his article on the modern poets, Cendrars reveals some of his debt to Whitman as one of the early "inventors" of the language and imagery, style and vision, of modern literature.

It may have been on one of his trips to the United States in 1910 and 1912 that Cendrars first became acquainted with the work of Whitman. When he returned from his second voyage in 1912, he carried his first major poem "Les Pâques à New York." This poem, with its innovative and Modernist spirit, along with "La Prose du Transsibérien et de la petite Jeanne de France," published in 1913, made Cendrars a central and inspirational figure among the writers of the new spirit.

In "Les Pâques à New York," Cendrars juxtaposes traditional and ritualistic images of Christ with images of poor, suffering humanity in the modern, urban world. Although there is a downbeat quality in the poem that is very unlike Whitman, it belongs to the Whitman tradition. Throughout the poem we hear the fraternal and humanitarian voice of Whitman as Cendrars sympathetically evokes the prostitutes, criminals, and opium eaters who people the same streets of New York through which Whitman tramped a half century before. In evoking the sights and sounds of New York, Cendrars also uses techniques that are reminiscent of Whitman. For example, we hear the cosmopolitan voice of Whitman in the following racial catalog:

> Il y a des Italiens, des Grecs, des Espagnols,
> Des Russes, des Bulgares, des Persans, des
> Mongols.
>
> (*Oeuvres*, I, p. 13)[24]

Cendrars uses the same series of end-stopped images, the same parallelism, enumeration, and initial repetition that are characteristic of Whitman's verse:

> Déjà un bruit immense retentit sur la ville.
> Déjà les trains bondissent, grondent, et
> défilent.
>
> Les métropolitains roulent et tonnent sous
> terre.
> Les ponts sont secoués par les chemins de
> fers.
>
> (*Oeuvres*, I, p. 18)

Although Cendrars employs a rather loose alexandrine throughout the poem, he has already begun moving toward the more liberated Whitmanian technique of his later verse.

It is in his 1913 poem, "Prose du Transsibérien et de la petite Jeanne de France," that we most feel Whitman's presence, in both the form and content of Cendrars' work. In this poem, Whitman's imaginary flight through time and space is made real through Cendrars' evocation of past and present to the beat of the Trans-Siberian Express as it rushes from Moscow to Paris. Cendrars expresses an infatuation with the speed and energy of the modern world through an apparently

---

Il y a . . . Mongols: There are Italians, Greeks, Spaniards,/ Russians, Persians, Mongols. ("Easter in New York")

Déjà . . . fers: Already a loud noise resounds through the city./ Already trains spring into action, rumble, and file out./ Metropolitans roll and thunder underground./ Bridges are shaken by railroads.

illogical flow of images and a free, prosy, unpunctuated verse line that represent a new departure—a departure that would lead to some of the more radical experiments of literary Cubism.

Cendrars described "Prose du Transsibérien" as a "livre simultané" after the model of the painter Madame Delaunay-Terk, who illustrated the first edition of the poem. In attempting to achieve the simultaneity of effect advocated by Delaunay and her group, Cendrars makes use of Whitmanian techniques. For example, in "Passage to India" we find a lyric notation of the multiple impressions received from a train speeding through the wilderness:

> I hear the locomotives rushing and roaring,
>   and the shrill steam-whistle,
> I hear the echoes reverberate through the
>   grandest scenery in the world,
> I cross the Laramie plains, I note the rocks
>   in grotesque shapes, the buttes.
>
> (50-52)
>
> ....
>
> I see in glimpses afar or towering immediately
>   above me the great mountains, I see the Wind
>   river and the Wahsatch mountains.
>
> (54)

In cataloguing the multiple impressions that flow simultaneously through man, Cendrars makes use of the same motif:

> Les rythmes du train
> La "moëlle chemin-de-fer" des psychiatres
>   américains
> Le bruit des portes des voix des essieux
>   grinçant sur les rails congelés
>
> ....

Les rythmes . . . descendent: The rhythms of the train/ The "railroad marrow" of American psychiatrists/ The noise of doors of voices of axles grinding on frozen rails/ . . . And the whistling of steam/ And the eternal noise of the wheels going wild in the grooves of the sky/ The windows are frozen/ No nature!/ And behind, the Siberian plains the low sky and the huge shadows of the Taciturns which climb and descend. ("Trans Siberian Prose")

Et le sifflement de la vapeur
Et le bruit éternel des roues en folie dans
  les ornières du ciel
Les vitres sont givrées
Pas de nature!
Et derrière, les plaines sibériennes le
  ciel bas et les grandes ombres des
  Taciturnes qui montent et qui
  descendent.

(*Oeuvres*, I, p. 23)

Cendrars, like Larbaud, found a symbol for the variety and dynamism of modern life in the "emblem of motion and power" that Whitman evoked in "To a Locomotive in Winter."

In recording the fragmentary and heterogeneous impressions from past and present that whirl through his mind as the Trans-Siberian Express speeds across Russia and Europe, Cendrars makes use of several Whitmanian devices. In "Salut Au Monde," Whitman, to organize the multiple images of the poem, uses an interrogatory refrain addressed to himself:

What widens within you Walt Whitman?
(5)

What do you hear Walt Whitman?
(22)

What do you see Walt Whitman?
(41)

Throughout "Prose du Transsibérien," Cendrars employs the same device in the recurrent question of his travelling mate Jeanne, "la petite prostituée":

Dis, Blaise, sommes-nous bien loin de
Montmartre?

As in Whitman, the recurrence of this interrogatory refrain inspires and structures the varied aural and visual impressions of the poem.

Dis . . . Montmartre: Tell me, Blaise, are we very far from Montmartre?

Cendrars uses a similar melange of Whitmanian motifs in the following passage:

> J'ai aussi joué aux courses à Auteuil et à
> Longchamp
> Paris-New York
> Maintenant j'ai fait courir tous les trains
> tout le long de ma vie
> Madrid-Stockholm
> Et j'ai perdu tous mes paris
> Il n'y a plus que la Patagonie, la Patagonie,
> qui convienne à mon immense tristesse, la
> Patagonie, et un voyage dans les mers du
> Sud,
> Je suis en route
> J'ai toujours été en route.
>
> (*Oeuvres*, I, pp. 24-25)

We find the same alternation of long- and short-lined image units, the same urban and geographic catalogs, the same infatuation with voyage, and impressionism of great spaces, that characterize Whitman's verse.

For Cendrars, as for Whitman, the locomotive is the voice and symbol of a new and secular worship. He says of the train in "Prose du Transsibérien":

> Le train avait ralenti son allure
> Et je percevais dans le grincement
> perpétuel des roues
> Les accents fous et les sanglots
> D'une éternelle liturgie.
>
> (*Oeuvres*, I, p. 30)

J'ai . . . route: I also played the races at Auteuil and at Longchamp/ Paris-New York/ Now I have made all the trains run throughout my life/ Madrid-Stockholm/ And I lost my bets/ There is nothing but Patagonia, Patagonia, which suits my immense sadness, Patagonia, and a voyage to the South Seas,/ I am on the road/ I have always been on the road.

Le train . . . liturgie: The train had slowed down its pace/ And I perceived in the perpetual creaking of the wheels/ The frantic ring and the tears/ Of an eternal liturgy.

With "Prose du Transsibérien et de la petite Jeanne de France," Cendrars began that Whitmanian hymn to transportation and intercommunication that is present throughout his work. In his next poem, for example, "Le Panama ou les aventures de mes sept oncles" (1918), Cendrars continues his celebration of transportation, voyage, and adventure. Whitman had the Suez canal as a subject for his poem; Cendrars had the Panama canal: "le Canal de Panama est intimement lié à mon enfance" (p. 34), he announces at the outset of the poem. Whitman celebrated such means of communication as the canal, the ferry boat, the railroad, and the electric telegraph; Cendrars found even greater cause for celebration in such modern inventions as the steamship, the automobile, and the telephone. Like Whitman, Cendrars delights in enumerating the technological achievements of the modern world:

> C'est en 1901 que j'ai vu la première
> automobile,
> En panne,
> Au coin d'une rue
> Ce petit train que les Soleurois appellent
> un fer à repasser
> Je téléphonerai à mon consul
> Délivrez-moi immédiatement un billet de 3e
> classe
> The Uranium Steamship Co.
> (*Oeuvres*, I, p. 39)

Whitman, in imaginary flight, could rest his elbows in sea-gaps and skirt sierras; Cendrars could dream of underwater tunnels and airplanes:

> J'ai réservé ma place dans le premier train
> qui passera le tunnel sous la Manche

Le Canal . . . enfance: The Panama Canal is intimately linked with my childhood. ("Panama, or the Adventures of My Seven Uncles")

C'est . . . Steamship Co: It is in 1901 that I saw the first automobile,/ Broken down,/ On the street corner/ This little train that the Sunkings call an iron/ I will telephone my Consul/ Bring me at once a 3rd class ticket/ The Uranium Steamship Co.

Je suis le premier aviateur qui traverse
  l'Atlantique en monocoque
900 millions.

(*Oeuvres*, I, p. 48)

In these lines, as throughout "Le Panama," Cendrars, like Whitman, makes use of cosmic and comic exaggeration in his attempt to give a legendary dimension to the modern technological world. Similarly, in such lines as the following,

La voie lactée autour du cou
Les deux hémisphères sur les yeux
A toute vitesse

(*Oeuvres*, I, p. 48),

we find a rather Surrealistic echo of Whitman's comic evocation of stellar flight in "Song of Myself":

Speeding through space, speeding through
  heaven and the stars,
Speeding amid the seven satellites and the
  broad ring, and the diameter of eighty
  thousand miles,
Speeding with tail'd meteors, throwing fireballs
  like the rest,
Carrying the crescent child that carries its
  own full mother in its belly.

(790-794)

Like Whitman, Cendrars was fascinated by speed, numbers, and planetary vistas. He flew Whitman's "flights of a fluid and swallowing soul"; and for him, as for Whitman, it was through the advances in modern communication that time and space could be literally transcended and the flight of the soul made real.

J'ai . . . millions: I have reserved my place on the first train that will go through the tunnel under the English Channel/ I am the first aviator who will cross the Atlantic in a monocoque/ 900 million.

La voie . . . vitesse: The Milky Way around the neck/ The two hemispheres in the eyes/ At top speed.

What is perhaps the most interesting aspect of the relationship between Cendrars and Whitman is Cendrars' experimentation with essentially Whitmanian motifs and themes. Whitman's lyric and impressionistic evocation of the modern landscape, his apparently illogical enumerations, his total freedom of form, the detours, parentheses, and digressions that are part of his "indirection," anticipated, if not directly inspired, the Cubist technique of Cendrars in such volumes as *Dix-Neuf Poèmes élastiques* (1919). In his effort to adapt to literature the methods of the Cubist painters, Cendrars makes use of Whitmanian techniques. The following passage from "Contrastes," for example, is an unpunctuated and modernized version of Whitman's urban catalogs:

> Il pleut les globes électriques
> Montrouge Gare de l'Est Métro Nord-Sud bateaux-
> mouches monde
> Tout est halo
> Profondeur
> Rue de Buci on crie "L'Intransigeant" et
> "Paris-Sports."
>
> (*Oeuvres*, I, p. 57)

In this poem, as throughout the volume, we see how Whitman's enumerative technique, his juxtaposition of diverse objects, events, sensations, and images, could become, *in extremis*, a part of the willful distortion and dislocation of Cubist art.

In his attempt to record the variety and immediacy of modern life, Whitman, like the Cubist painters, occasionally incorporated bits and pieces of local news in the body of his work. For example, as part of the lengthy catalog in section 33 of "Song of Myself," Whitman includes a description of a shipwreck that was reported in the *New York Weekly Tribune*.[25] In *Dix-Neuf Poèmes élastiques*, Cendrars similarly makes use of a news story in the poem "Dernière Heure." In this poem, which closes with the line "Télégramme-poème copié dans *Paris-Midi*" (*Oeuvres*, I, p. 68), Cendrars describes the events of a prison

---

Il pleut . . . "Paris-Sports": It is raining electric lights/ Montrouge East Station Metro North-South passenger-boats world/ All is halo/ Profundity/ On Buci Street one cries "The Intransigent" and "Paris-Sports." ("Contrasts")

escape. Although Whitman may be criticized for incorporating direct transcriptions from books and newspapers in his writing, his technique, for better or for worse, directly anticipated the methods of the Cubist painters and writers.

Cendrars also reveals the way Whitman's non-spatial and non-temporal poetic "I" anticipated the dynamic camera eye of the cinema. In 1920, Cendrars collaborated with Abel Gance in making the experimental film *La Roue*. For the visual center of this film, he again made use of the train, Whitman's symbol of motion and power. By juxtaposing in rapid succession a series of images of a train speeding through the countryside, Cendrars showed how Whitman's enumerative technique could be applied to the art of film. Whitman's poetic technique has frequently been compared to the art of cinematic montage, and Cendrars has actually demonstrated how this technique could be used in editing what was at the time one of the most *avant-garde* pieces of montage in the French cinema.

Cendrars continued to make use of a kind of photographic montage in his two 1924 volumes of poems, *Kodak* and *Feuilles de route*. He described *Kodak* as "des photographies 'mentales,' une sorte de cinéma, des photographies du voyage"; he described *Feuilles de route* as "des cartes postales que j'envoyais à mes amis, que je destinais à mes amis."[26] In these two works, as in such later prose works as *Aujourd'hui* (1931), *L'Homme foudroyé* (1945) and *La Grande Route* (1952), Cendrars continued to cast a Whitmanian shadow as he chronicled his experiences on the open road of life.

In the Preface to his *Poésies complètes*, Cendrars says: "Mes poèmes sont tous des poèmes de circonstance, ils s'inspirent de la réalité, c'est sur elle qu'ils se fondent et reposent."[27] By totally immersing himself in the life of his time, he, like Whitman, strove to uncover the poetry at the heart of the universe. As Whitman had envisioned "the popular tastes and employments taking precedence in poems or anywhere,"

Des photographies . . . voyage: 'Mental' photographs, a kind of cinema, photographs of travel.

Des cartes . . . amis: Postcards that I used to send to my friends, that I intended for my friends.

Mes poèmes . . . reposent: My poems are all occasional poems; they are inspired by reality; they are founded upon and rest upon reality.

Cendrars declared "la Poésie est dans la rue."[28] In their drive to rediscover the poetry of the present and the real, both poets were led to the kind of comic extravagance that is so characteristic of the Cubist perspective. If Whitman found literary masterpieces in tree-toads,

> And the tree-toad is a chef-d'oeuvre for
> the highest
> ("Song of Myself," 665),

Cendrars found the new poetry in menus:

> Tes menus
> Sont la poésie nouvelle.
> ("Le Panama," *Oeuvres*, I, p. 43)

Both poets rejected the traditional products of literary culture. Just as Whitman had exclaimed,

> Away with old romance!
> Away with novels, plots and plays of
> foreign courts,
> Away with love-verses sugar'd in rhyme,
> the intrigues, amours of idlers
> ("Song of the Exposition," 131-133),

so Cendrars declared:

> Je n'ai jamais aimé Mascagni
> Ni l'art ni les Artistes
> Ni les barrières ni les ponts.
> ("Bombay-Express," *Oeuvres*, p. 69)

In their desire to destroy all structures that might inhibit one's total experience of reality, both poets look forward to the spirit of Dadaism and Surrealism. Beneath the constructive negativism of Cendrars and the negativism *tout court* of Tristan Tzara, we hear a common reverberation of Whitman's cry:

Tes menus . . . nouvelle: Your menus/ Are the new poetry.

Je n'ai . . . ponts: I never liked Mascagni/ Nor art or Artists/ Nor barriers or bridges. ("Bombay-Express")

> Unscrew the locks from the doors!
> Unscrew the doors themselves from their
> jambs!
> ("Song of Myself," 501-502)

If it was Blaise Cendrars who removed the locks, it was the Dadaists and Surrealists who finally took the doors from their jambs.

III. Guillaume Apollinaire

According to Guillaume Apollinaire, it was "en presence d'un jeune poète de talent M. Blaise Cendrars"[29] that he first heard the extravagant account of Whitman's funeral that he later wrote for the *Mercure de France* in 1913.[30] Under the heading "Funérailles de Walt Whitman racontées par un témoin," Apollinaire describes the funeral of "Walt Whitman, the good gray," as "une grande fête populaire," complete with circus tents, rag-time, pederasty, and orgiastic brawling:

"Tous ceux que Walt avait connus étaient là . . . les stagedrivers (cochers d'omnibus) de Broadway, des nègres, ses anciennes maîtresses et ses comerados [sic]. . . . Les pédérastes étaient venus en foule. . . . Tout le monde but énormément. Il y eut soixante pugilats et la police, qui intervint, arrêta cinquante personnes. . . . On pense que plusieurs enfants de Whitman étaient là avec leurs mères, blanches ou noires" (pp. 658-59).

Despite the obvious hoax, which was typical of the Cubist milieu in which Apollinaire circulated, Apollinaire's comic account of Whitman's funeral inspired a series of defenses and rebuttals, which appeared in the French journals over a period of months.[31] The question of Whitman's homosexuality became the central issue, with Stuart Merrill and Léon Bazalgette defending Whitman's good gray image, and Harrison Reeves and the German Edouard Bertz defending Whitman's pederasty.[32]

Tous . . . noires: Everyone that Whitman had known was there . . . the stagedrivers of Broadway, negroes, his old mistresses and his comerados [sic]. . . . Pederasts came in great numbers. . . . Everyone drank a lot. There were sixty brawls and the police, who broke it up, arrested fifty people. . . . It is believed that several of Whitman's children were there, with their mothers, white or black.

After the controversy had raged for several months in the French journals, Apollinaire withdrew his initial account of the funeral: "Ne pouvant livrer un nom qu'il ne m'appartient pas de donner, je prie qu'on efface l'anecdote que j'ai racontée."[33] In his usual Cubist good cheer, Apollinaire does not recant, however, without striking a final blow for what he calls "l'unisexualité":

"Néanmoins, il me semble que M. Stuart Merrill fait dans sa réfutation définitive d'étranges confusions. C'est ainsi qu'il confond l'unisexualité avec la débauche la plus crapuleuse. . . . Puisque la législation barbare et injuste de certains Etats condamne avec sévérité les unisexuels, M. Merrill ne pense-t-il pas qu'il est du dernier intérêt de montrer qu'il a pu y avoir des hommes de génie parmi les unisexuels?"[34]

Whitman, we remember, consistently associated the French with a liberated attitude toward sexuality and the body. It is a kind of poetic justice that France should be the first country to make Whitman's sexuality a *cause célèbre*.

Apollinaire's comic description of Whitman's funeral was inspired by a desire to eradicate the good gray colors of the Whitman legend in favor of the equally legendary, but more flesh-colored, image of the eater, drinker, and breeder who tramps through *Leaves of Grass*. It was to this same good gray image that Apollinaire chanted "Merde" in the "Antitradition futuriste," which appeared a few months after his account of Whitman's funeral. In a kind of incantation, Apollinaire sings:

MER . . . DE aux
Dante Shakespeare Tolstoy
Goethe
Dilettantismes merdoyants

Ne pouvant . . . racontée: Not being able to produce a name that it is not in my power to give, I beg that everyone forget the anecdote that I told.

Néanmoins . . . unisexuels: Nevertheless, it seems to me that Mr. Stuart Merrill reveals some strange confusions in his definitive refutation. It is for this reason that he mistakes unisexuality for the most filthy debauchery. . . . Since the barbaric and unjust legislation of certain states severely condemns unisexuals, doesn't Mr. Merrill think that it is of the utmost importance to show that there could be men of genius among the unisexuals?

Eschyle et théâtre d'orange
Inde Egypte Fiesole et la
théosophie scientisme
Montaigne Wagner Beethoven
Edgar Poe Walt Whitman et
Baudelaire.

ROSE à
Marinetti Picasso Boccioni Apollinaire
Paul Fort
Mercereau Max Jacob Carrà Delaunay
Henri-Matisse Braque.[35]

The extent to which Whitman had entered the mainstream of French literature is perhaps best indicated by the fact that he is one of the forces that Apollinaire must purge in his Futurist renunciation of tradition. The rebellious "rowdy" of the Second Empire in France had slipped into the ranks of the traditionalists!

Despite this rather unpromising prelude, the more un-traditional, rose-colored image of Whitman had a considerable impact on Apollinaire. Apollinaire had an acquaintance with Whitman as early as 1904, when Valery Larbaud did some Whitman translations for Apollinaire's *Festin d'Esope*. Apollinaire may also have had some familiarity with Léon Bazalgette's laudatory study *Walt Whitman: l'homme et son oeuvre*, which appeared in 1908. He became involved with Jules Romains and the unanimists in 1908, and he may have been among those friends of Romains who were so enthusiastic about Bazalgette's Whitman translation.

Apollinaire's major volume of poems, *Alcools*, was published in 1913, the same year as his account of Whitman's funeral and his "Antitradition futuriste." The volume contains a number of traditional lyrics that were written in the years 1901-1906. In such poems from this period as "Rhénanes" and "La Chanson du mal-aimé," Apollinaire expresses conventional themes of love, loss, and nostalgia

---

MER...DE . . . Braque: *Merde* to Dante Shakespeare Tolstoy Goethe/ Annoying dilettantisms/ Eschylus and the theatre of orange/ India Egypt Fiesole and theosophy scientism/ Montaigne Wagner Beethoven Edgar Poe Walt Whitman and Baudelaire. Rose to Marinetti Picasso Boccioni Apollinaire Paul Fort/ Mercereau Max Jacob Carrà Del'aunay Henri-Matisse Braque. ("Futurist Antitradition") in classic octosyllabic or alexandrine form. In 1908, however, he began moving toward the Whitmanian form and vision that would become the characteristic note of his more experimental verse. For example, in the 1908 poem, "Les Fiançailles," Apollinaire mixes octosyllabic and alexandrine verse with a more irregular, long-lined verse that is reminiscent of Whitman:

> Toute la sainte journée
> Toute la sainte journée j'ai marché en chantant
> Une dame penchée à sa fenêtre m'a regardé longtemps
> M'éloigner en chantant
>
> (*Oeuvres*, p. 134)[36]

Apollinaire fully adopted the long-lined, Whitmanian *verset* to celebrate the marriage of a friend and fellow poet in the 1909 "Poème lu au mariage d'André Salmon":

> En voyant des drapeaux ce matin je ne me suis pas dit
> Voilà les riches vêtements des pauvres
> Ni la pudeur démocratique veut me voiler sa douleur
> Ni la liberté en honneur fait qu'on imite maintenant
> Les feuilles ô liberté végétale ô seule liberté terrestre
>
> ....
>
> Ni même on renouvelle le monde en reprenant la Bastille
> Je sais que seuls le renouvellent ceux qui sont fondés
> en poésie
> On a pavoisé Paris parce ce que mon ami André Salmon s'y
> marie
>
> (*Oeuvres*, p. 83)

Toute . . . chantant: All the blesséd day/ All the blesséd day I walked along singing/ A woman leaning out of her window looked at me for a long time/ Move off into the distance singing. ("The Bethrothal")

En voyant . . . marie: When I saw flags hung this morning I did not say/ Here we have the rich clothes of the poor/ Or democratic modesty wants to conceal its sadness from me/ Or in honor of liberty one must now imitate/ The leaves O vegetable liberty the only earthly liberty/ . . . Or even the world is being renewed by retaking the Bastille/ I know that the only ones to renew it are those who are grounded in poetry/ Paris has been decorated because my friend André Salmon is getting married there. ("Poem Read at the Marriage of André Salmon")

In this poem, Apollinaire not only expresses a Whitmanian confidence in the role of the poet, he also makes use of the same breath-oriented, enumerative rhythms, the same parallelism, participles, and initial repetitions that are so characteristic of Whitman's free verse technique. The poem is even accompanied with a Whitmanian story. According to Philippe Soupault, the poem was written atop an omnibus as Apollinaire bounced along on his way to the wedding of his friend.[37]

In several of the later poems of *Alcools,* Apollinaire continued to explore the Whitmanian form and vision of "Poème lu au mariage d'André Salmon." "Zone," "Cortège," and "Vendémiare," all of which were composed in 1912, are particularly reminiscent of Whitman. In "Zone," which opens the volume of *Alcools,* Apollinaire expresses a mixed mood of pain and joy, contemplative sadness and Whitmanian confidence, as he drinks in images of the modern landscape mingled with memories of his own and the Christian past. If Whitman's muse was "bluff'd not a bit by drainpipe, gasometers, artificial fertilizers,"[38] Apollinaire similarly found the new poetry in catalogs of the factual and the real:

> Tu lis les prospectus les catalogues les affiches qui
> chantent tout haut
> Voilà la poésie ce matin et pour la prose il y a les
> journaux
> Il y a les livraisons à 25 centimes pleines
> d'aventures policières
> Portraits des grands hommes et mille titres divers
> (*Oeuvres,* p. 39)

Like Whitman, Apollinaire delights in cataloguing the sights and sounds of the city; he even sings a kind of song for occupations:

> Les directeurs les ouvriers et les belles
> sténo-dactylographes
> Du lundi matin au samedi soir quatre fois par jour
> y passent

Tu lis . . . divers: You read the handbills catalogs posters that sing very loudly/ Here is the morning's poetry and for prose there are the newspapers/ There are dime novels full of police adventures/ Portraits of great men and a thousand other titles. ("Zone")

Le matin par trois fois la sirène y gémit
Une cloche rageuse y aboie vers midi
Les inscriptions des enseignes et des murailles
(*Oeuvres*, p. 39)

In his attempt to recreate verbally a kind of Cubist-simultanist collage of the urban landscape, Apollinaire, like Cendrars, makes use of the same rhythmic flow of end-stopped images and enumerations that is characteristic of Whitman's style.

If Apollinaire was fascinated with the grit and grind of modern life, he was also, like Whitman, both materialist and mystic. He consistently transforms material facts into spiritual events. Just as in "Passage to India," Whitman finds symbols of spiritual unity in the train, the cable, and the canal, so in "Zone," through a kind of Futurist leap, Apollinaire associates the airplane with Christ:

C'est Dieu qui meurt le vendredi et ressuscite le
dimanche
C'est le Christ qui monte au ciel mieux que les aviateurs
Il détient le record du monde pour la hauteur
(*Oeuvres*, p. 40)

Throughout the poem, Apollinaire evokes the airplane as a modern continuation of a long line of winged creatures, which includes legendary birds, Icarus, and Christ himself. For Apollinaire, as for Whitman, flight, whether mythic or real, becomes the symbol both for mystic transcendence and for the spiritual union of the globe.

In both Whitman and Apollinaire the poetic "I" itself embodies this same mystic capacity for flight. Whitman celebrates his simultaneous "presence" in various cosmopolitan centers throughout the world in "Salut Au Monde":

I see the cities of the earth and make myself at
random a part of them,

Les directeurs . . . murailles: Directors workers beautiful stenographers/ From Monday morning to Saturday night pass by four times per day/ In the morning the siren bellows three times/ A distempered clock barks about midday/ The inscriptions on signs and walls.

C'est . . . hauteur: It is God who dies on Friday and rises on Sunday/ It is Christ who flies higher than the aviators/ He holds the world's record for altitude.

I am a real Parisian,
I am a habitan of Vienna, St. Petersburg, Berlin, Constantinople,
....
I belong in Moscow, Cracow, Warsaw, or northward in
   Christiania or Stockholm, or in Siberian Irkutsk, or in
   some street in Iceland,
I descend upon all those cities, and rise from them again.
(129-31; 136-37)

Apollinaire's poetic "I" is also temporally and spatially plastic. He echoes Whitman when he addresses his poetic self in "Zone":

Te voici à Marseille au milieu des pastèques
Te voici à Coblence à l'hôtel du Géant
Te voici à Rome assis sous un néflier du Japon
Te voici à Amsterdam avec une jeune fille que tu
   trouves belle et qui est laide
(*Oeuvres*, p. 42)

Delighting in geographic displacement, Apollinaire moves from one time and place to another with Whitmanian fluidity.

In "Cortège" there is a similarly Whitmanian exploration of the expansive and all-inclusive properties of the self. At the outset of the poem, Apollinaire addresses himself in words that recall Whitman's invitation to his soul in "Song of Myself".

Un jour
Un jour je m'attendais moi-même
Je me disais Guillaume il est temps que tu viennes
Pour que je sache enfin celui-là que je suis
(*Oeuvres*, p. 74)

Apollinaire's use of an intimate, first name address to himself echoes "Song of Myself":

Te voici . . . laide: You are in Marseille among the watermellons/ You are in Coblence at the Hotel of the Giant/ You are in Rome seated under a Japanese medlar tree/ You are in Amsterdam with a young girl you find pretty and who is ugly.

Un jour . . . suis: One day/ One day I was waiting for myself/ I said to myself William it is time that you come out/ So I will finally know who I am. ("Procession")

My voice goes after what my eyes cannot reach,
With the twirl of my tongue I encompass worlds and
volumes of worlds.

Speech is the twin of my vision, it is unequal to
measure itself,
It provokes me forever, it says sarcastically,
Walt you contain enough, why don't you let it out then?
(564-68)

Apollinaire asserts a similar power to recreate worlds and volumes of worlds:

Moi qui connais les autres
Je les connais par les cinq sens et quelques autres
Il me suffit de voir leurs pieds pour pouvoir refaire
ses gens à milliers
(*Oeuvres*, pp. 74-75)

In this passage, as throughout "Cortège," Apollinaire describes his embodiment of all people and all time, past and present, in language and imagery strongly reminiscent of Whitman.

If in the opening poem of *Alcools*, "Zone," Apollinaire fluctuated between doubt and confidence, in the final poem of the volume, "Vendémiare," he surrenders himself fully to a Whitmanian mood of joyous, cosmopolitan lyricism. The central image of the poem is the wine harvest: the poet, as "le gosier de Paris," drinks the wine of the universe that comes to him from the cities of France and Europe. The motif of absorbing the universe parallels Whitman. The poet harvests the cities of Europe, the people, landscapes, histories, and myths:

Les villes répondaient maintenant par centaines
....
L'univers tout entier concentré dans ce vin
Qui contenait les mers les animaux les plantes

Moi . . . milliers: I who know others/ I know them by my five senses and by some others/ It is enough to see their feet to be able to recreate these people by the thousands.

Les villes . . . ciel: The cities now responded by the hundreds/ . . . The universe totally concentrated in this wine/ Containing seas animals plants/ Cities fates and stars that sing/ Men kneeling upon the banks of heaven. ("Vendémiare")

Les cités les destins et les astres qui chantent
Les hommes à genoux sur la rive du ciel
(*Oeuvres*, p. 153)

In much the same way, Whitman expands with the latitude and longitude of the universe in "Salut Au Monde":

What widens within you Walt Whitman?
What waves and soils exuding?
What climes? what persons and cities are here?
(5-7)

As Apollinaire receives the chants and cries of the cities,

Et j'écoutai longtemps tous ces chants et ces cris
Qu'éveillait dans la nuit la chanson de Paris

J'ai soif villes de France et d'Europe et du monde
Venez toutes couler dans ma gorge profonde
(*Oeuvres*, p. 149),

he recalls Whitman drinking in the sounds of the universe in "Proud Music of the Storm":

Give me to hold all sounds, (I madly struggling cry,)
Fill me with all the voices of the universe,
Endow me with their throbbings, Nature's also,
The tempests, waters, winds, operas and chants, marches and dances,
Utter, pour in, for I would take them all!
(138-142)

Apollinaire's central vision is, like Whitman's, both ethical and aesthetic. In the "chants d'universelle ivrognerie" in "Vendémiare" and in several of the *Alcools* poems, Apollinaire, by absorbing the

Et j'écoutai . . . profonde: And I listened a long time to all these songs and cries/ That were awakened in the night by the song of Paris/ I am thirsty cities of France and of Europe and of the world/ Come all of you flow down my deep throat.

wine of the universe, brings about the ethical renewal of society in universal communion and the aesthetic renewal of art through ecstatic contact with life.

It is in the poetry of *Calligrammes* (1918) that Apollinaire fully developed the experimental form and content toward which he began moving in the later poems of *Alcools*. It is also in this volume that Apollinaire reveals his more striking antecedents in the Modernist themes and free-verse techniques of Whitman. In the opening poem, "Liens," Apollinaire announces his poetic program in words that echo Whitman's celebration of the senses:

> J'écris seulement pour vous exalter
> O sens ô sens chéris
> (*Oeuvres*, p. 167)

He catalogues the bonds that unite men in images that are reminiscent of Whitman's technological and fraternal themes:

> Rails qui ligotez les nations
> Nous ne sommes que deux ou trois hommes
> Libre de tous liens
> Donnons-nous la main
> ....
> Cordes tissées
> Câbles sous-marins
> Tours de Babel changées en ponts
> (Oeuvres, p. 167)

Calligrammes abounds with similar images of trains, cables, bridges, and telegraph poles, which for Apollinaire, as for Whitman, were the poetry of the modern world.

In exalting the life of the senses amid the flux of the modern world, Apollinaire consistently uses a long-lined, enumerative verse technique that has direct antecedents in Whitman's free verse. For

---

J'écris . . . chéris: I write only to exalt you/ O senses O cherished senses. ("Ties")

Rails . . . ponts: Rails that link the nations/ We are only two or three men/ Free of all ties/ Let's shake hands/ . . . Woven ropes/ Underwater cables/ Towers of Babel turned into bridges.

example, in "Les Fenêtres" he employs a Whitmanian catalog to record the sights glimpsed from the window of a moving train:

> Vancouver
> Où le train blanc de neige et de feux nocturnes fuit l'hiver
> O Paris
> Du rouge au vert tout le jaune se meurt
> Paris Vancouver Hyères Maintenon New-York et les Antilles
> La fenêtre s'ouvre comme une orange
> Le beau fruit de la lumière
>
> (*Oeuvres*, p. 169)

In this passage, as throughout *Calligrammes*, we see the way Whitman's enumerative and impressionistic technique could be extended into the illogical flow of images, the distortion, dislocation, and surprise of Cubist art. Even the ideogrammic method of such poems as "Paysage" and "Lettre-Océan" is a kind of visual extension of Whitman's catalog technique.

Throughout *Calligrammes* Apollinaire echoes Whitman's cosmic and prophetic voice as he announces the exploration of new horizons in the psychic and planetary universe. Like Whitman, Apollinaire makes use of an imaginary stellar flight to suggest the undiscovered forces in man and the world. If in "Song of Myself" Whitman could go "speeding with tail'd meteors" through time and space, Apollinaire in the poem "Toujours" envisions himself as the Don Juan of a thousand and three comets:

> Et de planète en planète
> De nébuleuse en nébuleuse
> Le don Juan des mille et trois comètes
> Même sans bouger de la terre

Vancouver . . . lumière: Vancouver/ Where the train white with snow and with nocturnal fires escapes the winter/ O Paris/ From red to green all the yellow is dying/ Paris Vancouver Hyères Maintenon New-York and the Antilles/ The window opens like an orange/ The lovely fruit of the light. ("The Windows")

Et de . . . fantômes: And from planet to planet/ From nebula to nebula/ The Don Juan of a thousand and three comets/ Even without moving from the earth/ Looks for new forces/ And takes phantoms seriously. ("Forever")

Cherche les forces neuves
Et prend au sérieux les fantômes
(*Oeuvres*, p. 237)

Both poets reveal a Modernist infatuation with energy, speed, and the power of sheer numbers. Unlike Whitman, however, Apollinaire gives greater emphasis to the inner life. He says in the poem "Les Collines":

Profondeurs de la conscience
On vous explorera demain
Et qui sait quels êtres vivants
Seront tirés de ces abîmes
Avec des univers entiers
(*Oeuvres*, p. 172)

Although Whitman records in "The Sleepers" the illogic and unreality of the dream consciousness in a way that anticipates later writers, it is Apollinaire who invented the term *Surréalisme* to describe the modern artistic exploration of inner, psychic space.[39]

In addition to the more free-swinging poems of the modern world, *Calligrammes* includes several patriotic poems in which Apollinaire describes his experiences as a soldier on the front during World War I. Again Apollinaire had the example of Whitman's poems, particularly the poetry of *Drum-Taps* (1865), very much in mind. The *Drum-Taps* poems are a painfully graphic record of the scenes of grief and affliction, courage and heroism, that Whitman witnessed as a medical attendant during the Civil War. Like Whitman's "Wound-Dresser," Apollinaire expresses compassion for those who suffer, at the same time that he views the war effort as an adventurous, national renewal. Such poems as "Veille," "Ombre," and "Désir" are reminiscent of Whitman's realistic descriptions of war and the memories of war in "Vigil Strange I Kept on the Field One Night" and "The Artilleryman's Vision." In several of his war poems, Apollinaire reveals a direct debt to Whitman. For example in his patriotic call to the future in the poem "Chant de l'honneur,"

Profondeurs . . . entiers: Depths of the conscience/ We will explore you tomorrow/ And who knows what living beings/ Will be drawn from those depths/ With complete universes. ("Hills")

O poètes des temps à venir ô chanteurs
Je chante à la beauté de toutes nos douleurs
J'en ai saisi des traits mais vous saurez bien mieux
Donner un sens sublime aux gestes glorieux
Et fixer la grandeur des ces trépas pieux
(*Oeuvres*, p. 306),

Apollinaire directly echoes Whitman's "Poets to Come," which opens with the lines:

Poets to come! orators, singers, musicians to come!
Not to-day is to justify me and answer what I am for,
But you, a new brood, native, athletic, continental,
greater than before known,
Arouse! for you must justify me.
(1-4)

Just as Apollinaire was part of the new and continental "brood" who justified Whitman's songs, so Apollinaire looked to future generations to justify his own poems "en l'honneur de l'Honneur la Beauté du Devoir."

T. S. Eliot once said that a good artist does not borrow, he steals, and this is precisely what Apollinaire did; he lifted one of Whitman's *Drum-Taps* poems and included it among his own war poetry in *Calligrammes*. No critic has ever noticed the fact that Apollinaire's "Les Feux du bivouac" is a thinly disguised, Surrealistic adaptation of Whitman's "By the Bivouac's Fitful Flame." Apollinaire's poem opens with the following lines:

Les feux mouvants du bivouac
Eclairent des formes de rêve
Et le songe dans l'entrelacs
Des branches lentement s'élève
(*Oeuvres*, p. 250)

O poètes . . . pieux: O poets to come O singers/ I sing of the beauty of all our pains/ I have captured certain traits but you will know better how/ To give a sublime sense to these glorious exploits/ And to capture the greatness of these revered deaths. ("Song of Honor")

Les feux . . . s'élève: The fitful flames of the bivouac/ Light up the forms of reverie/ And the dream in the intertwining/ Of branches slowly arises. ("The Bivouac's Flames")

These lines are a condensed and elliptic version of the following passage from Whitman's poem:

> By the bivouac's fitful flame,
> A procession winding around me, solemn and sweet and slow—
>   but first I note,
> The tents of the sleeping army, the fields' and woods' dim
>   outline.
>
> (1-3)
>
> ....
>
> While wind in procession thoughts, O tender and wondrous
>   thoughts,
> Of life and death, of home and the past and loved, and
>   of those that are far away;
> A solemn and slow procession there as I sit on the ground,
> By the bivouac's fitful flame.
>
> (7-10)

In the final lines of his poem, Apollinaire gives a haunting, surreal dimension to Whitman's vision of the soldiers' thoughts and dreams circling amid the darkness and flame of an army bivouac:

> Voici les dédains du regret
> Tout écorché comme une fraise
> Le souvenir et le secret
> Dont il ne reste que la braise
>
> (*Oeuvres*, p. 250)

Like Whitman, Apollinaire was intrigued by spirit life, the phantom presence that he felt around him, and it was probably this visionary reality that drew him to Whitman's poem. Aside from the fact that he essentially borrowed the substance of Whitman's poem, it is important to note that it was again Whitman who broke the new ground of the dream landscape that we find in Apollinaire's Surrealistic poem. That Apollinaire could take one of Whitman's poems, edit it according to his own purposes, and call it his own is another telling indication of the close literary relations not only

---

Voici . . . braise: Here is the disdain of regret/ All rough like a strawberry/ The memory and the secret/ Of which only a cinder remains.

between Whitman and Apollinaire, but between America and France.

In "L'Esprit nouveau et les poètes," which Apollinaire wrote shortly before his death in 1918, he pays tribute to Walt Whitman and his compatriot Edgar Allan Poe as the "grands pionniers de la poésie."[40] Apollinaire's discussion fully reveals some of the Whitmanian antecedents of the new spirit in modern poetry. The entire document reads like a Modernist "revision" of Whitman's poetic theory and practice.

At the very outset Apollinaire announces that it is the primary function of literature to "exalter la vie sous quelque forme qu'elle se présente" (p. 385), words that echo Whitman's "Song of the Exposition":

> I raise a voice for far superber themes
> for poets and for art,
> To exalt the present and the real.
> (137-138)

In the attempt to exalt the present and the real, Apollinaire, like Whitman, proclaims a new formal liberty: "Le vers libre donna un libre essor au lyrisme; mais il n'était qu'une étape des explorations qu'on pouvait faire dans le domaine de la forme" (p. 386). Like Whitman, the poets of the new spirit did not aim mainly toward art or aestheticism. According to Apollinaire, "L'esprit nouveau est avant tout ennemi de l'esthétisme, des formules et de tout snobisme" (p. 395). For the new poets, as for Whitman, beauty is subordinated to truth. Apollinaire asserts: "Les poètes ne sont pas seulement les hommes du beau. Ils sont encore et surtout les hommes du vrai, en tant qu'il permet de pénétrer dans l'inconnu, si bien que la surprise, l'inattendu est un des principaux ressorts de la poésie d'aujourd'hui"

Le vers . . . forme: *Vers libre* gave full scope to lyricism; but it was only one stage in the explorations that one could make in the domain of form.

L'esprit . . . snobisme: The new spirit is above all an enemy of aestheticism, formulas, and all snobbery.

Les poètes . . . d'aujourd'hui: Poets are not only the followers of beauty. They are also, and in particular, followers of the truth; insofar as it permits the penetration of the unknown, the unexpected, along with surprise, is one of the mainsprings of today's poetry.

(p. 393). In their attempt to initiate what Apollinaire describes as "un nouveau réalisme," the new poets had discovered the elements of humor, surprise, and the unexpected that were also part of Whitman's miraculous penetration of reality:

> I find I incorporate gneiss, coal, long-
> threaded moss, fruits, grains, esculent
> roots,
> And am stucco'd with quadrupeds and birds
> all over.
> ("Song of Myself," 670-671)

As Whitman's poet-prophet "places himself where the future becomes present,"[41] so Apollinaire announces the prophetic role of the new poets: "Les poètes modernes sont donc des créateurs, des inventeurs et des prophètes" (p. 394). And finally, just as Whitman declared the necessity of opening poetry to the Kosmic Spirit, "the vastness and splendor and reality with which Scientism has invested Man and the Universe,"[42] so Apollinaire announces a similar need to explore the new realms discovered by the scientists and inventors: "Les savants scrutent sans cesse de nouveaux univers qui se découvrent à chaque carrefour de la matière, et il n'y aurait rien de nouveau sous le soleil. Pour le soleil, peut-être. Mais pour les hommes!" (P. 391). Like Whitman, Apollinaire proclaims the love between the poet and the scientist: "Les merveilles nous imposent le devoir de ne pas laisser l'imagination et la subtilité poétique derrière celle des artisans qui améliorent une machine" (p. 396). In his own imaginative exploration of the machine age and in his exuberantly "Kosmic" spirit, Apollinaire continued Whitman's pioneering effort to open the new matter and vision of modern literature.

In defining the aesthetics of the new spirit, Apollinaire combines elements of Futurist, Cubist, and Surrealist thought. The fact that his

---

Les poètes . . . prophètes: The modern poets are thus creators, inventors, and prophets.

Les savants . . . hommes: Scholars endlessly examine the new universes that are discovered at each crossroads of matter, and there should be nothing new under the sun. For the sun, perhaps. But for men!

Les merveilles . . . machine: Miracles impose upon us the duty of not leaving the imagination and poetic subtlety behind the skills of the craftsmen who perfect a machine.

description of the new spirit so closely resembles Whitman's poetic theory and practice is yet another indication of Whitman's important anticipation of the whole Modernist movement in art.

IV. Saint-John Perse

The poet Alexis Saint-Léger Léger, who adopted the name Saint-John Perse in order to keep his work as a career diplomat separate from his work as a literary artist, might also be included among the poets of the new spirit who received impressions from Walt Whitman. His exaltation of life, his cosmic spirit, and his use of a "liberated," rhythmic *verset* in such early volumes as *Eloges* (1911) and *Anabase* (1924), place him in rapport with the Whitmanian currents of *l'esprit nouveau*. Although Perse's work as a diplomat, from the years 1914 to 1940, kept him isolated from the literary milieu of his time, he was in close communication with several of Whitman's French admirers. He was a good friend of Paul Claudel and Valery Larbaud, and he was closely associated with André Gide, Léon-Paul Fargue, and other writers involved with the *Nouvelle Revue Française*; in fact, it was this review that published his first poem, "Images à Crusoé," in 1909.

Perse's rhythmic *verset* and his affirmative vision seem, at first glance, very close to Whitman. In his early poem "Pour fêter une enfance" (1910), for example, Perse praises the magical world of childhood in accents that are suggestive of Whitman:

> Ô j'ai lieu! ô j'ai lieu de louer!
> Il y avait à quai de hauts navires à musique. Il y avait des promontoires de campêche; des fruits de bois qui éclataient... Mais qu'a-t-on fait des hauts navires à musique qu'il y avait à quai?
>
> (*Oeuvres*, p. 28)[43]

The evocation of the child's world, the tone of wonder, the catalogs of the physical world, the repetitions, parallelisms, and suspension points are all reminiscent of Whitman's poetry. In another early

Ô j'ai . . . quai: O I have reason! I have reason to praise!/ There were high musical ships on the wharf. There were capes of logwood trees; wooden fruits that split open...But what has become of the high musical ships that were on the wharf? ("In Celebration of Childhood")

poem, "Eloges," Perse describes his love for the horse in words that are again reminiscent of Whitman:

> J'ai aimé un cheval—qui était-ce? —il m'a bien
> regardé de face, sous ses mèches.
> Les trous vivants de ses narines étaient deux choses
> belles à voir—avec ce trou vivant qui gonfle au-dessus
> de chaque oeil.
> Quand il avait couru, il suait: c'est briller! —et j'ai
> pressé des lunes à ses flancs sous mes genoux d'enfant...
> J'ai aimé un cheval—qui était-ce? —et parfois (car
> une bête sait mieux quelles forces nous vantent)
> il levait à ses dieux une tête d'airain: soufflante, sillonnée
> d'un pétiole de veines.
>
> (*Oeuvres*, p. 34)

Perse's words bear an extraordinary likeness in tone and image to Whitman's similar evocation of a horse in "Song of Myself":

> A gigantic beauty of a stallion, fresh and responsive to my caresses,
> Head high in the forehead, wide between the ears,
> Limbs glossy and supple, tail dusting the ground,
> Eyes full of sparkling wickedness, ears finely cut, flexibly moving.
>
> His nostrils dilate as my heels embrace him,
> His well-built limbs tremble with pleasure as we race around and
> return.
>
> (701-706)

Like Whitman, Perse looked upon the horse as an embodiment of the mystic energy and movement that are central to his view of the universe.

But though they share an attitude of praise for the universe, Whitman and Perse differ greatly in the verse forms they employ.

J'ai . . . veines: I loved a horse—who was he? —he looked me straight in the face, under his forelock./ The quivering holes of his nostrils were two beautiful things to see—with that quivering hole that expands over each eye./ When he had run, he sweated; it is to shine! —and I pressed moons in his flancs under my child's knees.../ I loved a horse—who was he? —and at times (because an animal knows better the forces that praise us)/ he lifted to his gods a head of bronze: panting, furrowed with a petiole of veins.

Perse's *verset* has a rhythmic unity, based on such devices as balanced phrasing, syllabic regularity, assonance, alliteration, and internal rhyme, that sets it apart from both Whitman's free verse and Claudel's *iambe fondamental.* In a letter to his American friend Katherine Biddle, Perse pointed up the difference between his technique and Whitman's. He says that his verse: "n'a absolument rien de commun avec les conceptions courantes du 'vers libre', du 'poème en prose' ou de la grande 'prose poétique.' C'est même de tout le contraire qu'il s'agit là. Et c'est encore, m'a-t-il semblé, ce que vous avez su bien voir vous-même, mieux qu'aucun critique américain, en opposant à l'art poétique d'un Walt Whitman les exigences rythmiques 'of such a rigorous metrique: an internal metrique so exacting and precise, although kept inapparent in its enclosed order, that not one syllable of the text could be changed or displaced without serious damage...' " (*Oeuvres*, p. 922).

In addition to his "rigorous metrique," Perse brings to his poetry an aristocratic and impersonal posture quite alien to Whitman's democratic stance. His poetry is characterized by an imagistic density, a use of ambiguity and ellipsis, and an almost cavalier avoidance of discursive material that make it different from and much more obscure than the poetry of Whitman.

In executing his "internal metrique," however, Perse frequently makes use of Whitmanian procedures. His verse abounds in the exclamations, parentheses, dashes, present participles, conjunctions, prepositions, initial repetitions, and catalogs that we associate with Whitman's poetic technique. The French critic Roger Caillois describes Perse's verse as "une poésie encyclopédique,"[44] and it is this characteristic feature of Perse's verse, his enumerative style, that most closely resembles the technique of Whitman's poetry.

For example, in *Anabase* (1924) Perse catalogues a variety of human activities in order to evoke the epic spectacle of mankind in its march toward the future: "ha! toutes sortes d'hommes dans leurs voies et façons: mangeurs d'insectes, de fruits d'eau; porteurs d'emplâtres,

---

N'a . . . rythmiques: Has absolutely nothing in common with current conceptions of "*vers libre*," the "prose poem" or the great "poetic prose." In fact, their concerns are exactly the opposite of mine. And again, it seems to me, it is what you were able to see, better than any other American critic, when you opposed to the poetic art of a Walt Whitman, rhythmic exigencies . . .

de richesses! l'agriculteur et l'adalingue, l'acuponcteur et le saunier; le péager, le forgeron . . . les ramasseurs de cailles dans les plis de terrains, ceux qui récoltent dans les broussailles les oeufs tiquetés de vert . . . ceux qui peignent en sifflant des coffrets en plein air, l'homme au bâton d'ivoire, l'homme à la chaise de rotin, l'ermite orné de mains de fille . . ." (*Oeuvres*, pp. 112-113). Whitman's famous long catalog in "Song of Myself" contains a similarly panoramic vision of life. He envisions himself:

Scaling mountains, pulling myself cautiously up, holding on by low
  scragged limbs,
Walking the path worn in the grass and beat through the leaves of
  the brush,
Where the quail is whistling betwixt the woods and the wheat-lot,

. . . .

Where the cheese-cloth hangs in the kitchen, where andirons
  straddle the hearth-slab, where cobwebs fall in festoons
  from the rafters;
Where trip-hammers crash, where the press is whirling its cylinders,
Wherever the human heart beats with terrible throes under its
  ribs,
Where the pear-shaped balloon is floating aloft, (floating in it my-
  self and looking composedly down,)
Where the life-car is drawn on the slip-noose, where the heat
  hatches pale-green eggs in the dented sand.

(731-733; 737-741)

Whereas Whitman is primarily a lyricist of the self and is thus personally present in his enumerations, Perse is a lyricist of the universe and tends to remain outside his verse. But both poets bring a microscopic eye to their inventories of the world: Perse's notation of such details as the green-speckled eggs is similar to Whitman's image

---

Ha! . . . fille: Ah! All kinds of men in their ways and their manners: eaters of insects, of waterfruits; bringers of plasters, of riches! the husbandman and the noble horseman; the acupuncturist and the salt-maker; the toll collector, the blacksmith . . . gatherers of quail in the folds of the ground, those who collect eggs speckled with green in the underbrush . . . those who paint small chests and whistle in the open air, the man with the ivory staff, the man in the wicker chair, the hermit adorned with a girl's hands . . . (*Anabasis*) of the "pale-green eggs in the dented sand." Both poets also strive to expand the frontiers of poetry by incorporating specialized skills and technical and scientific terms into their verse. In the above catalog, Perse includes such specialized occupations as *l'acuponcteur* and *le saunier*, and Whitman includes such technical terms as trip-hammers and cylinders, the life-car and the slip-noose.

The parallels between Whitman and Perse are particularly evident in Perse's later volume of poems *Vents* (1946), where he celebrates the western movement across the American continent. At the time that he wrote this epic poem, Perse was living in the United States because he had been exiled from his own country; nevertheless, the poem reads as a testament of hope and faith. The wind of the title is a symbol for Perse of the perpetual motion of the universe and of the forces of destruction and creation that will ultimately bring about the renewal of the world. His description of the western movement brings to mind Whitman's own celebration of westward expansion in such poems as "Pioneers! O Pioneers!" Perse asserts:

> Nos routes dures sont en Ouest, où court la pierre à son afflux. S'émacier, s'émacier jusqu'à l'os! à bout de vol et d'acier fin, à bout d'antennes et de rémiges, vers ce pays de pierre et d'os où j'ai mes titres et créances.
>
> Là vont toutes choses s'élimant, parmi les peuplements d'oponces, d'aloès, et tant de plantes à plumules; parmi l'orage magnétique, peignant au soufre de trois couleurs l'exhalaison soudaine d'un monde de stupeur.
>
> ("Vents," *Oeuvres*, p. 211)

Unlike Whitman, however, who tended to focus upon the western movement as a realization of the manifest destiny of the United States, Perse's treatment of the movement westward is linked to a more universal vision of cosmic evolution and perpetual renewal.

Perse's descriptions of the American land strike a particularly

---

Nos routes . . . stupeur: Our difficult route is Westward, where stone flows to its afflux. To emaciate, to emaciate down to the bone! at the edge of flight and of low steel, at the edge of antennae and wingtips, toward this country of stone and of bone where I have my titles and my trusts./ There all things are wearing down, amidst the population of cacti, of aloes, and so many plants with plumules; amidst the magnetic storm, painting with sulfur of three colors the sudden exhalation of a stupefied world. (*Winds*)

Whitmanian chord. For example, he evokes the swamp lands of the South in the following words:

> ...Guidez, ô chances, vers l'eau verte les grandes îles alluviales arrachées à leur fange! Elles sont pétries d'herbage, de gluten; tressées de lianes à crotales et de reptiles en fleurs. Elles nourrissaient à leurs gluaux la poix d'un singulier idiome.
>
> Coiffées de chouettes à présages, aimantées par l'oeil noir du Serpent, qu'elles s'en aillent, au mouvement des choses de ce monde, ah! vers les peuplements de palmes, vers les mangles, les vases et les évasements d'estuaires en eau libre."
>
> ("Vents," *Oeuvres*, p. 207)

Perse's description is suggestive of Whitman's vision of the "dense swamps" in "O Magnet-South":

> O the strange fascination of these half-known half-impassable
> swamps, infested by reptiles, resounding with the bellow
> of the alligator, the sad noises of the night-owl and the
> wild-cat, and the whirr of the rattlesnake.
>
> (16)

Both poets focus on similar images of snakes, reptiles, and owls in their attempt to evoke a Southland that is at once ominous and foreboding, but also lush, fertile, and magnetically appealing.

The entire movement of *Vents* is unified by the same vision of physical and spiritual renewal that characterizes such later Whitman poems as "Prayer of Columbus," "Passage to India," and "Proud Music of the Storm." Like Whitman, Perse was particularly fascinated by the figure of the explorer; his poetry abounds in catalogs of the adventurers, conquistadors, and navigators who pushed forward into new frontiers:

> Des hommes dans le temps ont eu cette façon de tenir face au vent:

Guidez . . . libre: ...Guide us, O chances, toward the green water, the great alluvial islands drawn from their sludge! They are molded from herbage, from gluten; interwoven with rattlesnake lianas and reptiles in bloom. Amid their lime twigs they nourish the pitch of a singular idiom./ Covered with portentious owls, magnetized by the black eye of the Serpent, let them go along, with the movement of the things of this world. Ah! toward the populations of palms, toward the mangroves, the silt, and the openings of estuaries into free water.

Chercheurs de routes et d'eaux libres, forceurs de pistes en Ouest, par le cañons et par les gorges et les raillères chargées d'ans—Commentateurs de chartes et de bulles, Capitaines de corvée et Légats d'aventure, qui négociaient au prix du fer les hautes passes insoumises, et ces gisements au loin de mers nouvelles en plein ciel. . . .

(*Oeuvres*, p. 217)

For Perse, as for Whitman, the explorer is a symbol of "The urge, the ardor, the unconquerable will,/ The potent, felt, interior command, stronger than words" that continually drives mankind forward from the known to the unknown ("Prayer of Columbus," 26-27).

Just as Whitman saw in Columbus' discovery of the new world a projection of his own role as poet-prophet, so Perse saw the explorer as an embodiment of the restless energy that urges the poet ever forward to push back the frontiers of the known world. For Perse, as for Whitman, it is the poet-explorer who must communicate to the world his prophetic vision of universal harmony and renewal. In *Vents*, for example, it is the poet who unifies the diverse and apparently fragmented pursuits of men. He arrives

...Avec tous hommes de douceur, avec tous hommes de patience aux chantiers de l'erreur,

Les ingénieurs en balistique, escamoteurs sous roche de basiliques à coupoles,

---

Des hommes . . . ciel: Throughout time men have had this manner of facing up to the wind:/ Seekers of routes and free waters, forcers of trails to the West, by canyons and by gorges and slopes weighted down by years—Commentators on charters and edicts, Captains of forced labor and Legates of adventure, who negotiated the high, unconquered passes for the price of a sword, and those faraway expanses of new seas in the open sky. . . .

Avec . . . nouvelle: With all men of gentleness, with all men of patience in the workshops of error,/ Ballistic engineers, conjurers under rock of domed basilicas,/ Manipulators of switches and keys at beautiful white marble tables, inspectors of powders and inventions, and correctors of aviation charts,/ The Mathematician in search of a solution at the end of his halls of mirrors, and the Algebraist at the knot of his *chevaux-de-frise;* the redressers of celestial wrongs, opticians in the cellar and *philosophe* lense polishers./ . . . With his mass of servants, with his mass of followers, and all his rags trailing in the wind, O smile, O gentleness,/ The Poet himself at the gangway of the Century!/ —Welcome to the causeway of men, and the wind bending the new grass a hundred leagues away.

Les manipulateurs de fiches et manettes aux belles tables de marbre blanc, les vérificateurs de poudres et d'artifices, et correcteurs de chartes d'aviation,

Le Mathématicien en quête d'une issue au bout de ses galeries de glaces, et l'Algébriste au noeud de ses chevaux de frise; les redresseurs de torts célestes, les opticiens en cave et philosophes polisseurs de verres.

....

...Avec son peuple de servants, avec son peuple de suivants, et tout son train de hardes dans le vent, ô sourire, ô douceur,

Le Poète lui-même à la coupée du Siècle!

—Accueil sur la chaussée des hommes, et le vent à cent lieues courbant l'herbe nouvelle.

(*Oeuvres*, pp. 225-226)

Perse's ballistic engineers, manipulators of switches, and correctors of aviation charts are a modern version of the engineers, inventors, and scientists who precede the poet in "Passage to India":

After the seas are all cross'd, (as they seem already cross'd,)
After the great captains and engineers have accomplish'd their
 work,
After the noble inventors, after the scientists, the chemist, the
 geologist, ethnologist,
Finally shall come the poet worthy that name,
The true son of God shall come singing his songs.

(101-105)

Like Whitman, Perse envisioned the poet working along with the scientist (and sometimes in advance of him) to penetrate the mystic sources of Being.

The final lines of *Vents* contain a vision of renewal brought to the poet by the winds:

Des Messagers encore s'en iront aux filles de la terre,
et leur feront encore des filles à vêtir pour le délice du poète.

Et nos poèmes encore s'en iront sur la route des hommes, portant semence et fruit dans la lignée des hommes d'un autre âge—

Une race nouvelle parmi les hommes de ma race, une race

nouvelle parmi les filles de ma race, et mon cri de vivant sur la chaussée des hommes, de proche en proche, et d'homme en homme,

Jusqu'aux rives lointaines où déserte la mort!...

(*Oeuvres*, p. 250)

In "Proud Music of the Storm," Whitman receives a similar message of renewal from the wind:

And I said, moreover,
Haply what thou hast heard O soul was not the sound of winds,
Nor dream of raging storm, nor sea-hawk's flapping wings nor
harsh scream,
....
Nor flutes, nor harps, nor the bugle-calls of camps,
But to a new rhythmus fitted for thee,
Poems bridging the way from Life to Death, vaguely wafted in
night air, uncaught, unwritten,
Which let us go forth in the bold day and write.

(155-157; 161-164)

Like Whitman's "new rhythmus," Perse's "cri de vivant" carries a message of renewal that bridges the way from life to death.

Although it is in *Vents* that the similarities between Perse and Whitman are most apparent, there are Whitmanian echoes throughout Perse's poetry. Even the titles of Perse's final volumes of poems, *Amers* (1957) and *Oiseaux* (1962), bear a rather remarkable likeness to the titles of two of the major groups of poems, "Sea-Drift" and "Birds of Passage," in the final version of *Leaves of Grass* (1881). But these similar titles are not so unusual. The sea and the bird are central images in the poetry of Whitman and Perse. It is in and through the sea and the bird that both poets discover not only the sources of their poetry, but also the mystic sources of life.

Des Messagers . . . mort: Once again Messengers will go to the daughters of earth, and will make more daughters to be dressed for the poet's delight./ And once again our poems will go on the road of men, bearing seed and fruit to the lineage of men of another age—/ A new race amidst the men of my race, and the cry of my being upon the causeway of men, nearer and nearer, from man to man,/ To the distant shores where death deserts!....

The suggestive parallels between Whitman and Perse might tempt one to assert that Whitman had some direct influence on the French poet. But at the time Perse began writing, Whitman had so penetrated the French tradition that it would be difficult to pinpoint any direct influence he might have had on Perse. It may be that in his early years Perse had some firsthand acquaintance with Whitman's work, but it is also possible that he received indirect impressions from Whitman through such works as Maeterlinck's *Serres chaudes*, Gide's *Les Nourritures terrestres*, and Claudel's *Cinq Grandes Odes*.[45]

Regardless of whether or not Whitman had any direct impact on his poetry, Saint-John Perse is, in many ways, the finest literary product of the liberating seeds that Whitman had planted in France at the end of the nineteenth century. The essentially Whitmanian vision of Perse is nowhere more apparent than in his 1960 Nobel Prize acceptance speech. From the podium in Stockholm, Perse announces the religious role of poetry, the union of the poet and the scientist, the universal law of harmony and renewal, and the opening of new vistas in the human and spiritual world, in words that remind us that, even amidst the prospect of nuclear annihilation, Whitman's affirmative and progressive vision is still alive in the modern world. In fact, Perse's description of the regenerative function of poetry sounds like an exact summary of Whitman's poetic program:

"La poésie moderne s'engage dans une entreprise dont la poursuite intéresse la pleine intégration de l'homme. Il n'est rien de pythique dans une telle poésie. Rien non plus de purement esthétique. Elle n'est point art d'embaumeur ni de décorateur. Elle n'élève point des perles de culture, ne trafique point de simulacres ni d'emblèmes, et d'aucune fête musicale elle ne saurait se contenter. . . . Se refusant à dissocier l'art de la vie, ni de l'amour la connaissance, elle est action, elle est passion, elle est puissance, et novation toujours qui déplace les bornes" (*Oeuvres*, p. 445).

La poésie . . . bornes: Modern poetry is engaged in a task, the pursuit of which concerns the full integration of man. There is nothing at all Pythian about such a poetry, nor anything that is purely aesthetic. This poetry is not in the least the art of the embalmer or the decorator. It does not raise cultured pearls or traffic in simulacrums and emblems; nor would it be content with any mere musical feast. . . . Refusing to separate art from life and love from knowledge, this poetry is action, it is passion, it is power, and continual innovation that expands the boundaries.

Like Whitman before him, and like such of his compatriots as Paul Claudel, André Gide, Valery Larbaud, and Guillaume Apollinaire, Saint-John Perse sought through his poetry to release man into the plenitude of being. When Perse goes on to assert of poetry that "c'est d'une même étreinte, comme une seule grande strophe vivante, qu'elle embrasse au présent tout le passé et l'avenir, l'humain avec le surhumain, et tout l'espace planétaire avec l'espace universel," we are reminded once again that Whitman's "Kosmic" spirit is still alive in the global and visionary poetry of Saint-John Perse (*Oeuvres*, p. 445).

Upon the death of John Kennedy in 1963, Perse again revived the spirit of Whitman for the modern world. In an article entitled "Grandeur de Kennedy," which appeared on the front page of *Le Monde*, Perse describes Kennedy as a "soldat d'humanité," who fought for the rights of man not only in America but throughout the world. Searching for the appropriate words to express his grief, Perse refers his readers to Whitman's threnody for Lincoln in "When Lilacs Last in the Dooryard Bloom'd": "Lincoln pleuré par Walt Whitman éveille encore dans nos coeurs le très long thrène du martyr" (*Oeuvres*, p. 640). The fact that Perse, seemingly at a loss for words, would look to Whitman's funeral song to express his own and the universal grief at the death of Kennedy is one final indication of the rapport between the American bard and the French poet laureate.

V. New Directions

In Sylvia Beach's book *Shakespeare and Company*, a memoir of the Paris literary scene in the 1920's, Beach gives an account of how she put on a Whitman exhibition in her American bookstore on the Left Bank in Paris. Writing of the period around 1925, she says: "It was about this time, too, that I put on an exhibition in honor of Walt Whitman. Whitman was anything but the style. 'The Crowd' couldn't put up with him, especially after T. S. Eliot aired *his* views

---

C'est . . . universel: It is in the same embrace, like a single, great living strophe, that poetry joins all the past and the future to the present, the human with the superhuman, and all planetary space with universal space.

Lincoln . . . martyr: Walt Whitman's mourning for Lincoln awakens once again in our hearts the very long threnody for the martyr.

about Walt. Only Joyce and the French and I were still old fashioned enough to get along with Whitman. I could see with half an eye Whitman's influence on Joyce's work—hadn't he recited some lines to me one day?"[46] Sylvia Beach's Whitman exhibition provides a telling contrast with the empty corridors of the Whitman exhibition that Romains attended in New York.[47] The Whitman exhibition at 12 rue de l'Odéon in Paris became an occasion for Whitman's French translators, critics, and admirers to pay hommage to the American poet, whom many regarded as one of the seminal forces in modern literature, not only in France and America but throughout the world. According to Beach, the exhibition "was a great success, and in a Ulysses-sized morocco-bound book I have the signatures, headed by that of Paul Valéry, of the many visitors who came to see it."[48]

By the time of Sylvia Beach's exhibition, Whitman had come to filter and fiber the blood of French literature. Although the automatism and dreams of the Surrealists and the nausea and the absurd of the Existentialists were essentially alien to Whitman's solar vision, Whitman continued to be a vital presence for those poets who placed themselves confidently at the crossroads between the material and the spiritual, the real and the unreal. We still feel Whitman's breath and spirit in the cosmopolitan vision of André Salmon, in the urban and planetary themes of Léon-Paul Fargue, in Jules Supervielle's mystic embrace with the universe, and in Paul Eluard's cosmic love poetry. But in the years following the war, it becomes increasingly difficult to speak of direct influence. The Whitmanian form and content that we find in many of the modern French writers—the rhythmic free verse, the repetitive and enumerative style, the barbaric yawp and the blab of the pave, the exaltation of the present and modern, the fraternal and cosmopolitan vision, the vagabonding and loafing, the physical joy and extravagance, the Adamic mood and confidential tone, the mystic and cosmic "I," the flights into psychic and planetary space—all these Whitmanian characteristics had been thoroughly absorbed into the mainstream of French literature.

Although the Whitman cult of the pre-war period in France waned considerably in later years, several of the new generation of post-war writers continued to express an enthusiastic interest in his work. For example, in a broadcast for French radio in 1934, Marcel Martinet, the former editor of *L'Humanité* and author of a Whitmanian volume of poems entitled *Eux et moi: chants d'identité*, expressed the debt that he and his countrymen owed to Whitman. He says: "Assuredly Whitman's name is not so well known as that of a general or a boxer, but it can be said that since Bazalgette, French poetry has been secretly impregnated with his works and in so far as poetry secretly influences the general sensibility of people, his works have stamped our sensibility as much as any French works and even more sometimes."[49] Martinet's words again suggest the extent to which Whitman's works had become a literary as well as a cultural force in France.

Among the post-war generation of French writers, it is perhaps the novelist Jean Giono who reveals the most direct debt to Whitman. According to Giono's biographer Christian Michelfelder, Giono kept a copy of Whitman's works beside his work desk.[50] Throughout his work Giono makes direct and indirect allusions to Whitman. For example, Giono's autobiographical novel, *Le Serpent d'étoiles*, is headed by the following epigraph from Whitman: "Votre oeuvre peut-elle faire vis-à-vis à la pleine campagne et au bord de la mer."[51] In such works as *Présentation de Pan* (1930), *Le Chant du Monde* (1934), and *Les Vraies Richesses* (1936), Giono's celebration of the natural world and the life of the senses is clearly reminiscent of Whitman. As William Starr says in his article "Jean Giono and Walt Whitman":

"Certain ideas are important in the works of both men. Such are their ideas concerning life and the place of death and creation in the process of life; the interior unity of all existing things, the relations between man, animals, and the less conscious world; the need for close communion between man and nature. . . . In the case of the expression of the identity of the poet with humanity, of their attitude towards death, and towards animals, the similarity is still greater. These comparisons seem to point rather conclusively to the importance of the American poet in the writings of Jean Giono."[52]

Although Mr. Starr discusses only those works which appeared before the publication of his article in 1940, in such later works as *Les Grands Chemins* (1951) and *Le Bonheur fou* (1965), Giono continues

---

Votre . . . mer: Can your work stand in the open country and by the seashore?

to evoke a similarly Whitmanian vision of physical and spiritual reality.

The influence of Whitman on Jean Giono is only one instance of Whitman's continuing importance for modern French writers. The extent to which he remains a viable force in contemporary French literature is best indicated by the regular appearance of new translations of his work by the young French poets. In 1948, the poet Paul Jamati published a study of Whitman and a selection of his poems for the *Poètes d'aujourd'hui* series.[53] Whitman is among the few foreign poets to be included in this series. The young French poet Alain Bosquet also published a selection of Whitman's poetry and prose in 1959.[54] In his biographical-critical introduction, Bosquet comments upon Whitman's vital role in emancipating the language and content of contemporary French literature. According to Bosquet, "sa poésie sera toujours un message, que les autres pourront suivre; une leçon de sagesse, de grandeur, de puissance."[55]

In recent years, the French critic and poet Roger Asselineau has come to play a role similar to the role played by Léon Bazalgette, over fifty years before, in making Whitman known to contemporary French audiences. Like Bazalgette, Asselineau began by writing a biography of Whitman and then went on to do a translation of Whitman's poems. Asselineau's biography, *L'Evolution de Walt Whitman*, appeared in 1954; his translation, *Feuilles d'herbe*, in 1956.[56] Since that time, Asselineau's warmth and generosity as a person and his continued work in translation and criticism have been instrumental in keeping Whitman studies alive in France, America, and throughout the world.[57]

It is in large part the work of Roger Asselineau that has made Whitman available to contemporary French writers. These writers continue to express their debt of gratitude to Whitman. For example, the French poet Roger Ninck commemorated the centennial of *Leaves of Grass* by including an "Ode à Walt Whitman" in his 1956 volume of poems entitled *Les Couteaux du destin*. More recently, in 1971, the contemporary novelist Jean-Marie Le Clezio has commented upon Whitman's importance for the young French writers:

Sa poésie . . . puissance: His poetry will always be a message that others will be able to follow; it is a lesson of wisdom, of greatness, of power.

"There cannot be another poetry now," says Le Clezio, "because the explosion of consciousness and language, which Walt Whitman and his fellow-men have set in, is still lasting. . . . He is still among us. His eyes and his voice still invent our shapes and our words. He is even the most alive of us all."[58] Perhaps better than any other contemporary French writer, Le Clezio suggests the extent to which Whitman remains and will remain a vital presence in the French literary tradition.

EPILOGUE

> Failing to fetch me at first keep
> encouraged,
> Missing me one place search another,
> I stop somewhere waiting for you.
> "Song of Myself"

AT THE END of the 1855 Preface to *Leaves of Grass*, Whitman says: "The proof of a poet is that his country absorbs him as affectionately as he has absorbed it" (*LG*, p. 729). But by the beginning of the twentieth century, it was France, not America, that had absorbed Whitman as affectionately as he had absorbed it. From the Symbolist period to the Modern period, the French writers responded most sympathetically to those very poems that Whitman associated with the French; "O Star of France," the *Children of Adam* poems, and poems with French in the title or content such as "Salut Au Monde" were early favorites. The ideas that Whitman associated with France—the physiological and sexual interest, the democratic and fraternal impulse, and the urban, cosmopolitan, and scientific themes—were precisely what most attracted such French writers as Jules Laforgue, André Gide, Jules Romains, and Guillaume Apollinaire.

But Whitman's recurrent image of the circle must be completed. If in the opening decades of the twentieth century Whitman had not been fully absorbed by "literary" America, he would be smuggled back into the country via his French connections. To be sure, such writers as Carl Sandburg, Hart Crane, Wallace Stevens, and William Carlos Williams found certain roots in the native ground of Walt Whitman, but the major spokesmen for American letters in the early part of the century, T. S. Eliot and Ezra Pound, resisted Whitman's full impact until he, like Poe, had been given a French face.

It is the Frenchman Charles Baudelaire, and not the American Walt Whitman, whom Eliot regarded as the seminal figure in modern literature. In an essay on Baudelaire, written in 1930, Eliot praised the French poet for his renovation of the language of verse; for his imagery of the modern, metropolitan world; and for his introduction of a new attitude toward life.[1] It is odd that Eliot did not recognize Whitman's similar renewal of the language, imagery, and attitude of modern literature. But Eliot could not stomach Whitman. He once confessed that he "had to conquer an aversion to his form as well as to much of his matter" before he could read him at all.[2] The fact that his own religious, social, political, and aesthetic views seemed the exact antithesis of Whitman's vision prevented Eliot's recognizing Whitman's real contributions to modern literature.

Eliot consistently dismissed the whole question of Whitman's impact on contemporary writing. For example, in his review of Emory Holloway's *Walt Whitman*, Eliot opens with the following remarks:

"This book is in no way a critical examination of Whitman's work; it has nothing to say—thank God—about Whitman's influence upon 'vers-libre' and contemporary American verse; it is silent about Whitman's present standing in American literature. Mr. Van Wyck Brooks would have made the subject the occasion for an elegy, Mr. Mencken for a diatribe upon democracy. Mr. Holloway's subject is 'Whitman the Man' and his environment, and he keeps to the matter in hand."[3]

Amy Lowell, in her article "Walt Whitman and the New Poetry," similarly denies Whitman's contribution to the development of English vers-libre: "Often and often I read in the daily, weekly, and monthly press, that the modern *vers-libre* writers derive their form from Walt Whitman. As a matter of fact, most of them got it from the French Symbolist poets, they were nearest to our time."[4]

What T. S. Eliot and Amy Lowell did not know was that Whitman had gotten to the French Symbolists before they had.

The irony, of course, is that in their attempt to renovate American and English letters by drinking at the source of modern French literature, Eliot and his coterie were absorbing the very same French tradition that Whitman had nourished. The early relationship between Whitman and Laforgue casts an ironic shadow over Eliot's later relationship to Laforgue, the poet with whom Eliot felt the strongest personal and poetic affinity.[5] The free verse rhythms, the novelty, the modernity that Eliot imitated and admired in Laforgue were, in fact, Whitman refined. A further irony is that Eliot also found models in such French writers as Arthur Rimbaud, Guillaume Apollinaire, and Saint-John Perse, all of whom had important antecedents in Whitman.[6] Similarly, the six poets whom Amy Lowell sets forth as models for her own work and that of others in her critical anthology *Six French Poets* include such figures as Emile Verhaeren, Remy de Gourmont, Francis Jammes, and Paul Fort, all of whom received impressions from Whitman.[7]

Unlike Eliot and Lowell, Pound in his early years acknowledged Whitman as a spiritual father. In an essay entitled "What I Feel About Walt Whitman" (1909), Pound admitted that "the vital part of my message, taken from the sap and fibre of America, is the same as his." But Pound still felt the shadows of Theocritus, Dante, and Shakespeare hovering over his shoulder, and he hastened to add: "Mentally I am a Walt Whitman who has learned to wear a collar and a dress shirt (although at times inimical to both)."[8] In 1915, in the volume of poems entitled *Lustra*, Pound made a similar pact with Whitman:

> It was you that broke the new wood,
> Now is a time for carving.
> We have one sap and one root—
> Let there be commerce between us.[9]
> ("A Pact")

In his desire to refine Whitman's "barbaric yawp," Pound reveals all the usual insecurity of the American in the face of European tradition.

Even William Carlos Williams, for all his efforts to ground his writing in the idioms and rhythms of American experience, reveals a similar complex in his attitude toward Whitman. All of Williams' discussions of Whitman center around Whitman's technical breakthrough, and in this Williams finds him lacking. Summing up his attitude to Whitman in 1955, he says: "He had seen a great light but forgot almost at once after the first revelation everything but his 'message,' the idea which originally set him in motion, the idea on which he had been nurtured, the idea of democracy—and took his eye off the words themselves which should have held him."[10] Williams never did see what the French recognized from the start: that Whitman's "message" was organically related to his form, and that both represented a radical renewal in the technique and attitude of modern literature. It was Poe and not Whitman whom Williams named as the true American original.[11]

But, once again, literary history reveals unexpected associations. While Pound and Williams were busy apologizing for Whitman, they were announcing the very same kind of renewal in literature and in life that the French writers had found in Whitman over a generation before. The Imagist program that Pound sets forth in "A Few Don'ts by an Imagiste" (1913)[12] exactly corresponds with the post-Symbolist return to directness in language and imagery. Many of the major French writers who were associated with this movement in the 1890's—Francis Jammes, Paul Fort, André Gide, and Marcel Schwob—were animated by a strong Whitmanian impulse. In his Imagist manifesto, Pound also suggests *Notes sur la technique poétique*, by Georges Duhamel and Charles Vildrac, as a guide for contemporary experiments in verse rhyme and rhythm. Both of these writers, we remember, had the theory and example of Whitman's free verse very much in mind when they composed their own treatise on vers-libre technique.

In his early writings, Pound consistently proposed Whitman's French followers and admirers as models for literary America. He wrote laudatory articles on Jules Laforgue, Remy de Gourmont, Charles Vildrac, and Jules Romains.[13] The critical selection of French poetry that Pound published in *The Little Review* in 1918 included such writers as Rimbaud, Laforgue, de Gourmont, Vielé-Griffin, Merrill, Jammes, Spire, Vildrac, and Romains.[14] Pound recommended all of these French writers, many of whom had important antecedents in Whitman, as vital models for contemporary experiments in the form and content of literature. For example, Pound says of Jules Romains and unanimism: "He has felt this general replunge of mind into instinct, or this development of instinct to cope with a metropolis and with metropolitan conditions. . . . Romains had made a new kind of poetry. . . . His work is perhaps the fullest statement of the poetic consciousness of our time, or the scope of that consciousness."[15] And yet, unlike Romains, Pound failed to recognize the "en-masse" of the original unanimist, Walt Whitman, who remained securely tucked beneath Pound's collar and dress shirt.

It is in William Carlos Williams that native Whitmanism and French Whitmanism began to converge. Just as Whitman had helped Laforgue to rediscover his senses, so Williams found fresh evidence of the importance of sensation in both Whitman and Laforgue.

Williams says in an article he wrote for *Contact* in 1921: "I begin to feel that there is in Laforgue a something, a very simple and direct thing, without which his ironic talent would have gone for nothing. It is his clear use of sensation. It is a building upon the basis of what is observed, what is proved, what is of value to the man in the welter as he found it, and a rigid exclusion of everything else. It makes the efforts of an Eliot to escape the influence of Laforgue most silly. Why escape influences unless one has imitated the wrong thing?" [16]

For all his loyalty to the American ground, Williams was in some ways an internationalist in spite of himself. His imagist or objectivist phase has antecedents in the return to the direct and concrete that characterized French post-Symbolist writings in the 1890's. Williams' attempt to root literature in the native ground of Whitman also brings him into direct relation with the similarly Whitmanian attempt by such Naturist writers as Jammes and Fort to renew literature through a return to the local and the native.

In his effort to reinvent the form and substance of modern literature, Williams again comes into contact with the liberating impulse that Whitman brought to the French writers. Williams describes his new mode of composition in the Prologue to *Kora in Hell* (1920): "The attention has been held too rigid in one plane instead of following a more flexible, jagged resort. It is to loosen the attention, my attention since I occupy part of the field, that I write these improvisations." [17] But Williams' ideas on broken composition had been anticipated not only by Gide's attempt to record the simultaneity and immediacy of man "feeling," but also by the literary Cubism of Apollinaire and Cendrars. The visionary flow of *Kora in Hell* also has direct links with Rimbaud's *Illuminations* and the language experiments of the Surrealists, whom Williams consistently evoked in defining his new credo.

Williams is also a distant relative of Jules Romains, whose play about a small town doctor, *Knock, ou le triomphe de la médecine* (1923), he saw during his trip to Paris in 1924. One does not have to strain to hear echoes of Romains and his philosophy of unanimism in Williams' work. Even in the long poem *Paterson*, Williams' development of Paterson both as the single consciousness of a man and as the collective consciousness of the city is an imaginative embodiment of Romains' unanimist theories.

During his stay in Paris in 1924, Williams met Valery Larbaud, another of Whitman's French followers. Williams was puzzled by Larbaud's eager desire to speak with him. In his transcription of their conversation in *In the American Grain* Williams says: "Who is this man Larbaud who has so little pride that he wishes to talk with me? . . . He is a student, I am a block, I thought. I could see it at once: he knows far more of what is written of my world than I. But he is a student while I am—the brutal thing itself."[18] What Williams did not realize is that in some ways he represented that poet, who was "le successeur à la fois de Laforgue, de Rimbaud, et de Whitman," of whom Larbaud dreamed as a youth. Williams may have been the "brutal thing itself," but he was also Barnabooth!

Despite Williams' attempt to work the new ground that had been broken by Whitman, after the publication of *The Waste Land* in 1922, Eliot's distaste for Whitman prevailed in American letters. It was not until the 1950's that American writers and critics began to reassess Whitman's real contributions to the renewal of literature and art in the modern world.[19] Gregory Corso spoke for the new generation of American poets when, in an article entitled "Variations on a Generation," he evoked Whitman as a kind of orphic figure who presided over the renovation of American prosody: "In America Walt Whitman the mountain too vast to be seen broods over the dance of the walls that agitates her meadows—and his children Pound Williams Eliot have sat under his shadow inhabiting his beard like butterflies. A whole new generation of prosody has wept and wailed in the solitudinous cities of the West."[20]

As usual, the Americans were a half century behind the French, even in their discovery of Whitman as a vital source of renewal in modern literature. Whitman had opened the field that would be worked by such new American writers as Charles Olson, Henry Miller, Allen Ginsberg, Lawrence Ferlinghetti, Jack Kerouac, Robert Duncan, Denise Levertov, Gary Snyder, Robinson Jeffers, Robert Creeley, and Saul Bellow, as a few generations before that field had been worked by such *avant-garde* French writers as Jules Laforgue, André Gide, Paul Claudel, Georges Duhamel, Jules Romains, Valery Larbaud, Blaise Cendrars, and Guillaume Apollinaire.

If the social impulse that animates the writers associated with Ferlinghetti's City Lights publications revives the spirit of the French artists of the Abbaye and if Ginsberg's description of his measure as "one physical-mental inspiration of thought contained in the elastic of a breath"[21] evokes shades of Claudel's breath-oriented *verset*, it is because Whitman's *Leaves of Grass*, after several years of exile in France, had at last taken root in American soil. The new generation of American writers had finally absorbed the strain of native defiance and extravagance, the organic and rhythmic form, the joyous Adamic mood, the comic and cosmic vision, the urban and cosmopolitan themes, the democratic and fraternal impulse, the personal and confessional voice, the songs of body and soul, the flights through space and time that the French had absorbed from Whitman a half century earlier.

But Whitman's circle again repeats itself. At the same time that the new American writers drank at the native source of Whitman, they repeated his earlier attempt to break through the encrustations of the English tradition by turning to the thinkers and writers of France. If Whitman found vital models for himself and America in such French writers as Volney and Rousseau, Michelet and Hugo, Taine and Sainte-Beuve, the new American writers found equally vital models in such *avant-garde* French writers as Baudelaire and Rimbaud, Apollinaire and Cendrars, Eluard and Breton.

Ultimately, Whitman's circumnavigation, from America to France, from France back to America again, becomes part of the new trend toward an international community of art. As Ezra Pound announced at the beginning of his study of the French poets: "The time when the intellectual affairs of America could be conducted on a monolingual basis is over."[22]

APPENDIX I

CHRONOLOGICAL LIST OF FRENCH CRITICISM OF WHITMAN SINCE 1861

1861

Etienne, Louis. "Walt Whitman, poète, philosophe et 'rowdy.' " *La Revue Européene*, 1 Nov. 1861, pp. 104-17.

1868

Pichot, A. "Correspondance de Londres." *Revue Britannique*, May 1868, pp. 267-68.

1872

Bentzon, Thérèse. "Un Poète américain—Walt Whitman: 'Muscle and Pluck Forever.' " *Revue des Deux Mondes*, 1 June 1872, pp. 565-82.

Blémont, Emile. "La Poésie en Angleterre et aux Etats-Unis." *Renaissance Littéraire et Artistique*, No. 7 (June 1872), pp. 54-56; No. 11 (July 1872), pp. 86-87; No. 12 (July 1872), pp. 90-91.

1877

Cochin, Henri. "Un Poète américain: Walt Whitman." *Le Correspondant*, 25 Nov. 1877, pp. 634-35.

1882

Bentzon, Thérèse. *Littérature et moeurs étrangeres*, II. Lévy, 1882. (Reprint of 1872 article.)

Quesnel, Léo. "La Littérature aux Etats-Unis." *La Nouvelle Revue*, 1 May 1882.

1884

Quesnel, Léo. "Poètes américains—Walt Whitman." *Revue Politique et Littéraire*, 7 (Feb. 1884), 212-17.

1886

Bentzon, Thérèse. "Les Poètes américains." *Revue des Deux Mondes*, 17 (May 1886), 80-115.

Quesnel, Léo. "Walt Whitman." *Bibliothèque Universelle et Revue Suisse*, Feb. 1886, pp. 277-307.

1888

Sarrazin, Gabriel. "Poètes modernes de l'Amérique—Walt Whitman." *Nouvelle Revue*, 52 (May 1888), 164-84.

1889

Sarrazin, Gabriel. *Renaissance de la poésie anglaise*. Paris, 1889. (Reprint of 1888 article.)

1890

Gourmont, Remy de. "The New Spirit, H. Ellis." *Mercure de France*, 1 (June 1890), 220-21.

1892

Béranger, Henri. "Walt Whitman." *L'Ermitage*, June 1892.

Desjardins, Paul. "Walt Whitman." *Journal des Débats*, April 1892.

Gausseron, B. H. "Walt Whitman." *Revue Encyclopédique*, 2, No. 35 (May 1892), 721-26.

Valette, A. "Autobiographie de Walt Whitman que rapporte M. Francis Vielé-Griffin." *Mercure de France*, 2 (May 1892), 85-86.

———. "Article by H. Ellis on Whitman." *Mercure de France*, 5 (May 1892), 368.

Vielé-Griffin, Francis. "Autobiographie de Walt Whitman." *Entretiens Politiques et Littéraires*, 4, No. 25 (April 1892), 166-69.

Wyzewa, Teodor de. "Notes sur les littératures étrangères—Walt Whitman 1819-1892." *Revue Politique et Littéraire*, 49, No. 17 (April 1892) 513-19.

1897

Davray, Henry D. "Lettres anglaises." *Mercure de France*, 41 (June 1897), 585.

1898

Albert, Henri. "Walt Whitman et Johannes Schlaf." *Mercure de France*, 48 (Aug. 1898), 582.

1902

Davray, Henry D. "Lettres anglaises." *Mercure de France*, 51 (Jan. 1902), 261.

———. "Walt Whitman." *L'Ermitage*, 2 (Dec. 1902), 401-19.

Norvins, L. de. "Le Mouvement littéraire aux Etats-Unis." *La Revue des Revues*, Jan. 1902.

1903

Couvert, J. C. *Quelques Poètes américains: Longfellow, Whitman, Poe*. Lyons, 1903.

1904

Blémont, Emile. *Beautés étrangères*. Paris, 1904. (Reprint of 1872 article.)

Davray, Henry D. "Walt Whitman Seer, Henry Wallace." *Mercure de France*, 57 (Nov. 1904), 534.

1906

Davray, Henry D. "Lettres anglaises." *Mercure de France*, 62 (July 1906), 132.

1907

Masson, Elsie. "Walt Whitman, ouvrier et poète." *Mercure de France*, 68 (Aug. 1907), 385-404.

1908

Bazalgette, Léon. *Walt Whitman, l'homme et son oeuvre*. Paris, 1908.

Davray, Henry D. "Walt Whitman, l'homme et son oeuvre, Léon Bazalgette." *Mercure de France*, 74 (July 1908), 335-38.

Lebesgue, Philéas. "Le Livre pour toi, par Marguerite Burnat-Provins." *La Phalange*, Feb. 1908, pp. 755-57.

———. "Léon Bazalgette: Walt Whitman, l'homme et son oeuvre." *La Phalange*, 15 June 1908, pp. 1160-63.

Le Conte, Joseph. "Un Poète américain: Walt Whitman." *La Vie*

Intellectuelle, 1, No. 1 (Feb. 1908). Lecture given at the Université populaire in the North East quarter of Brussels on 2 Feb. 1907.

Nicolas, Pierre. "Lectures étrangères: Walt Whitman." *Pages Libres*, July 1908.

1909

Anon. "Notes." *La Phalange*, 20 April 1909, p. 959.

Larbaud, Valery. "Lettres anglaises: Walt Whitman en français." *La Phalange*, 20 April 1909, pp. 952-55.

Lasserre, Pierre. "Walt Whitman." *Action Française*, April 1909.

Mende, Louis. "Acclimation." *Journal du Soir*, May 1909.

Muselli, V. "Commémoration de la mort de Whitman." *La Phalange*, 20 April 1909.

Royère, J. "Francis Vielé-Griffin: Thrène pour le Président Lincoln." *La Phalange*, February 1909, pp. 739-40.

1910

Alain-Fournier, Henri. "Le Président Roosevelt à la Sorbonne." *Nouvelle Revue Française*, 1 June 1910, pp. 806-08.

Delattre, Floris. "Un Poète de la démocratie: Walt Whitman." *Revue Pédagogique*, 56 (May 1910), 402-20.

Guilbeaux, Henri. *Walt Whitman*. Paris, 1910.

Hirsch, Charles H. "Traduction par L. Bazalgette des propos de Walt Whitman recueillis par H. Traubel à l'insu du poète." *Mercure de France*, 86 (July 1910), 155-56.

1911

Maury, Lucien. *Figures littéraires, écrivains français et étrangers*. Paris, 1911.

Lebesgue, Philéas. "Walt Whitman et la poésie contemporaine," in *Essai d'expansion d'une esthétique*. Tours, 1911, pp. 5-26.

1912

Duhamel, Georges. "*L'Anthologie de l'Effort*." *Mercure de France*, 96 (April 1912), 583.

Ghéon, Henri. "Les Poèmes: le whitmanisme." *Nouvelle Revue Française*, 14 (June 1912), 1053-71.

Guilbeaux, Henri. "Whitmanisme." *Effort Libre*, May-June 1912.

Maury, Lucien. "Figures littéraires: Walt Whitman." *Mercure de France*, 95 (Jan. 1912), 152.

Merrill, Stuart. "Walt Whitman." *Le Masque*, Nos. 9-10 (1912), pp. 303-07.

1913

Anon. "Les Humbles: Revue whitmaniste de Roubaix." *Mercure de France*, 106 (Dec. 1913), 627.

Anon. "Whitman en Italie." *Mercure de France*, 103 (June 1913), 645; "L'Homosexualité de Whitman." *Mercure de France*, 103 (June 1913), 893-95.

Apollinaire, Guillaume. "Funérailles de Walt Whitman racontées par un témoin." *Mercure de France*, 102 (April 1913), 658-59.

______. "La Vie anecdotique: A propos de Walt Whitman." *Mercure de France*, 106 (Dec. 1913), 864-65.

Arcos, René. "A propos de quelques poètes modernes." *Mercure de France*, 105 (Oct. 1913), 697-713.

Bazalgette, Léon. "Le Document de M. Apollinaire." *Effort Libre*, April 1913.

Bazalgette, Léon. "Une Lettre à propos de Walt Whitman." *Mercure de France*, 105 (Sept. 1913), 221-22.

______. "Une Lettre à propos de Walt Whitman." *Mercure de France*, 105 (Oct. 1913).

______. "Les Petits-fils de l'honorable James Harlan." *Effort Libre*, Nov. 1913.

Bekhoud, Georges. "Chronique de Bruxelles." *Mercure de France*, 101 (Jan. 1913).

Bertz, Edouard. "A propos de Walt Whitman: les funérailles, l'homosexualité de Whitman." *Mercure de France*, 104 (July 1913), 204-10.

______. "Lettre à la rédaction à propos de Walt Whitman." *Mercure de France*, 105 (Oct. 1913), 654-55.

______. "Lettre à la rédaction à propos de Walt Whitman." *Mercure de France*, 106 (Nov. 1913), 219.

Casseres, Benjamin de. "Lettre à la rédaction à propos de Walt Whitman." *Mercure de France*, 103 (June 1913), 67.

Duhamel, Georges. "Mallarmé, Whitman, Rimbaud." *Mercure de France*, 102 (April 1913), 76-79.

Merrill, Stuart. "Une Lettre à la rédaction à propos de Walt Whitman."*Mercure de France*, 102 (April 1913), 890-92.

______. "La Question Walt Whitman." *Mercure de France*, 106 (Nov. 1913), 329-36.

Reeves, Harrison. "Lettre à la rédaction à propos de Walt Whitman." *Mercure de France*, 103 (June 1913), 68.

Stanton, Théodore. "Lettres américaines," *Mercure de France*, 105 (Sept. 1913), 668.

Vildrac, Charles. "La Leçon de Walt Whitman." *Les Feuilles de Mai*, No. 3 (April-June), pp. 143-49.

Wilde, Oscar. "La Renaissance anglaise de l'art." *Mercure de France*, 105 (Sept. 1913), 286.

1914

Bertz, Edouard. "Lettre à la rédaction à propos de Walt Whitman." *Mercure de France*, 107 (Jan. 1914), 222-23.

Schinz, Albert. "Lettre à la rédaction à propos de Walt Whitman." *Mercure de France*, 107 (Feb. 1914), 669-71.

1916

Anon. "Walt Whitman et Kennerley." *Mercure de France*, 132 (March 1916), 154-55; "Whitman et Emerson." *Mercure de France*, 132 (March 1916), 237-38.

Stanton, Théodore. "Lettres américaines." *Mercure de France*, 114 (March 1916), 153.

1917

Pilon, Edmond. "Walt Whitman et la France." in *Pèlerinages de guerre jadis et de nos jours*. Paris, 1917.

1918

Cestre, Charles. "Walt Whitman, poète de l'Amérique en guerre." *Revue des Nations Latines*, Oct. 1918, pp. 168-83.

Chadbourne, Louis. "La Pensée américaine et la France." *La Revue*, 125 (Aug. 1918), 274-85.

Davray, Henry D. "Lettres anglaises." *Mercure de France*, 129 (Oct. 1918).

Figuière, Eugène. *Walt Whitman*. Paris, 1918.

Hermant, Abel. "Walt Whitman et Christophe Colomb." *Le Figaro*, 15 Oct. 1918.

Hirsch, Charles H. "Les Revues: les humbles, revue littéraire." *Mercure de France*, 125 (Feb. 1918), 505-10.

Larbaud, Valery. Préface to Walt Whitman: *Oeuvres choisies*. Paris, 1918.

Loyson, Paul-Hyacinth and Longworth Chambrun. "Les Maquilleurs de cadavres; sur la tentative de conversion posthume de Walt Whitman, d'Emile Verhaeren et d'Octave Mirbeau." *La Revue des Revues*, 122 (Jan. 1918), 51-92; 331-43.

Michaud, Regis. "Walt Whitman, poète cosmique," in *Mystiques et réalistes anglo-saxons d'Emerson à Bernard Shaw*. Paris, 1918, pp. 75-104.

Richepin, Jean. "Walt Whitman," in *L'Ame américaine à travers quelques-uns de ses interprètes*. 1918-19, Paris. Twelve Lectures.

1919

Cestre, Charles. "Le Lyrisme de Walt Whitman." *Anglo-French Review*, June 1919, pp. 395-408.

Erkskine, John. *Walt Whitman*. Dijon, 1919. Lecture given in Dijon on June 10, 1919.

______. "Walt Whitman." *Revue de Bourgogne*, 10 June 1919.

Guehenno, Jean. "Whitman, Wilson et l'esprit moderne." *Revue de Paris*, 26 (Jan. 1919), 107-30.

O'Sullivan, Vincent. "La Littérature américaine." *Mercure de France*, 130 (Jan. 1919), 246.

1920

Catel, Jean. "La Poésie américaine d'aujourd'hui." *Mercure de France*, 138 (March 1920), 601.

Cé, Camille. "Le Poète-prophète Walt Whitman." *La Grande Revue*, 101 (Feb. 1920), 573-99.

1921

Bazalgette, Léon. *Le Poème-évangile de Walt Whitman*. Paris, 1921.

Dujardin, Edouard. "Les Premiers poètes du vers libre." *Mercure de France*, 144 (March 1921), 577-621.

Riley, Issac W. *Le Génie américain*. Paris, 1921.

Schoell, Marie. "Walt Whitman et la jeune poésie américaine." *Les Tablettes*, July 1921.

Tonqueduc, Joseph de. "Walt Whitman: un poète de la nature aux Etats-Unis." *Etudes*, 164 (Jan. 1921), 190-207.

1922

Braga, Dominique. "Walt Whitman." *Europe Nouvelle*, No. 35 (Aug. 1922), p. 1042.

Gourmont, Remy de. "Version nouvelle des 'Dormeurs' de Whitman par Bazalgette." *Mercure de France*, 159 (Nov. 1922), 739.

Guehenno, Jean. "Feuilles d'herbe de Walt Whitman." *La Grande Revue*, Nov. 1922, pp. 147-57.

Merrill, Stuart. *Walt Whitman*. Toronto, 1922.

Van Eeden, F. "Walt Whitman." *Le Monde Nouveau*, 4 (May 1922), 1-6.

1923

Catel, Jean. "Walt Whitman, puritain." *Mercure de France*, 167 (Oct. 1923), 289-313.

Villard, Léonie. "Tendances nouvelles de la littérature américaine." *Mercure de France*, 165 (May 1923), 577-617.

1924

Catel, Jean. "Lettres anglo-américaines." *Mercure de France*, 169 (Feb. 1924), 259-60.

———. "Le Roman d'amour de Walt Whitman." *Revue Anglo-Américaine*, Feb. 1924, pp. 197-212.

1926

Catel, Jean. "Walt Whitman." *Mercure de France*, 190 (Sept. 1926), 470-75.

———. "Walt Whitman pendant la guerre de la sécession." *Revue Anglo-Américaine*, 3 (June 1926), 410-19.

Hirsch, Charles H. "Jean Catel: Walt Whitman pendant la Guerre de Sécession." *Mercure de France*, 189 (Aug. 1926), 716.

Michaud, Regis. "Walt Whitman." *Nouvelles Littéraires*, 6 Nov. 1926.

Rogers, C. *La Vie de Walt Whitman*, trans. H. Pierrot. Paris, 1926.

1927

Blaizot, G. "Pages de journal traduits par L. Bazalgette." *Europe*, 2 (1927), 265-67.

Catel, Jean. "La Véridique histoire de Walt Whitman." *Rabelais*, Feb.-Mar. 1927.

Eastman, Max. "Poe, Whitman et la poésie des temps nouveaux." *Europe*, 10 (1927), 443-62.

1928

Lecomte, J. "Un Poète américain, Walt Whitman." *La Vie Intellectuelle*, No. 1 (Feb. 1928).

1929

Catel, Jean. "L'Atelier de Walt Whitman." *Revue Anglo-Américaine*, 6 (Aug. 1929), 527-29.

______. *Walt Whitman: la naissance du poète*. Paris, 1929.

Figuière, Eugène. *Walt Whitman: poète américain*. Paris, 1929.

1930

Catel, Jean. *Rythme et langage dans la première édition de Leaves of Grass*. Montpellier, 1930.

Cestre, Charles. "Walt Whitman, l'inadapté." *Revue Anglo-Américaine*, 6 (June 1930), 385-408.

______. "Walt Whitman, le mystique." *Revue Anglo-Américaine*, 7 (Aug. 1930), 481-501.

______. "Walt Whitman, le poète." *Revue Anglo-Américaine*, 8 (Oct. 1930), 19-41.

1931

Jacoby, John E. *Le Mysticisme dans la pensée américaine*. Paris, 1931.

Lafourcade, Georges. "Swinburne et Walt Whitman." *Revue Anglo-Américaine*, 14 (Oct. 1931), 49-51.

1932

Exideuil, Pierre d'. "Walt Whitman et la poésie." *Cahiers du Sud*, July 1932, pp. 453-69.

1933

Catel, Jean. "Poésie moderne aux Etats-Unis." *Revue des Cours et Conférences*, May 1933, pp. 21-24; 345-57.

1934

Catel, Jean. "Whitman et la Guerre Civile." *Revue Anglo-Américaine*, 10 (June 1934), 434-39.

1935

Cestre, Charles. "Un Intermède de la renommée de Walt Whitman en France." *Revue Anglo-Américaine*, 9 (Dec. 1935), 136-40.

Maratray, R. de. *Whitmaniana, réflexions d'un adepte de la morale ouverte*. Paris, 1935.

1939

Hercourt, Jean. *Primauté de Walt Whitman, essai*. Genève, 1939.

1946

Neveu, Charles. *L'Enigme de Nouveau Monde*. Paris, 1946

1948

Asselineau, Roger. "A propos de Walt Whitman." *Langues Modernes*, 42 (Aug.-Oct. 1948), 62-65.

Billy, A. "Le Plus Grand Génie du XIXe siècle." *Figaro Littéraire*, May 1948, p. 2.

Cestre, Charles. "Walt Whitman, 1819-1892," in *Les Poètes américains*. Paris, 1948, pp. 61-85.

Morgan, Claude. "Walt Whitman et Howard Fast." *Parallèle*, 50, No. 108 (Oct. 1948), 5.

1950

Jamati, Paul. *Walt Whitman, une étude, un choix de poèmes*. Paris, 1950.

1951

Arnavon, Cyrille. *Les Lettres américaines devant la critique française 1887-1917*. Paris, 1951, pp. 51-70.

1952

Asselineau, Roger. "Compte-rendu du *Walt Whitman* de F. Schyberg." *Revue de Littérature Comparée*, Jan.-Mar. 1952, pp. 155-56.

1953

De Graaf, Daniel A. "Arthur Rimbaud et Walt Whitman." *Levende Talen* (Nov. 1953), pp. 363-72.

1954

Asselineau, Roger. *L'Evolution de Walt Whitman*. Paris, 1954.

______. "Un Poète cosmique américain: Walt Whitman." *Mystère Solitaire,* Nos. 13-14 (Jan. 1954).

______. "La Thème de la mort dans l'oeuvre de Walt Whitman," *La Revue des Lettres Modernes,* Nov. 1954, pp. 33-48.

1955

Anon. "Walt Whitman, poète insolite." *Informations et Documents,* No. 25 (15 Mar. 1955), pp. 29-38.

Asselineau, Roger. "Whitman et Wordsworth—étude d'une influence indirecte." *Revue de Littérature Comparée,* 29 (1955), 505-12.

Guehenno, Jean. "Rousseau et Whitman." *Figaro,* 22 Nov. 1955, p. 1.

Hentges, Phyl et Pierre. "Walt Whitman, poète d'un nouveau monde." *Nouvelle Critique,* 7 (Sept.-Oct. 1955), 84-104.

Herra, Maurice. "Feuilles d'Herbe en Europe et en Amerique Latine." *Europe,* 33 (Nov.-Dec. 1955), 137-45.

Jamati, Paul. "Léon Bazalgette: Introducteur de Whitman." *Europe,* 33 (Nov.-Dec. 1955), 135-37.

Jouvenel, Renaud de. "Walt Whitman." *Europe,* 33 (Nov.-Dec. 1955), 91-107.

______. "Walt Whitman." *Lettres Françaises,* No. 586 (Sept. 1955), p. 1; p. 9.

1956

Lacote, René. "Le Chemin de Whitman." *Lettres Françaises* (March 1956), p. 2.

Messaien, Pierre. "Walt Whitman, poète des Etats-Unis et la démocratie." *Le Croix,* 24 March 1956, p. 3.

Sillen, Samuel. "Walt Whitman, poète de la democratie américaine." *La Pensée,* No. 69 (1956), pp. 71-91; No. 70 (1956), pp. 69-82.

1957

Asselineau, Roger. "Un Inédit de Walt Whitman: Taine's *History of English.*" *Etudes Anglaises,* 10 (1957), 128-38.

Cestre, Charles. "L'Evolution de Walt Whitman." *Les Langues Modernes,* 51 (1957), 158-60.

Remords, G. "Les Lettres américaines et la critique universitaire française." *Bulletin de la Faculté de Lettres de Strausbourg*. Jan. 1957.

Roddier, Henri. "Pierre Leroux, George Sand et Walt Whitman, ou l'éveil d'un poète. *Revue de Littérature Comparée*, 31 (1957), 5-33.

1958

Asselineau, Roger. "Etat présent des etudes Whitmaniennes." *Etudes Anglaises*, 11 (1958), 31-40.

1959

Bosquet, Alain. *Whitman*. Paris, 1959.

1962

Murciaux, Christian. "Walt Whitman, poète et prophète." *Revue des Deux Mondes*, 15 Nov. 1962, pp. 182-99.

1966

Brunel, Pierre. "A la recherche d'une influence: l'image de l'orchestre et la tentation symphonique chez Walt Whitman et Paul Claudel." *Revue des Lettres Modernes*, Nos. 134-36 (1966), pp. 49-63.

1967

Taylor, Paul. "Les Deux Faces de Walt Whitman." *Synthèses*, Nos. 251-52 (1967), pp. 104-07.

1969

Bordier, Roger. "Whitman et Lorca." *Europe*, 483 (1969) 188-91.

Bosquet, Alain. "Les Deux Visages de Walt Whitman." *Nouvelles Litteraires*, 21 Aug. 1969, p. 3.

1975

Asselineau, Roger. "Whitman et Millet." *La Quinzaine Littéraire*, 16 Nov. 1975, p. 18.

1976

Asselineau, Roger. "Jack London et Walt Whitman." *Europe: Revue Littéraire Mensuelle*, 54 (Jan.-Feb. 1976), 76.

APPENDIX II

CHRONOLOGICAL LIST OF FRENCH TRANSLATIONS OF WHITMAN SINCE 1886

1886

Laforgue, Jules. "*Les Brins d'herbe:* traduit de l'étonnant poète américain Walt Whitman—*Dédicaces.*" *La Vogue*, 1, No. 10 (June-July 1886), 325-28. (Includes "Je Chante le soi-même," "Aux Nations étrangères," "A Un Historien," "A Une Certaine Cantatrice," "Ne Fermez pas vos portes," "Poètes à venir," "A Vous," and "Toi lecteur.")

———. "O Etoile de France." *La Vogue*, 1, No. 11 (July 1886), 388-90.

———. "Une Femme m'attend." *La Vogue*, 2, No. 3 (August 1886), 73-76.

1888

Vielé-Griffin, Francis. "Walt Whitman: Poèmes—'Visages,' 'A Une Locomotive en hiver,' 'Un Monde.' " *Revue Indépendante*, 9, No. 25 (Nov. 1888), 279-86.

1889

Vielé-Griffin, Francis. "Walt Whitman: *Ruisseaux d'automne—'Il y avait un enfant qui partait chaque jour.'* " *La Cravache Parisienne*, No. 423 (June 1889).

1892

Vielé-Griffin, Francis. "Walt Whitman: 'A Quelque Révolutionnaire d'Europe dans la défaite.' " *Les Entretiens Politiques et Littéraires*, 5, No. 32 (Nov. 1892), 219.

1894

Jerrold, Laurence. "Walt Whitman: Poèmes." *Le Magasin Inter-*

national, No. 1 (Dec. 1894), pp. 5-12. (Includes "Qui que ce soit," "Le Poète," and "Chant au soleil.")

1896

Jerrold, Laurence. "Walt Whitman: *Les Feuilles d'herbe*, préface de la première édition de 1855." *Le Magazine International*, Jan. 1896, pp. 1-7.

______. "Walt Whitman: *Les Feuilles d'herbe*: préface (suite)." *Le Magazine International*, July 1896, pp. 267-70.

1899

Vielé-Griffin, Francis. "Walt Whitman: 'Le Chant de la hache.' " *L'Ermitage*, 1 (1899), 293-308.

1901

Davray, Henry. "Walt Whitman: 'Salut Au Monde!' " *La Plume*, 1 February 1901, pp. 67-70.

______. "Walt Whitman: *Brins d'herbe*." *La Plume*, 1 April 1901, pp. 194-96. (Includes "Aux Contrées étrangères," "Commençant mes études," "A Une Certaine Cantatrice," "One's self I sing," "Me Imperturbe," "Ne Fermez pas vos portes," and "Poètes à venir.")

Halévy, Daniel. "Walt Whitman: Chants démocratiques." *Pages Libres*, July 1901, pp. 75-80. (Includes "Aux Ouvriers," "A Un Révolté ou à une révoltée vaincue," "La Mère de toutes choses," and "Le Départ approche.")

1902

Davray, Henry. "Walt Whitman: *Specimen Days*." *L'Ermitage*, Dec. 1902, pp. 401-19.

1903

Davray, Henry. "Walt Whitman: *Specimen Days*, suite." *L'Ermitage*, Jan. 1903, pp. 60-72.

______. "Walt Whitman: *Specimen Days*, suite." *L'Ermitage*, Feb. 1903, pp. 112-33.

______. "Walt Whitman: *Specimen Days*, suite." *L'Ermitage*, March 1903, pp. 201-21. (Also includes six poems: "A Une Certaine Cantatrice," "Vocalisme," "Italian Music in Dakota," "Proud

Music of the Storm," "Cette Musique toujours autour de moi," and "Pour des voyages à travers les états.")

1904

Fabulet, Louis. "Walt Whitman: Poèmes." *L'Ermitage*, Mar. 1904, pp. 218-22. (Includes "O Sud-Aimant," "A Un Etranger," and "Quand j'appris à la chute du jour.")

1905

Fabulet, Louis. "Walt Whitman: Poèmes." *L'Ermitage*, 15 Dec. 1905, pp. 333-40. (Includes "J'ai traversé jadis une cité populeuse," "Battez! battez! tambours!," "Reviens des champs Père," "Mouvements primitifs," "Etrange Veillée que je fis sur le terrain une nuit," and "O Etoile de France 1870-1871.")

1908

Vielé-Griffin, Francis. *Walt Whitman: Thrène pour le président Lincoln*. Paris, 1908.

1909

Bazalgette, Léon. *Walt Whitman: Feuilles d'herbe*. Paris, 1909.

1910

Bazalgette, Léon. "Walt Whitman: Quelques propos." *Nouvelle Revue Française*, 1 June 1910. (Excerpts from *With Walt Whitman in Camden* by Horace Traubel.)

1911

Bazalgette, Léon. "Walt Whitman: Préface de la première édition de *Feuilles d'herbe* (1855)." *La Phalange*, March 1911.

1912

Bazalgette, Léon. "Walt Whitman: Poèmes choisis," in *L'Anthologie de l'Effort*, Paris, 1912, pp. 285-308.

1913

Bazalgette, Léon. "Walt Whitman: Pages de journal." *Effort Libre*, Feb. 1913.

1914

Bazalgette, Léon. *Poèmes de Walt Whitman*. Paris, 1914.

———.. "Walt Whitman: Pages de journal." *Effort Libre*, June 1914, pp. 550-61.

1916

Bazalgette, Léon. "Walt Whitman: Pages de journal." *Mercure de France*, Mar. 1916.

1917

Bazalgette, Léon. *Walt Whitman: Ode à la France*. Paris, 1917.

Bazalgette, Léon and A. M. Gossez. *Walt Whitman: Le Panseur de plaies, poèmes, lettres et fragments sur la guerre*. Paris. 1917.

1918

Gide, André, Jean Schlumberger, Jules Laforgue, Louis Fabulet, Francis Vielé-Griffin, and Valery Larbaud. *Walt Whitman: Oeuvres choisies*. Paris, 1918.

1919

Bazalgette, Léon. *Walt Whitman: Calamus*. Paris, 1919.

———. *Walt Whitman: Les Dormeurs*. Paris, 1919.

———. *Walt Whitman: Six Poèmes*. Paris, 1919.

1922

Bazalgette, Léon. *Walt Whitman: Feuilles d'herbe*. Paris, 1922.

1924

Bazalgette, Léon. *Walt Whitman: Les Dormeurs*. Paris, 1924. (Re-edition of 1919 volume.)

1926

Beach, Sylvia. "La Dix-huitième présidence." *Navire d'Argent*, 1 Mar. 1926.

L'Ane d'Or, Feb.-Mar. 1926 (special Whitman issue).

1930

Gide, André, et al. *Walt Whitman: Oeuvres choisies*. Paris, 1930. (Re-edition of 1918 volume.)

1936

Dion-Levesque, R. *Walt Whitman, ses meilleures pages*. Paris, 1936.

1946

Neveu, Charles. "Walt Whitman: *Perspectives démocratiques*," in *L'Enigme du nouveau monde*. Paris, 1946, pp. 41-72.

1947

Bokanowski, Hélène. *Walt Whitman: Choix des textes et traduction*. Paris, 1947.

1948

Jamati, Paul. *Walt Whitman: Une Etude, un choix de poèmes (Poètes d'aujourd-hui)*. Paris, 1948.

1951

Messiaen, Pierre. *Walt Whitman: Choix de poèmes*. Paris, 1951.

1955

"Walt Whitman: Fragments politiques inédits en français." *La Nouvelle Critique*, 7 (July-Aug. 1955), 239-56. (Extracts from "The Eighteenth Presidency!," *Democratic Vistas*, and a letter to a Russian translator).

1956

Asselineau, Roger. *Walt Whitman: Feuilles d'herbe* (Choix). Paris, 1956.

1959

Bosquet, Alain. *Whitman*. Paris, 1959. (Biographical and critical introduction with translations of selected poetry and prose.)

1960

Gide, André et al. *Walt Whitman: Poèmes et proses*. Paris, 1960. (Re-edition of 1918 volume.)

1966

Asselineau, Roger. *Walt Whitman: Chants de la terre qui tourne*. Paris, 1966.

1972

Asselineau, Roger. *Leaves of Grass: Feuilles d'herbe* (choix), Paris, 1972.

NOTES

INTRODUCTION

1. John Burroughs, *Notes on Walt Whitman as Poet and Person* (1867; rpt. New York, 1971), p. 80.

2. Walt Whitman, *Prose Works 1892*, ed. Floyd Stovall, II (New York, 1964), 523.

3. Matthew Arnold, "Letter to W. D. O'Connor" (Sept. 16, 1866), reprinted in *Walt Whitman*, ed. Francis Murphy (Baltimore, 1970), p. 89.

4. Walt Whitman, *Leaves of Grass: Comprehensive Readers Edition*, ed. Harold Blodgett and Sculley Bradley (New York, 1965), p. 709.

5. R. W. B. Lewis, *The American Adam* (Chicago, 1955), p. 50. See also the more recent study of Whitman by Edwin Haviland Miller, *Walt Whitman's Poetry: A Psychological Journey* (New York, 1968). Miller says of Whitman's relationship to other writers and thinkers: "Although the journey to self-awareness, and therefore to reality, has a long literary history, the past furnished Whitman with no usable models" (pp. 66-67).

CHAPTER I

1. Horace Traubel, *With Walt Whitman in Camden*, I (Boston, 1906), 461.

2. Howard Mumford Jones, *America and French Culture: 1750-1848* (Chapel Hill, 1927).

3. Cited in Gay Wilson Allen, *The Solitary Singer* (1955; rpt. New York, 1960), p. 72.

4. Traubel, IV (Philadelphia, 1953), 223.

5. Walt Whitman, *Prose Works 1892*, ed. Floyd Stovall, II (New York, 1964), 757. Subsequent references to this edition will appear in the text as *PW*.

6. Traubel, I, 467.

7. Walt Whitman, *Leaves of Grass: Comprehensive Readers Edition*, ed. Harold Blodgett and Sculley Bradley (New York, 1965). Unless otherwise indicated, all quotations of Whitman's poems are from this edition. Subsequent references to this edition will appear in the text as *LG*.

8. Edith Wharton, *A Backward Glance* (New York, 1934), p. 186.

9. Richard Maurice Bucke, *Walt Whitman* (Philadelphia, 1883), p. 52.

10. Traubel, I, 124.

11. *The Complete Writings of Walt Whitman: Notes and Fragments*, ed. R. M. Bucke et al. (New York, 1902), IX, 82.

12. *New York Dissected*, ed. Emory Holloway and Ralph Adimari (New York, 1936), pp. 70-71.

13. *Notes and Fragments*, p. 218.

14. Voltaire, *Philosophical Dictionary*, ed. Abner Kneeland (1824; rpt. Boston, 1852), II, 150. Whitman owned the 1836 reprint of this edition.

15. *LG*, p. 719.

16. *New York Dissected*, pp. 69-73. Subsequent references to this article will appear in the text.

17. Traubel, II (New York, 1908), 445.

18. Whitman, "Sun-down Papers," in *The Uncollected Poetry and Prose of Walt Whitman*, ed. Emory Holloway (New York, 1921), I, 37.

19. *Ibid.*

20. Constantin Volney, *The Ruins: or Meditations on the Revolutions of Empires*, trans. Joel Barlow (1802; rpt. New York, 1853), p. 35. Since it was probably Barlow's translation of *The Ruins* that Whitman owned, all quotes will be from this edition. Subsequent references to this work will appear in the text.

21. Preface 1855—*Leaves of Grass: Comprehensive Readers Edition*, p. 719; "Song of Myself" (1855), Line 429, in Walt Whitman's *Leaves of Grass: His Original Edition*, ed. Malcolm Cowley (New York, 1959). Subsequent references to the 1855 poems will be from this work and will appear in the text as *LG* 1855.

22. *Notes and Fragments*, p. 49.

23. *Ibid.*, p. 213.

24. David Goodale discusses some of Whitman's debt to Volney in "Some of Walt Whitman's Borrowings," *American Literature*, X (May 1938), 202-13.

25. Malcolm Cowley, ed., *Leaves of Grass*, p. xii.

26. *Uncollected Poetry and Prose*, I, 121.

27. "Notes on Rousseau," *Faint Clews and Indirections: Manuscripts of Walt Whitman and His Family*, ed. Clarence Gohdes and Rollo G. Silver (Durham, 1949), p. 41.

28. "Art and Artists" (1851), *Uncollected Poetry and Prose*, I, 243. The example of Rousseau's life and art figure importantly in this address to the Brooklyn Art Union.

29. *Notes and Fragments*, p. 80.

30. J-J Rousseau, *The Confessions*, trans. William Swinton (1856; rpt. New York, 1858), II, 395. Swinton was a friend of Whitman; this is the edition Whitman cites in his biographical note on Rousseau.

31. Rousseau, *The Confessions*, I, 191-92.

32. *Notes and Fragments*, p. 80.

33. *Ibid.*, p. 81.

34. Rousseau, *Confessions*, II, 395.

35. Walt Whitman, *The Correspondence* (1842-1892), III (1964, New York), 308.

36. Traubel, III (New York, 1914), 397.

37. *Ibid.*, p. 355.

38. Rousseau, *Confessions*, I, 21.

39. "A Backward Glance," *LG: Comprehensive Readers Edition*, pp. 573-74.

40. *Uncollected Poetry and Prose*, I, 125-37.

41. *Ibid.*, pp. 132-33.

42. *Notes and Fragments*, p. 63; the article was clipped from Charles Knight, *Half-Hours with the Best Authors* (Philadelphia, 1847-49), pp. 123-32.

43. Knight, *Half-Hours*, p. 124.

44. *Uncollected Poetry and Prose*, I, 134.

45. Jules Michelet, *History of France*, trans. G. H. Smith (New York, 1848), I, 4.

46. Gay Wilson Allen, "Walt Whitman and Jules Michelet," *Etudes Anglaises*, I (May 1937), 232.

47. Jules Michelet, *The People*, trans. G. H. Smith (New York, 1846), p. 6.

48. Adeline Knapp, "A Whitman Coincidence," *Critic*, 44 (1907), 467-68. In a recent article, "Whitman and Michelet—Continued," *American Literature*, 45 (Nov. 1973), 428-32, Gay Wilson Allen discusses the parallels between Michelet's *The Bird* and Whitman's mockingbird in "Out of the Cradle Endlessly Rocking"; Arthur Geffen also suggests Michelet's *La Femme* (*Women*, English trans. 1860) as a source for "Passage to India"; in "Walt Whitman and Jules Michelet—One More Time," *American Literature*, 45 (March 1973), 107-14.

49. Books that Whitman noticed or reviewed for the *Brooklyn Daily Eagle* include Dumas' *The Duke of Burgundy*, *The Count of Monte Christo*, *Diana of Meridor*, *Sylvandire*, and *Memoirs of a Physician*; Soulié's *Pastourel* and *Countess of Morion*; Sue's *Martin the Foundling* and *The Wandering Jew*; in *Uncollected Poetry and Prose*, I, 125-37. Whitman refers to the work of Paul de Kock in "Home Literature," *Brooklyn Daily Eagle* (1846); in *Uncollected Poetry and Prose*, I, 123.

50. Traubel, III, 422-23.

51. *Notes and Fragments*, p. 19.

52. Esther Shephard, *Walt Whitman's Pose* (New York, 1938), p. 140.

53. *Ibid.*, p. 221.

54. Whitman, "Lectures and Lessons," in Clifton Furness, *Walt*

Whitman's Workshop (Cambridge, 1928), p. 34.

55. Traubel, III, 35.

56. William Sloane Kennedy, *Conservator*, Feb. 1907, pp. 184-85, cited in *LG*, pp. 148-49n.

57. George Sand, *Consuelo*, trans. Francis G. Shaw (New York, 1846), pp. 423-24.

58. *Uncollected Poetry and Prose*, I, 135.

59. The subject has been discussed by G. R. Roy, "Walt Whitman, George Sand, and Certain French Socialists," *Revue de Littérature Comparée*, 29 (1955), 550-61; Henri Roddier, "Pierre Leroux, George Sand, et Walt Whitman, ou l'éveil d'un poète," *Revue de Littérature Comparée*, 31 (1957), 5-33.

60. Walt Whitman, "A Christmas Garland: Genius—Victor Hugo-George Sand-Emerson," *Christmas Graphic* (1874), in *Uncollected Poetry and Prose*, II, 53.

61. Furness, p. 207.

62. Cited in *Correspondence*, V (1969), 222n.

63. Traubel, II, 502.

64. *Notes and Fragments*, p. 81.

65. Walt Whitman, "The Moral Effect of the Cable," in *I Sit and Look Out* (New York, 1932), pp. 159-60.

66. *Ibid.*, p. 159.

67. Traubel, I, 443.

68. Traubel, IV, 281.

69. See Charles Lombard, "Whitman and Hugo," *Walt Whitman Review*, 19 (March 1973), 19-25. Lombard claims that Whitman became familiar with Hugo's works through his involvement with the New York literati in the 1840's and 1850's; however, this article is poorly researched and full of inaccuracies.

70. Cited in Shephard, pp. 135-36.

71. Traubel, II, 523.

72. Traubel, I, 119.

73. Traubel, V, (Illinois, 1964), 127.

74. Whitman, "Genius—Victor Hugo-George Sand-Emerson," in *Uncollected Poetry and Prose*, II, 53.

75. Traubel, II, 522.

76. *Ibid.*, p. 335.

77. See, for example: "Les Pauvres gens" and "Le Crapaud" for the same sympathy and compassion for common life, both human and natural, that is present throughout Whitman's poetry; "Dieu invisible au philosophe" and "Tout le passé et tout l'avenir" for the same contrast between man's constant

complaints and the faith of natural creation, particularly animals, in the order of things that is characteristic of Whitman's poetry; "L'Epopée du ver" for similarities between the protean qualities of the worm and Whitman's poetic "I."

78. Victor Hugo, *La Légende des siècles*, ed. Jean-louis Cornuz (Paris, 1968). All quotations of *La Légende* are from this edition.

79. *Correspondence*, III, 391.

80. Traubel, II, 522.

81. *Ibid.*, p. 335.

82. Traubel, III, 90.

83. *Ibid.*, p. 360.

84. Whitman's article on Taine was published by Roger Asselineau, "Un inédit de Walt Whitman: Taine's *History of English Literature*," *Etudes Anglaises*, 10 (1957), 128-38.

85. *Ibid.*, p. 131.

86. *Ibid.*, p. 135.

87. *Ibid.*, p. 129.

88. *Ibid.*, p. 136.

89. Traubel, III, 175.

90. Traubel, V, 496.

91. Traubel, III, 182.

92. *Ibid.*, p. 175. Whitman claimed that Zola's salutation was sent by way of a man named Minturn; I have found no record of this communication.

93. Sainte-Beuve's *Critiques et portraits littéraires* (1832) first appeared in English translation in 1839.

94. Whitman copied the passage from a review of Sainte-Beuve's *Nouveaux Lundis* (1868), which appeared in the *North American Review*, 108 (Jan. 1869), 296-99; see *Prose Works 1892*, II, 482n.

Chapter II

1. Teodor de Wyzewa, "Notes sur les littératures étrangères—Walt Whitman," *Revue Politique et Littéraire*, 23 April 1892, p. 513.

2. *Ibid.*, p. 513.

3. In *L'Evolution de Walt Whitman* (1954), Roger Asselineau points out the similarities between *Les Fleurs du mal* and the titles Whitman initially contemplated for *Leaves of Grass:* "Flames of Confession," "Drops of My Blood," "Drops of Evil," "Flames of Evil," "Verses of Evil." *The Evolution of Walt Whitman*, trans. Burton L. Cooper (Cambridge, 1962), II, 119.

4. Charles Baudelaire, *Les Fleurs du mal*, in *Oeuvres complètes*, ed. Jacques Crépet (Paris, 1923), V, 7.

5. See Chapter I, note 94.

6. Charles Baudelaire, "L'Art romantique," in *Oeuvres complètes*, II, 119.

7. Charles Baudelaire, "A Arsène Houssaye," in *Oeuvres complètes*, III, vi.

8. Emile Blémont, *Beautés étrangères* (Paris, 1904), p. 147.

9. For example: C. P. Cambiare, *The Influence of Edgar Allan Poe in France* (1927); Léon Lemonnier, *Edgar Poe et la critique française de 1845 à 1875* (Paris, 1928), *Les Traducteurs d'Edgar Poe en France* (Paris, 1928), *Edgar Poe et les poètes français* (Paris, 1932), *Edgar Poe et les conteurs français* (Paris, 1932); Louis Seylaz, *Edgar Poe et les premiers symbolistes français* (Lausanne, 1923); Joseph Chiari, *Symbolism from Poe to Mallarmé: The Growth of a Myth* (London, 1956); Patrick Francis Quinn, *The French Face of Edgar Poe* (Carbondale, 1957).

10. Louis Etienne, "Walt Whitman, poète, philosophe et rowdy," *La Revue Européene*, 1 Nov. 1861, pp. 104-17.

11. For a study of Whitman's reception among the French critics, see Oreste Pucciani, "The Literary Reputation of Whitman in France," Diss. Harvard, 1943.

12. Emile Blémont, "La Poésie en Angleterre et aux Etats-Unis, III, Walt Whitman," *Renaissance Artistique et Littéraire*, No. 7 (June 1872), pp. 54-56; No. 11 (July 1872), pp. 86-87; No. 12 (July 1872), pp. 90-91.

13. Thérèse Bentzon, "Un Poète américain, Walt Whitman; 'Muscle and Pluck Forever,' " *Revue des Deux Mondes*, 1 June 1872, pp. 565-82.

14. Blémont, "Walt Whitman," No. 7 (June 1872), p. 56.

15. Jean Richepin, "Walt Whitman," in *L'Ame américaine à travers quelques-uns des ses interprètes*, Douze conférences, 1918-1919 (Paris, 1920), p. 243.

16. *Ibid.*

17. Richepin, p. 242.

18. Arthur Rimbaud, *Correspondance inédite (1870-1875)*, ed. Roger Gilbert-Lecomte (Paris, 1929), p. 57. Subsequent references to this edition will appear in the text.

19. Speaking of Verlaine and Rimbaud in his article "Arthur Rimbaud et Walt Whitman," Daniel De Graff says: "Mais il suffisait que les deux poètes, avides de nouvelles inspirations d'origine étrangère, prissent connaissance de deux périodiques français tels que la *Revue des Deux Mondes* et la *Renaissance artistique et littéraire*, pour se renseigner sur l'homme [Whitman] et son oeuvre" (p. 363). Mr. De Graff also suggests that Blémont spoke with Rimbaud about Whitman when they posed for Fantin-Latour's picture "Coin de Table" in 1872; in *Levende Talen*, Nov. 1953, pp. 363-72. In *Rimbaud et Verlaine*

vivants (Paris, 1949), Robert Goffin suggests that Rimbaud and Verlaine became acquainted with Whitman's work during their several sojourns to England in the 1870's (pp. 270-71).

20. Bentzon, pp. 569-70.

21. Rimbaud, *Oeuvres*, ed. Suzanne Bernard (Paris, 1960). Subsequent references to this edition will appear in the text.

22. Bentzon, p. 568. For further discussion of the affinities between the mystic and primitive strains in Whitman and Rimbaud, see David Wells, "Whitman and Rimbaud," *Walt Whitman Review*, 19 (March 1973), 25-28.

23. De Graaf, p. 369.

24. Bentzon, p. 569.

25. Blémont, No. 11 (July 1872), 87.

26. *Ibid.*

27. Suzanne Bernard, ed., *Oeuvres de Rimbaud* (Paris, 1960), p. 532n.

28. Edouard Dujardin, *Les Premiers Poètes du vers libre* (Paris, 1936), p. 155.

29. Marcel Raymond, *From Baudelaire to Surrealism*, trans. G. M. (New York, 1950), p. 62.

30. Warren Ramsey, *Jules Laforgue and the Ironic Inheritance* (New York, 1953), p. 68. According to Ramsey, it was part of Laforgue's function to run through "numbers of the *Revue des deux mondes* for articles that the Empress might have missed. Dreary as this occupation must have been, it was not quite fruitless: one day in an old *Revue* he stumbled on an article about Walt Whitman—bad, scolding, but nevertheless an introduction to the American poet that had a far-reaching effect on his verse technique." The article was "Un Poète américain, Walt Whitman," by Thérèse Bentzon. See note 13 in this chapter.

31. Jules Laforgue, "*Les Brins d'herbe:* traduit de l'étonnant poète américain, Walt Whitman," *La Vogue*, 1, No. 10 (June 1886), 325-28; 1, No. 11 (July 1886), 388-90; 2, No. 3 (Aug. 1886), 73-76.

32. Traubel, IV, 266.

33. Laforgue, *La Vogue*, June 1886, p. 327.

34. *Lettres à un ami: Laforgue à Kahn*, ed. G. Jean-Aubry (Paris, 1941), p. 197.

35. Jules Laforgue, *Poésies complètes*, ed. G. Jean-Aubry (Paris, 1943). Subsequent references to this edition will appear in the text.

36. *Lettres à un ami*, p. 197.

37. Laforgue, "Une Femme m'attend," *La Vogue*, 2 (Aug. 1886), 73-76.

38. *Lettres à un ami*, p. 193.

39. Stuart Merrill, "Walt Whitman," trans. John J. Espey, *Walt Whitman Newsletter*, 3, No. 4 (Dec. 1957), 55-56. Originally appeared in *Le Masque*,

Nos. 9-10 (1912), pp. 303-07.

40. *Ibid.*, p. 57.

41. Cited in Marjorie-Louise Henry, *La Contribution d'un américain au symbolisme français: Stuart Merrill* (Paris, 1927), p. 149.

42 Stuart Merrill, "La Question Walt Whitman," *Mercure de France*, 106 (Nov. 1913), p. 334.

43. Cited in Henry, p. 188.

44. Traubel, I, 118-19.

45. *Ibid.*, p. 119.

46. *Ibid.*, p. 171.

47. Francis Vielé-Griffin, "Visages"; "A Une Locomotive en hiver"; "Un Monde"; *Revue Indépendante*, 9, No. 25 (Nov. 1888), 279-86.

48. In an article entitled "Autobiographie de Walt Whitman," in *Les Entretiens Politiques et Littéraires*, 4, No. 25 (April 1892), Vielé-Griffin says: "J'ai offert il y a deux ans pour rien une traduction de Whitman à l'editeur Savine, il me fut gracieusement répondu que l'auteur de Brins d'Herbe était 'trop peu connu' " (169).

49. Francis Vielé-Griffin, "Il y avait un enfant qui partait chaque jour," *La Cravache Parisienne*, No. 432 (June 1889); "A Quelque Révolutionnaire d'Europe dans la défaite," *Les Entretiens Politiques et Littéraires*, 5, No. 32 (Nov. 1892), 219-20; "Le Chant de la hache," *L'Ermitage* (April 1899), pp. 293-308.

50. Francis Vielé-Griffin, *Thrène pour le Président Lincoln, transposition du poème de Walt Whitman* (Paris, 1908).

51. Pucciani, p. 5.

52. Cited in Henry, *Stuart Merrill*, p. 213.

53. Stuart Merrill, "Les Poésies," *L'Ermitage* (April 1893), p. 272. Cited in Martin Kanes, "La Fortune de Walt Whitman en France," Diss. Sorbonne, 1953, p. 89.

54. Stuart Merrill, *Les Quatres Saisons* (Paris, 1900).

55. Stuart Merrill, *Une Voix dans la foule* (Paris, 1909). Subsequent references to this work will appear in the text.

56. Francis Vielé-Griffin, *Joies* (Paris, 1889). Subsequent references to this work will appear in the text.

57. Francis Vielé-Griffin, *Clarté de vie* (Paris, 1897).

58. Interview with Percy Mansell Jones, reported in P. M. Jones, *The Background of Modern French Poetry* (Cambridge, 1951), pp. 138-39.

59. Guy Michaud, *Message poétique du symbolisme* (Paris, 1947), II, 387.

60. Georges Duhamel, "Mallarmé, Whitman, Rimbaud," *Mercure de France*, 102 (April 1913), 577.

61. Jules Huret, *L'Enquête sur l'évolution littéraire* (Paris, 1891), p. 60.

62. Jethro Bithell, *The Life and Writings of Maurice Maeterlinck* (London, 1913).

63. Percy Mansell Jones, "Influence of Walt Whitman on the Origin of the 'Vers Libre'," *Modern Language Review*, 6 (1916), 191.

64. Vielé-Griffin, "Visages," *Revue Indépendante*, p. 279.

65. Maurice Maeterlinck, *Serres chaudes* (Bruxelles, 1900).

66. P. M. Jones, "Whitman and Verhaeren," *Aberystwyth Studies*, 2 (1914), 71-106; Huberta Randall, "Whitman and Verhaeren—Priests of Human Brotherhood," *French Review*, 16 (1942), 36-43.

67. P. M. Jones, "Memories of Emile Verhaeren," *Belgian Review* (June 1944), p. 29.

68. P. M. Jones, "Influence of Whitman on the Origin of 'Vers Libre'," *Modern Language Review*, 6 (1916), 186-94; "Whitman and the Origins of the Vers Libre," in *The Background of Modern French Poetry* (Cambridge, 1951), pp. 136-51.

69. Jones, "Influence of Whitman on the Origin of 'Vers Libre'," p. 188.

70. Gabriel Sarrazin, "Poètes modernes de l'Amérique, Walt Whitman," *La Nouvelle Revue*, 52 (May 1888), 164. Subsequent references to this article will appear in the text.

71. Whitman, *The Correspondence*, IV, 273.

72. Traubel, IV, 221.

73. *Ibid.*, p. 427.

74. Whitman, *The Correspondence*, IV, 278.

75. Traubel, IV, 221-22.

76. Whitman, *The Correspondence*, IV, 379.

77. Traubel, V, 408.

78. Traubel, V, 498.

CHAPTER III

1. *Documents sur le naturisme*, cited in Robert Mallet, *Le Jammisme* (Paris, 1961), p. 219.

2. *Ibid.*

3. Cited in Jones, "Whitman and the Symbolists," in *The Background of Modern French Poetry*, p. 84.

4. Paul Fort, *Ballades françaises*, XIV (Paris, 1912). All quotations from *Naissance du printemps* and *Vivre en Dieu* are from this volume.

5. Francis Jammes, "Un Manifeste littéraire de Monsieur Francis Jammes: le jammisme," *Mercure de France*, 40 (March 1897), 492-93.

6. *Oeuvres de Francis Jammes*, I (Paris, 1913). All quotations of the poems are from this volume.

7. Marcel Schwob, *Oeuvres complètes*, I (Paris, 1927).

8. Schwob, *Coeur double* (Paris, 1891), p. ix.

9. *Ibid.*, p. xxii.

10. Edmond and Jules Goncourt, *Journal: mémoires de la vie littéraire (1891-1904)*, ed. Robert Ricatte (Monaco, 1956), IV, 436.

11. *Oeuvres de Marcel Schwob*, II (Paris, 1921).

12. *Ibid.*, I, 174-75.

13. S. A. Rhodes, "The Influence of Walt Whitman on André Gide," *Romanic Review*, 31 (April 1940), 157.

14. André Gide, *Si le grain ne meurt* (1928; rpt. Paris, 1945), p. 246.

15. André Gide, *Les Nourritures terrestres*, in *Oeuvres complètes*, ed. Martin-Chauffier (Paris, 1932), II, 227. Subsequent references to this work will appear in the text.

16. *Nourritures*, p. 57; "So Long," 53-54; *Nourritures*, p. 58.

17. *Nourritures*, p. 61; "Song of Myself," 1281.

18. *Nourritures*, p. 178.

19. Yvonne Davet discusses this misunderstanding in *Autour des Nourritures terrestres* (Paris, 1948), p. 36.

20. For a detailed discussion of this controversy, see Martin Kanes, "Whitman, Gide and Bazalgette: An International Encounter," *Comparative Literature*, 14 (Fall 1962), 341-55.

21. André Gide, *Corydon* (Paris, 1925), p. 17. Subsequent references to this work will appear in the text.

22. Paul Claudel refers to the project in a letter to André Gide dated February 11, 1913; in Paul Claudel and André Gide, *Correspondance 1899-1926* (Paris, 1949), p. 210.

23. Jules Laforgue, "Dédicaces," "Une Femme m'attend," "O Etoile de France"; Vielé-Griffin, "Le Chant de la hache," "Un Monde," "Visages," *Walt Whitman: oeuvres choisies* (Paris, 1918).

24. See, for example: Pierre Brunel, "A la recherche d'une influence: l'image de l'orchestre et la tentation symphonique chez Walt Whitman et Paul Claudel," *La Revue des Lettres Modernes*, Nos. 134-36 (1966), 49-63; James Cappon, "New Systems of Verse: Whitman and Paul Claudel," in *Bliss Carmen* (New York, 1930), pp. 314-22; Jones, *The Background of Modern French Poetry*, p. 147; Claude-André Strauss, "Origine et sens du vers claudelien," *PMLA*, 64 (March 1949), 15-26.

25. Stanislas Fumet, ed., *Oeuvre poétique*, by Paul Claudel (Paris, 1957), p. xxix.

26. Jones, *Background*, p. 147.

27. Letter dated 21 April 1916, Rome; in Charles Saunders Collection at

Brown University. I am indebted to Roger Asselineau, who shared with me his transcription of this letter.

28. Claudel knew English at the time that he wrote *Tête d'Or* in 1889. He said in a broadcast for French radio: "J'ai appris l'anglais dans Shakespeare, je peux dire. Quand on voit ma première version de *Tête d'Or*, on retrouve partout l'influence de Shakespeare." In Paul Claudel, *Mémoires improvisés*, ed. Jean Amrouche (Paris, 1954), p. 33.

29. Jacques Madaule, *Le Génie de Paul Claudel* (Paris, 1933), p. 45.

30. Henri Guillemin, *Claudel et son art d'écrire* (Paris, 1955), p. 80.

31. "Positions et propositions sur le vers français," in Paul Claudel *Oeuvres en prose*, ed. Jacques Petit and Charles Galperine (Paris, 1965), pp. 33-34.

32. Remy de Gourmont, *Le Livre des masques* (1896; rpt. Paris, 1914), p. 198.

33. Paul Claudel, *Théâtre*, ed. Jacques Madaule and Jacques Petit (Paris, 1967), p. 41. Subsequent references to this edition will appear in the text.

34. "Visages," *Revue Indépendante*, p. 279.

35. "La Catastrophe d'Igitur," in *Oeuvres en prose*, p. 508.

36. Claudel, *Journal*, ed. François Varillon and Jacques Petit (Paris, 1968), I, 1020.

37. He bought the David McKay edition of *Leaves of Grass* on his first diplomatic mission to the U.S. in Jan. 1894. This volume is in the collection of Mme. Jacques de Massary in France. See Brunel, p. 50.

38. This play was not published until 1893.

39. "Art poétique," in *Oeuvre poétique*, pp. 203-04.

40. "Positions et propositions," in *Oeuvres en prose*, p. 33.

41. Roger Asselineau, *The Evolution of Walt Whitman* (Cambridge, 1962), II, 244-45.

42. Letter to Alexander Cordato (1948), cited in Brunel, p. 56.

43. Paul Claudel, *Oeuvre poétique*, p. 237. All quotations of *Cinq Grandes Odes* are from this edition, hereafter referred to in the text as *OP*.

44. Claudel-Gide, *Correspondance*, p. 210.

45. "Proud Music of the Storm" comes immediately to mind, but this poem is rather long. He may be referring to the short section in "Song of Myself" on tenors (600-10), or he may be thinking of "Vocalism" or "The Dead Tenor."

46. Paul Claudel and Jacques Rivière, *Correspondance* (Paris, 1955), p. 155.

47. Claudel-Rivière, *Correspondance*, p. 216.

48. Claudel-Gide, *Correspondance*, p. 222.

49. Claudel, *Oeuvres en prose*, pp. 865-66.

50. Charles Willard refers to this speech in *Whitman's American Fame* (Providence, 1950), p. 78.

51. Claudel, *Journal*, I, 1252.

52. *Oeuvres en prose*, p. 338.

53. André Spire, *Versets* (Paris, 1908), p. 64. Subsequent references to this work will appear in the text.

54. Martin Kanes discusses some of the parallels between Whitman and Péguy in his dissertation, "La Fortune de Walt Whitman en France," (Sorbonne 1953), pp. 210-18.

55. Georges Duhamel, *Paul Claudel suivi de Propos critiques* (Paris, 1919), p. 121.

56. Charles Vildrac, "La Leçon de Walt Whitman," *Les Feuilles de Mai* (April-June, 1913), p. 148.

57. Marie-Louise Bidal, *Les Ecrivains de l'Abbaye* (Paris, 1939), p. 41.

58. Bazalgette's biography *Walt Whitman: l'homme et l'oeuvre* was published in 1908; his translation *Feuilles d'herbe* was published in 1909.

59. *Propos critiques*, p. 138.

60. Georges Duhamel, *Le Temps de la recherche: Lumières sur ma vie* (Paris, 1947), III, 157.

61. René Arcos, "Quelques Poètes modernes," *Mercure de France*, 105 (Oct. 1913), 698.

62. *Propos critiques*, p. 131.

63. *Ibid.*, p. 139.

64. Charles Vildrac, "Le Mois du théâtre," *La Phalange* (20 May 1911), p. 455.

65. *Propos critiques*, p. 138.

66. Georges Duhamel, "Orgueil," *Mercure de France*, 107 (Feb. 1914), 577.

67. Vildrac, "La Leçon de Walt Whitman," p. 145.

68. *Ibid.*, p. 149.

69. René Arcos, *La Tragédie des espaces* (Paris: L'Abbaye, 1906).

70. Arcos, *Ce qui naît* (Paris, 1911). All quotations of this work are from this edition.

71. Arcos, "Quelques Poètes modernes," p. 700.

72. *Ibid.*

73. Charles Vildrac, *Poèmes de l'Abbaye* (Paris, 1925). Subsequent references to this work will appear in the text.

74. Vildrac, *Découvertes* (Paris, 1923), p. 11.

75. *Propos critiques*, p. 190.

76. *Ibid.*, p. 132.

77. Georges Duhamel, *Compagnons, poèmes (1910-1912)* (Paris, 1918). Subsequent references to this work will appear in the text.

78. *Propos critiques*, p. 136.

79. *Ibid.*, p. 138.

80. Georges Duhamel, "Mallarmé, Whitman, Rimbaud," *Mercure de France*, 103 (April 1913), 577.

81. Duhamel, "A Léon Bazalgette," *Europe* (15 May 1929), p. 160.

82. In *Walt Whitman in Europe Today*, ed. Roger Asselineau and William White (Detroit, 1972), p. 18.

83. Emile Henriot, *A quoi rêvent les jeunes gens* (Paris, 1913), p. 35.

84. Jules Romains, Préface, *Les Hommes de bonne volonté*, I (Paris, 1932), xiii.

85. *Ibid.*, p. v.

86. See André Cuisenier, *Jules Romains et l'unanimisme* (Paris, 1935), p. 74; Frederik Schyberg, *Walt Whitman*, trans. Evie Allison Allen (New York, 1951), p. 301; Gay Wilson Allen, *Walt Whitman Handbook* (1946; rpt. New York, 1962), p. 494.

87. Jules Romains, *La Vie unanime* (Paris, 1913), p. 136. Subsequent references to this work will appear in the text.

88. Cuisenier, *Jules Romains*, p. 74.

89. Jules Romains, "La Poésie immédiate," *Vers et prose*, 19 (1909), 95.

90. Préface, *Les Hommes de bonne volonté*, I, xx.

91. Romains, in *Whitman in Europe*, p. 18.

92. Chennevière, *Oeuvres poétiques*. All quotations of the poetry are from this edition.

93. André Cuisenier, ed., *Oeuvres poétiques*, by Chennevière, p. 41.

94. *Ibid.*, p. 51.

95. Philéas Lebesgue, *Aux Fenêtres de France* (Paris, 1906), p. 7.

96. Philéas Lebesgue, "Lettres étrangères: Walt Whitman," *La Phalange* (15 June 1908), p. 1161.

97. *Ibid.*, p. 1162.

98. Philéas Lebesgue, "Walt Whitman et la poésie contemporaine," in *Essai d'expansion d'une esthétique* (Tours, 1911), p. 12.

99. *Ibid.*, p. 13.

100. *Ibid.*, p. 16.

101. Lebesgue, *La Grande Pitié* (Paris, 1920). Subsequent references will appear in the text.

102. André Spire, Préface, *Lettres à quelques amis* (Paris, 1926), p. 50.

103. Roger Asselineau, in a review of Schyberg's *Walt Whitman*, first pointed out the Whitmanian antecedents of Franck; in *Revue de Littérature Comparée* (Jan.-Mar. 1952), pp. 155-56.

104. *La Danse devant l'arche* (Paris, 1921).

105. *Perspectives* (Paris, 1924), p. 7.

106. Jean-Richard Bloch, ed., *Anthologie de l'Effort* (Poitiers: Effort Libre,

1912). The tendency to include Whitman in anthologies of modern French poetry continues to this day. For example, in 1965, Henry Lemaitre included a poem from Walt Whitman in his collection of poetry entitled *La Poésie depuis Baudelaire* (San Francisco, 1965).

107. Jean-Richard Bloch, *Lévy* (Paris, 1912), p. 7.

108. Henri Ghéon, "Les Poèmes: le Whitmanisme," *Nouvelle Revue Française*, 12 (June 1912), 1053.

109. *Ibid.*, p. 1054.

110. *Ibid.*, p. 1055-56.

111. Daniel Halévy, "Chants démocratiques," *Pages Libres*, No. 30 (July 1901), 75-80.

112. *Ibid.*, p. 78.

113. Bazalgette stressed the social and political orientation of Whitman's work in *Walt Whitman: l'homme et l'oeuvre* (1908); see also F. Delattre, "Un Poète de la démocratie: Walt Whitman," *Revue Pédagogique*, 56 (May 1910), 407-20; Elsie Masson, "Walt Whitman, ouvrier et poète," *Mercure de France*, 68 (Aug. 1907), 385-90; Pierre Nicolas, "Lectures étrangères: Walt Whitman," *Pages Libres* (11 July 1908), pp. 38-45.

114. Valery Larbaud, "Lettres anglaises: Walt Whitman en français," *La Phalange* (20 April 1909), p. 952.

Chapter IV

1. Guillaume Apollinaire, "L'Esprit nouveau et les poètes," *Mercure de France*, 130 (Dec. 1918), 396.

2. Henri Guilbeaux, "Walt Whitman," *Portraits d'hier*, No. 37 (Paris, 1910), p. 26.

3. In a lecture on Dynamism that he gave at Rouen in 1909, A. M. Gossez named Whitman as a precursor of the Dynamist movement. This lecture, along with a lecture by Henri Strentz, and Lebesgue's lecture "Walt Whitman et la poésie contemporaine" are collected in *Essai d'expansion d'une esthétique* (Tours, 1911).

4. Filippo Marinetti, *Le Futurisme* (Paris, 1911), p. 89.

5. See Appendix II: 1914-1922.

6. Richepin, p. 242.

7. Jean Guehenno, "Whitman, Wilson et l'esprit moderne," *Revue de Paris*, 26 (Jan. 1919), 124.

8. *Ibid.*, p. 130.

9. See Appendices I and II.

10. Valery Larbaud, *Oeuvres*, eds. Georges Jean-Aubry and Robert Mallet (Paris, 1957), p. xxxvii. Subsequent references to this work will appear in the text.

11. Larbaud, "Lettres anglaises: Walt Whitman en français," p. 952.

12. See Chapter III, p. 174.

13. Georges Jean-Aubry, *Valery Larbaud, sa vie et son oeuvre* (Monaco, 1949), p. 97.

14. Larbaud, "Whitman en français," p. 952.

15. *Ibid.*, p. 955.

16. Larbaud, "Walt Whitman: Etude par V. Larbaud," in *Walt Whitman: poèmes et proses* (Poitiers: Nouvelle Revue Française, 1960). This is a re-edition of Gide's *Walt Whitman: oeuvres choisies* (1918). Subsequent references will be from the 1960 edition, hereafter referred to as *Poèmes*.

17. Aubry, *Valery Larbaud*, p. 97.

18. "Conversation" with Léon-Paul Fargue cited in *Larbaud: Oeuvres*, pp. 1132-33.

19. Cendrars, *La Vie dangereuse* (1938), in *Edition complète des oeuvres de Blaise Cendrars*, IV (Paris, 1965), p. 579. Subsequent references to Cendrars' work will be from this edition.

20. Critics frequently allude to the Whitmanian quality of Cendrars' work. See, for example: Jay Bochner, "From Whitman to Blaise Cendrars," *Calamus: Walt Whitman Quarterly*, No. 9 (May 1974), pp. 8-29; Jacques-Henri Lévesque, *Blaise Cendrars* (Paris, 1947), p. 27; Jean-Claude Lovey, *Situation de Blaise Cendrars* (Neuchâtel, 1965), p. 52; Louis Parrot, *Blaise Cendrars; Poètes d'aujourd'hui* (Paris, 1948), pp. 24-25.

21. Cendrars' collected poetry was published with the title *Du Monde entier au coeur du monde* (Paris, 1947).

22. Cendrars, *Aujourd'hui* (1931), in *Oeuvres*, IV, 213.

23. *Ibid.*, p. 208.

24. Cendrars, *Du Monde entier au coeur du monde*, in *Oeuvres*, I. Subsequent references to this work will appear in the text.

25. "Song of Myself," 822-32. Whitman describes the shipwreck of the *San Francisco*, which was reported in the *New York Weekly Tribune* of January 21, 1854.

26. Cendrars, *Oeuvres*, VIII (Paris, 1965), 549.

27. Cendrars, *Poésies complètes* (Paris, 1944).

28. Whitman, "A Song for Occupations," line 141; Cendrars, *Blaise Cendrars vous parle* (1950), in *Oeuvres*, VIII, 564.

29. Guillaume Apollinaire, "A propos de Walt Whitman," *Mercure de France*, 106 (Dec. 1913), 864.

30. Apollinaire, "Funérailles de Walt Whitman racontées par un témoin," *Mercure de France*, 102 (April 1913), 658-59.

31. See Appendix I.

32. Harrison Reeves, "Lettre à la rédaction à propos de Walt Whitman," *Mercure de France*, 103 (June 1913), 893-95.

Edouard Bertz, "A propos de Walt Whitman: les funérailles, l'homosexualité de Whitman," *MF*, 104 (July 1913), 204-10; "Lettre à la rédaction à propos de Walt Whitman," *MF*, 105 (Oct. 1913), 654-55; "Lettre à la rédaction à propos de Walt Whitman," *MF*, 106 (Nov. 1913), 219.

Léon Bazalgette, "Le Document de M. Apollinaire," *Effort Libre* (April 1913), 513; "Une Lettre à propos de Walt Whitman," *MF*, 105 (Sept. 1913), 221-22; "Les Petits-fils de l'honorable James Harlan," *Effort Libre* (Nov. 1913); "Lettre à propos de Walt Whitman," *MF*, 105 (Oct. 1913), 877.

Stuart Merrill, "Une Lettre à la rédaction à propos de Walt Whitman," *MF*, 102 (April 1913), 890-92; "La Question Walt Whitman," *MF*, 106 (Nov. 1913), 329-36.

33. Apollinaire, "A propos de Whitman," p. 865.

34. *Ibid.*, pp. 864-65.

35. Apollinaire, "L'Anti-tradition futuriste," in *Manifestes futuristes* (Milan, 1913).

36. Guillaume Apollinaire, *Oeuvres poétiques*, eds. Marcel Adéma and Michel Décaudin (Paris, 1959). All quotations of Apollinaire's poetry are taken from this edition; subsequent references to this edition will appear in the text.

37. In Michel Décaudin, *Le Dossier d'Alcools* (Paris, 1960), p. 138.

38. Whitman, "Song of the Exposition," line 57.

39. Apollinaire first used the term *Surréalisme* in 1917 to describe the play *Parade*, for which he wrote the program on opening night. He also used the term to describe his play *Les Mamelles de Tirésias*, which also appeared in 1917. See Roger Shattuck, *The Banquet Years* (New York, 1968), p. 294.

40. Apollinaire, "L'Esprit nouveau," p. 395. Subsequent references to this article will appear in the text.

41. 1855 Preface, *LG*, p. 716.

42. 1876 Preface, *LG*, p. 752.

43. Saint-John Perse, *Oeuvres complètes* (Paris, 1972). All quotations of Perse's work are taken from this edition; subsequent references will appear in the text.

44. Roger Caillois, *Poétique de St.-John Perse* (Paris, 1954), pp. 185-90.

45. Yves-Alain Favre, *Saint-John Perse: le langage et le sacré* (Paris, 1977), pp. 11-14.

46. Sylvia Beach, *Shakespeare and Company* (New York, 1959), p. 128.

47. See Chapter III, p. 164.

48. Beach, p. 129.

49. Marcel Martinet, in *Walt Whitman in Europe*, p. 17.

50. Christian Michelfelder, *Jean Giono et les religions de la terre* (Paris, 1938), p. 14.

51. Jean Giono, *Le Serpent d'étoiles* (Paris, 1933).

52. William T. Starr, "Jean Giono and Walt Whitman," *French Review*, 14 (Dec. 1940), 128-29.

53. Paul Jamati, *Walt Whitman: une étude, un choix de poèmes: poètes d'aujourd'hui* (Paris, 1948).

54. Alain Bosquet, *Whitman* (Paris, 1959).

55. *Ibid.*, p. 83.

56. Roger Asselineau, *L'Evolution de Walt Whitman* (Paris, 1954); *Whitman: Feuilles d'herbe* (Paris, 1956).

57. Asselineau's works on Whitman include: "A propos de Walt Whitman," *Langues Modernes*, 42 (Aug.-Oct. 1948), 62-65; "La Thème de la mort dans l'oeuvre de Walt Whitman," *La Revue des Lettres Modernes* (Nov. 1954), pp. 33-48; "Un Poète cosmique américain: Walt Whitman," *Mystère Solaire*, Nos. 13-14 (Jan. 1954); "Whitman et Wordsworth—étude d'une influence indirecte," *Revue de Littérature Comparée*, 29 (1955), 505-12; "Walt Whitman—or Nature Imitates Art," *Walt Whitman Newsletter*, 3 (1957), 22-24; "Whitman Agonistes," *Walt Whitman Newsletter*, 3 (1957), 3-5; "Whitman in France in 1960," *Walt Whitman Review*, 6 (1960), 4-5; "If Walt Lived Today," *American Dialog*, 2 (Oct.-Nov. 1965), 3-6; "Walt Whitman from Paumanok to More Than America," *Papers on Language and Literature*, 5 (1969), 18-39; Walt Whitman, *Leaves of Grass: Feuilles d'herbe*, trans. Roger Asselineau (Paris, 1972); *Walt Whitman in Europe Today*, ed. Roger Asselineau (Detroit, 1972); "Walt Whitman's Humor," *American Transcendental Quarterly*, 22 (Spring 1974), 86-91; "Whitman et Millet," *La Quinzaine Littéraire* (Nov. 1975), p. 18; "Jack London et Walt Whitman," *Europe: Revue Littéraire Mensuelle*, 54 (Jan.-Feb. 1976), 76; "Whitman in France in 1976," *The Bicentennial Walt Whitman* (Detroit, 1976), pp. 13-14.

58. Le Clezio, in *Whitman in Europe*, p. 7.

Epilogue

1. T. S. Eliot, "Baudelaire," in *Selected Essays* (1932; rpt. London, 1950), pp. 371-81; see also "Baudelaire in our Time," in *Essays Ancient and Modern* (London, 1936), pp. 89-106.

2. T. S. Eliot, Introduction to Ezra Pound's *Selected Poems* (London, 1928), pp. x-xi.

3. T. S. Eliot, "Whitman and Tennyson," a review of Emory Holloway's *Whitman: An Interpretation in Narrative*, *The Nation and the Athenaeum*, 18 (Dec. 1926), 426.

4. Amy Lowell, "Walt Whitman and the New Poetry," *Yale Review*, n.s., 16 (1926-27), 509.

5. Eliot expressed his debt to Laforgue in several essays, including: "The Metaphysical Poets," in *Homage to John Dryden* (London, 1924), pp. 24-33; his introduction to Pound's *Selected Poems;* "Donne in Our Time," in A *Garland for John Donne* (Cambridge, 1931), pp. 2-19.

6. René Taupin discusses the influence of the French writers on Eliot in *L'Influence du symbolisme français sur la poésie américaine* (Paris, 1929); see also Bruce Morrissette, "T. S. Eliot and Guillaume Apollinaire," *Comparative Literature* 5 (Summer 1953), 262-68. Eliot introduced and translated an edition of St.-John Perse's *Anabase* (New York, 1948).

7. Amy Lowell, *Six French Poets* (New York, 1915).

8. Pound, "Walt Whitman," *American Literature,* 27 (1955), 60.

9. Pound, *Personae* (New York, 1926), p. 89.

10. William Carlos Williams, "An Essay on Leaves of Grass," in *Leaves of Grass: One Hundred Years After*, ed. Milton Hindus (Stanford, 1955), p. 22.

11. See "Edgar Allan Poe," in *In the American Grain* (Norfolk, 1925), pp. 216-34.

12. Pound, "A Few Don'ts by an Imagiste," *Poetry*, 1, No. 6 (March 1913), 200-06.

13. See "Remy de Gourmont," *Poetry*, 7, No. 4 (Jan. 1916), 197-202; "Monsieur Romains, Unanimist," *New Age*, 13, No. 21 (Sept. 1913), 607-09; "*Odes et prières*, par J. Romains," *Poetry*, 2, No. 5 (Aug. 1913), 187-89; "Charles Vildrac," *New Age*, 13, No. 22 (Sept. 1913), 631-33; "Remy de Gourmont" (1920), "The Hard and Soft in French Poetry" (1918), and "Irony, Laforgue, and Some Satire" (1917), in *Literary Essays of Ezra Pound* (New York, 1935).

14. Pound, "French Poets," in *Make it New* (London, 1934), pp. 159-251.

15. *Ibid.*, pp. 211-13.

16. Williams, "Yours, O Youth" (1921), in *Selected Essays* (1931; rpt. New York, 1954), p. 36.

17. Williams, Prologue to *Kora in Hell* (Boston, 1920).

18. "Père Sebastian Rasles," in *In the American Grain*, p. 107.

19. See, for example: Malcolm Cowley, Introduction to *Leaves of Grass: His Original Edition* (New York, 1959); Richard Chase, *Walt Whitman Reconsidered* (New York, 1955); Milton Hindus, ed., *Leaves of Grass One Hundred Years After* (Stanford, 1955); James E. Miller, Karl Shapiro, and Bernice Slote, *Start with the Sun: Studies in Cosmic Poetry* (Lincoln, 1960); Edwin H. Miller, ed., *The Artistic Legacy of Walt Whitman* (New York, 1970).

20. Gregory Corso, "Variations on a Generation," in A *Casebook on the Beat*, ed. Thomas Parkinson (1961; rpt. New York, 1967), p. 91.

21. Allen Ginsberg, "Notes Written on Finally Recording 'Howl,' " in *Casebook*, p. 28.

22. Pound, "French Poets," in *Make it New*, p. 159.

BIBLIOGRAPHY

Allen, Gay Wilson. *The Solitary Singer: A Critical Biography of Walt Whitman*. 1955; rpt. New York: The Macmillan Company, 1960.

———. *Walt Whitman Handbook*. 1946; rpt. New York: Hendricks House, 1962.

———. "Walt Whitman and Jules Michelet." *Etudes Anglaises*, 1 (1937), 230-37.

———. "Whitman and Michelet—Continued." *American Literature*, 45 (Nov. 1973), 428-32.

Apollinaire, Guillaume. "L'Antitradition futuriste." *Manifestes Futuristes*, 20 June 1913.

———. "L'Esprit nouveau et les poètes." *Mercure de France*, 130 (Dec. 1918), 385-96.

———. "Funérailles de Walt Whitman racontées par un témoin." *Mercure de France*, 102 (April 1913), 658-59.

———. *Oeuvres poètiques*. Ed. Marcel Adéma and Michel Décaudin. Paris: Gallimard, 1959.

———. "A Propos de Walt Whitman." *Mercure de France*, 106 (Dec. 1913), 864-65.

Arcos, René. *Ce qui naît*. Paris: Figuière, 1911.

———. "Quelques Poètes modernes." *Mercure de France*, 105 (Oct 1913), 696-713.

———. *La Tragédie des espaces*. Paris: L'Abbaye, 1906.

Asselineau, Roger. "Compte-rendu du *Walt Whitman* de F. Schyberg." *Revue de Littérature Comparée*, Jan.-Mar. 1952, pp 155-56.

———. *The Evolution of Walt Whitman*. 2 vols. Cambridge: Harvard University Press, 1962.

———. "Un Inédit de Walt Whitman: Taine's *History of English Literature*." *Etudes Anglaises*, 10 (1957), 128-38.

✓ Asselineau, Roger and William White, eds. *Walt Whitman in Europe Today*. Detroit: Wayne State University Press, 1972.

Baudelaire, Charles. *Oeuvres complètes*. 19 vols. Ed. Jacques Crépet. Paris: Louis Conard, 1923-1953.

Bazalgette, Léon. "Le Document de M. Apollinaire." *Effort Libre*, April 1913, p. 513.

———. "Une Lettre à propos de Walt Whitman." *Mercure de France*, 105 (Sept. 1913), 221-22.

———. "Une Lettre à propos de Walt Whitman." *Mercure de France*, 105 (Oct. 1913), 877.

———. "Les Petits-fils de l'honorable James Harlan." *Effort Libre*, Nov. 1913.

———. *Walt Whitman: l'homme et son oeuvre*. Paris: Mercure de France, 1908.

———, trans. *Feuilles d'herbe*. Paris: Mercure de France, 1909.

Beach, Sylvia. *Shakespeare and Company*. New York: Harcourt Brace, 1959.

Bentzon, Thérèse. "Un Poete américain, Walt Whitman: 'Muscle and Pluck Forever.' " *Revue des Deux Mondes*, 42 (June 1872), 565-82.

Bertz, Edouard. "Les Funérailles, l'homosexualité de Whitman." *Mercure de France*, 104 (July 1913), 204-210.

———. "Lettre à la rédaction à propos de Walt Whitman." *Mercure de France*, 105 (Oct. 1913), 654-55.

———. "Lettre à la rédaction à propos de Walt Whitman." *Mercure de France*, 106 (Nov. 1913), 219.

Bidal, Marie-Louise. *Les Ecrivains de l'Abbaye*. Paris: Boivin, 1939.

Bithell, Jethro. *The Life and Writings of Maurice Maeterlinck*. London: Walter Scott Publishing Co., 1913.

Blémont, Emile. *Beautés étrangères*. Paris: Lemerre, 1904.

———. "La Poésie en Angleterre et aux Etats-Unis, III, Walt Whitman." *La Renaissance Artistique et Littéraire*, No. 7 (June 1872), pp. 54-56; No. 11 (July 1872), pp. 86-87; No. 12 (July 1872), pp. 90-91.

Bloch, Jean. *Lévy*. Paris: Gallimard, 1912.

Bochner, Jay. "From Whitman to Blaise Cendrars." *Calamus: Walt Whitman Quarterly, International*, No. 9 (May 1974), pp. 8-29.

Bosquet, Alain. *Whitman*. Paris: Gallimard, 1959.

Brunel, Pierre. "A La Recherche d'une influence: l'image de l'orchestre et la tentation symphonique chez Walt Whitman et

Paul Claudel." *La Revue des Lettres Modernes*, Nos. 134-36 (1966), pp. 49-63.

Bucke, Richard M. *Walt Whitman*. Philadelphia: David McKay, 1883.

Burroughs, John. *Notes on Walt Whitman as Poet and Person*. 1867; rpt. New York: Haskell House, 1971.

Caillois, Roger. *Poétique de St.-John Perse*. Paris: Gallimard, 1954.

Cappon, James. *Bliss Carmen and the Literary Currents and Influences of His Time*. New York: L. Carrier & A. Isles, 1930.

Cendrars, Blaise. *Edition complète des oeuvres*. Paris: Denoël, 1960-1965.

Chennevière, Georges. *Oeuvres poétiques*. Ed. André Cuisenier and R. Maublanc. Paris: Gallimard, 1929.

Claudel, Paul. *Journal*. 2 vols. Ed. François Varillon and Jacques Petit. Paris: Gallimard, 1968.

______. *Mémoires improvisés*. Ed. Jean Amrouche. Paris: Gallimard, 1954.

______. *Oeuvre poétique*. Ed. Stanislas Fumet. Paris: Gallimard, 1957.

______. *Oeuvres en prose*. Ed. Jacques Petit and Charles Galperine. Paris: Gallimard, 1965.

______. *Théâtre*. 2 vols. Ed. Jacques Madaule and Jacques Petit. Paris: Gallimard, 1967.

Claudel, Paul and André Gide. *Correspondance: 1899-1926*. Paris: Gallimard, 1949.

Claudel, Paul and Jacques Rivière. *Correspondance: 1907-1914*. Paris: Gallimard, 1955.

Cuisenier, André. *Jules Romains et l'unanimisme*. Paris: Flammarion, 1935.

Davet, Yvonne. *Autour des Nourritures terrestres*. Paris: Gallimard, 1948.

Décaudin, Michel. *Le Dossier d'Alcools*. Paris: Minard, 1960.

De Graaf, Daniel. "Arthur Rimbaud et Walt Whitman." *Levende Talen*, Nov. 1953, pp. 363-72.

Delattre, F. "Un Poète de la démocratie: Walt Whitman." *Revue Pédagogique*, 56 (May 1910), 407-20.

Duhamel, Georges. *Compagnons, poèmes (1910-1912)*. Paris: Rivière, 1912.

———. "A Léon Bazalgette." *Europe*, 15 May 1929, p. 160.

———. "Mallarmé, Whitman, Rimbaud." *Mercure de France*, 102 (April 1913), 576-79.

———. "Orgueil." *Mercure de France*, 107 (Feb. 1914), 577.

———. *Paul Claudel suivi de Propos critiques*. Paris: Mercure de France, 1919.

———. *Le Temps de la recherche*. Paris: P. Hartman, 1947.

Dujardin, Edouard. *Les Premiers Poètes du vers libre*. Paris: Messein, 1936.

Durtain, Luc. *Perspectives*. Paris: Stock, 1924.

Eliot, T. S. *Essays Ancient and Modern*. London: Faber and Faber, 1936.

———. *A Garland for John Donne*. Cambridge: Harvard University Press, 1931.

———. *Homage to John Dryden*. London: L. and Virginia Woolf, 1924.

———. *Selected Essays*. 1932; rpt. London: Faber and Faber, 1950.

———. "Whitman and Tennyson." *The Nation and the Athenaeum*, 18 (Dec. 1926), 426.

Etienne, Louis. "Walt Whitman, poète, philosophe et rowdy." *La Revue Européene*, 1 Nov. 1861, pp. 104-17.

Favre, Yves-Alain. *Saint-John Perse: le langage et le sacré*. Paris: Librairie José Corti, 1977.

Fort Paul. *Ballades françaises*. 14 vols. Paris: Mercure de France, 1912.

Franck, Henri. *La Danse devant l'arche*. Paris: Gallimard, 1921.

———. *Lettres à quelques amis: préface par André Spire*. Paris: Grasset, 1926.

Geffen, Arthur. "Walt Whitman and Jules Michelet—One More Time." *American Literature*, 45 (Mar. 1973), 107-14.

Ghéon, Henri. "Les Poèmes: le whitmanisme." *Nouvelle Revue Française*, 12 (June 1912), 1053-59.

Gide, André. *Corydon*. Paris: Gallimard, 1925.

———. *Oeuvres complètes*. 15 vols. Ed. Martin-Chauffier. Paris: Nouvelle Revue Française, 1932-1939.

———. *Si le grain ne meurt*. 1928; rpt. Paris: Gallimard, 1945.

Giono, Jean. *Le Serpent d'étoiles*. Paris: Grasset, 1933.

Goffin, Robert. *Rimbaud et Verlaine vivants*. Paris: Editions L'Ecran du monde, 1949.

Goncourt, Edmond and Jules. *Journal: mémoires de la vie littéraire (1891-1904)*. 4 vols. Monaco: Fasquelle and Flammarion, 1956.

Goodale, David. "Some of Walt Whitman's Borrowings." *American Literature*, 10 (May 1938), 202-13.

Gourmont, Remy de. *Le Livre des masques*. 2 vols. 1896; rpt. Paris: Mercure de France, 1914.

Guehenno, Jean. "Whitman, Wilson et l'esprit moderne." *Revue de Paris*, 26 (Jan. 1919), 107-30.

Guilbeaux, Henri. *Walt Whitman: portraits d'hier*. Paris: Fabre, 1910.

Guillemin, Henri. *Claudel et son art d'écrire*. Paris: Gallimard, 1955.

Halévy, Daniel. "Chants démocratiques." *Pages Libres*, No. 30 (July 1901), pp. 75-80.

Henriot, Emile. A *Quoi rêvent les jeunes gens*. Paris: Champion, 1913.

Henry, Marjorie-Louise. *La Contribution d'un américain au symbolisme français: Stuart Merrill*. Paris: Champion, 1927.

Hindus, Milton, ed. *Leaves of Grass: One Hundred Years After*. 1955; rpt. Stanford: Stanford University Press, 1966.

Hugo, Victor, *La Légende des siècles*. 2 vols. Ed. Jean-Louis Cornuz. Paris: Editions Rencontre, 1968. Vols. 21-22 of *Oeuvres complètes*.

Huret, Jules. *L'Enquête sur l'évolution littéraire*. Paris: Charpentier, 1891.

Jamati, Paul. *Walt Whitman: une étude, un choix de poèmes*. Paris: Poètes d'aujourd'hui, 1948.

Jammes, Francis. "Un Manifeste littéraire de monsieur Francis Jammes: le jammisme." *Mercure de France*, 40 (Mar. 1897), 492-93.

______. *Oeuvres*. 5 vols. Paris: Mercure de France, 1913-1926.

Jean-Aubry, Georges. *Valery Larbaud: sa vie et son oeuvre d'après des documents inédits*. Monaco: Editions du Rocher, 1949.

Jones, Howard M. *America and French Culture: 1750-1848*. Chapel Hill: University of North Carolina Press, 1927.

Jones, Percy M. *The Background of Modern French Poetry*. Cambridge: Cambridge University Press, 1951.

———. "Influence of Walt Whitman on the Origin of the 'Vers libre'." *Modern Language Review*, 6 (1916), 186-94.

———. "Memories of Emile Verhaeren." *Belgian Review*, June 1944, pp. 29-36.

———. "Whitman and Verhaeren." *Aberystwyth Studies*, 2 (1914), 71-106.

Kanes, Martin. "La Fortune de Walt Whitman en France." Diss. Sorbonne, 1953.

———. "Whitman, Gide and Bazalgette: An International Encounter." *Comparative Literature*, 14 (Fall 1962), 341-55.

Knapp, Adeline. "Walt Whitman and Jules Michelet, Identical Passages." *Critic*, 44 (1907), 467-68.

Knight, Charles. *Half-Hours with the Best Authors*. 6 vols. Philadelphia: Porter and Coates, 1847-49.

Laforgue, Jules. *Lettres à un ami: Laforgue à Kahn*. Ed. Georges Jean-Aubry. Paris: Mercure de France, 1941.

———. *Poésies complètes*. 2 vols. Ed. Georges Jean-Aubry. Paris: Edition de Cluny, 1943.

———, trans. "*Les Brins d'herbe:* traduit de l'étonnant poète américain, Walt Whitman." *La Vogue*, 1, No. 10 (June-July 1886), 325-28; 1, No. 11 (July 1886), 388-90; 2, No. 3 (Aug. 1886), 73-76.

Larbaud, Valery. "Lettres anglaises: Walt Whitman en français." *La Phalange*, 20 April 1909, pp. 952-55.

———. *Oeuvres*. Ed. Georges Jean-Aubry and Robert Mallet. Paris: Gallimard, 1957.

Lebesgue, Philéas. *Aux Fenêtres de France*. Paris: Sansot, 1906.

———. *La Grande Pitié*. Paris: Sansot, 1920.

———. "Walt Whitman." *La Phalange*, 15 June 1908, pp. 1160-63.

Lebesgue, Philéas, et al. *Essai d'expansion d'une esthétique*. Tours: Editions de la Province, 1911.

Lévesque, Jacques-Henri. *Blaise Cendrars*. Paris: La Nouvelle Revue Critique, 1947.

Lewis, R. W. B. *The American Adam*. Chicago: University of Chicago Press, 1955.

Lombard, Charles. "Whitman and Hugo." *Walt Whitman Review*, 19 (Mar. 1973), 19-25.

Lovey, Jean-Claude. *Situation de Blaise Cendrars*. Neuchâtal: La Baconnière, 1965.

Lowell, Amy. *Six French Poets*. New York: The Macmillan Company, 1916.

______. "Walt Whitman and the New Poetry." *Yale Review*, n.s., 16 (1926-27), 502-19.

Madaule, Jacques. *Le Génie de Paul Claudel*. Paris: Desclée de Brauwer, 1933.

Maeterlinck, Maurice. *Serres chaudes*. Bruxelles: Paul Lacomblez, 1900.

Mallet, Robert. *Le Jammisme*. Paris: Mercure de France, 1961.

Marinetti, Filippo. *Le Futurisme*. Paris: Sansot, 1911.

Masson, Elsie. "Walt Whitman, ouvrier et poète." *Mercure de France*, 68 (Aug. 1907), 385-90.

Merrill, Stuart. "Une Lettre à la rédaction à propos de Walt Whitman." *Mercure de France*, 102 (April 1913), 890-92.

______. *Les Quatre Saisons*. Paris: Mercure de France, 1900.

______. "La Question Walt Whitman." *Mercure de France*, 106 (Nov. 1913), 329-36.

______. *Une Voix dans la foule*. Paris: Mercure de France, 1909.

______. "Walt Whitman." Trans. John J. Espey. *Walt Whitman Newsletter*, 3 (1957), 55-57.

Michaud, Guy. *Message poétique du symbolisme*. 3 vols. Paris: Nizet, 1947.

Michelet, Jules. *History of France*. 2 vols. Trans. G. H. Smith. 1846; rpt. New York: Appleton, 1848.

______. *The People*. Trans. G. H. Smith. New York: Appleton, 1846.

Michelfelder, Christian. *Jean Giono et les religions de la terre*. Paris: Gallimard, 1938.

Miller, Edwin H. *Walt Whitman's Poetry: A Psychological Journey*. New York: New York University Press, 1968.

Morrissette, Bruce A. "T. S. Eliot and Guillaume Apollinaire." *Comparative Literature*, 5 (Summer 1953), 262-68.

Murphy, Francis, ed. *Walt Whitman*. Baltimore: Penguin, 1970.

Nicholas, Pierre. "Lectures étrangères: Walt Whitman." *Pages Libres*, 11 July 1908, pp. 38-45.

Parkinson, Thomas, ed. *A Casebook on the Beat*. 1961; rpt. New York: Thomas W. Crowell Co., 1967.

Perse, Saint-John. *Oeuvres complètes*. Paris: Gallimard, 1972.

Parrot, Louis. *Blaise Cendrars*. Paris: P. Seghers, 1948.

Payne, Richard M. "Blaise Cendrars: From Action to Contemplation." Diss. Stanford, 1960.

Pound, Ezra. "A Few Don'ts by an Imagiste." *Poetry*, 1, No. 6 (Mar. 1913), 200-206.

———. *Make it New*. London: Faber and Faber, 1934.

———. *Personae*. New York: New Directions, 1926.

———. *Selected Poems*, with an Introduction by T. S. Eliot. London: Faber & Gwyer, 1928.

———. "Walt Whitman." *American Literature*, 27 (1955), 59-61.

Pucciani, Oreste F. "The Literary Reputation of Whitman in France." Diss. Harvard, 1943.

Ramsey, Warren. *Jules Laforgue and the Ironic Inheritance*. New York: Oxford University Press, 1953.

Randall, Huberta F. "Whitman and Verhaeren—Priests of Human Brotherhood." *French Review*, 16 (1942), 36-43.

Raymond, Marcel. *From Baudelaire to Surrealism*. Trans. G. M. New York: Wittenborn, Schultz, 1950.

Reeves, Harrison. "A Propos de Walt Whitman." *Mercure de France*, 103 (June 1913), 893-95.

Rhodes, S. A. "The Influence of Walt Whitman on André Gide." *Romanic Review*, 31 (April 1940), 156-71.

Richepin, Jean. *L'Ame américaine à travers quelques-uns de ses interprètes*. Paris: Flammarion, 1920.

Rimbaud, Arthur. *Correspondance inédite (1870-1875)*. Ed. Roger Gilbert-Lecomte. Paris: Cahiers Libres, 1929.

———. *Oeuvres*. Ed. Suzanne Bernard. Paris: Garnier, 1960.

Roddier, Henri. "Pierre Leroux, George Sand et Walt Whitman, ou l'éveil d'un poète." *Revue de Littérature Comparée*, 31 (1957), 5-33.

Romains, Jules. *Les Hommes de bonne volonté*. 27 vols. Paris: Flammarion, 1932-1946.

———. "La Poésie immédiate." *Vers et prose*, 19 (1909), 90-95.

———. *La Vie unanime*. Paris: L'Abbaye, 1908.

Rousseau, Jean-Jacques. *The Confessions*. 2 vols. Trans. Swinton. New York: C. Blanchard, 1856-1857.

Roy, G. R. "Walt Whitman, George Sand, and Certain French Socialists." *Revue de Littérature Comparée*, 29 (1955), 550-61.

Sand, George. *Consuelo.* 3 vols. Trans. Francis G. Shaw. New York: Ticknor, 1846.

Sarrazin, Gabriel. "Poètes modernes de l'Amérique, Walt Whitman." *La Nouvelle Revue,* 52 (May 1888), 164-84.

Schwob, Marcel. *Coeur double.* Paris: Ollendorf, 1891.

______. *Oeuvres.* 2 vols. Paris: Mercure de France, 1921.

______. *Oeuvres complètes.* 10 vols. Paris: Bernouard, 1927-1930.

Schyberg, Frederik. *Walt Whitman.* Trans. Evie Allison Allen. New York: Columbia University Press, 1951.

Shattuck, Roger. *The Banquet Years.* 1955; rpt. New York: Random House, 1968.

Shephard, Esther. *Walt Whitman's Pose.* 1936; rpt. New York: Harcourt Brace, 1938.

Spire, André. *Versets.* Paris: Mercure de France, 1908.

Starr, William T. "Jean Giono and Walt Whitman." *French Review,* 14 (Dec. 1940), 118-29.

Strauss, Claude-André. "Origine et sens du vers claudelien." *PMLA,* 64 (Mar. 1949), 15-26.

Taupin, René. *L'Influence du symbolisme français sur la poésie américaine (de 1910 à 1920).* Paris: Champion, 1929.

Traubel, Horace. *With Walt Whitman in Camden.* Vol. 1. Boston: Small Maynard, 1906; Vol. 2. New York: Appleton, 1908; Vol. 3. New York: M. Kennerley, 1914; Vol. 4. Philadelphia: University of Pennsylvania Press, 1953; Vol. 5. Carbondale: Southern Illinois University Press, 1964.

Vielé-Griffin, Francis. *Oeuvres.* 2 vols. Paris: Mercure de France, 1924-1926.

______. *Thrène pour le Président Lincoln, transposition du poème de Walt Whitman.* Paris: Bibliotèque de l'Occident, 1908.

______, trans. "A Quelque Révolutionnaire d'Europe dans la défaite." *Les Entretiens Politiques et Littéraires,* 5, No. 32 (Nov. 1892), 219.

______, trans. "Autobiographie de Walt Whitman." *Les Entretiens Politiques et Littéraires,* 4, No. 25 (April 1892), 166-69.

______, trans. "Le Chant de la hache." *L'Ermitage,* April 1899, pp. 293-308.

______, trans. "Il y avait un enfant qui partait chaque jour." *La Cravache Parisienne,* 9, No. 432 (June 1889).

———, trans. "Poèmes de Walt Whitman." *Revue Indépendante*, 9, No. 25 (Nov. 1888), 279-86.

Vildrac, Charles. *Découvertes*. Paris: Gallimard, 1912.

———. "La Leçon de Walt Whitman." *Les Feuilles de Mai*, April-May-June 1913, pp. 143-49.

———. "Le Mois du théâtre." *La Phalange*, 20 May 1911, p. 455.

———. *Poèmes de l'Abbaye suivis de Esquisse d'un Pégase*. Paris: Sablier, 1925.

Volney, Constantin F. *The Ruins, or Meditations on the Revolutions of Empires*. Trans. C. Volney and Joel Barlow. 1802; rpt. New York: C. Blanchard, 1853.

Voltaire, François. *Philosophical Dictionary*. 1824; rpt. Boston: J. P. Mendum, 1852.

Wells, David J. "Whitman and Rimbaud." *Walt Whitman Review*, 19 (Mar. 1973), 25-28.

Wharton, Edith. *A Backward Glance*. New York: Appleton, 1934.

Whitman, Walt. *The Complete Writings*. 10 vols. Ed. Richard Maurice Bucke et al. New York: Putnam's, 1902.

———. *The Correspondence (1842-1892)*. 5 vols. Ed. Edwin H. Miller. New York: New York University Press, 1961-1969. Vol. 1 of *The Collected Writings of Walt Whitman*. Ed. Gay Wilson Allen and Sculley Bradley.

———. *Faint Clews and Indirections: Manuscripts of Walt Whitman and His Family*. Ed. Clarence Gohdes and Rollo G. Silver. Durham: Duke University Press, 1949.

———. *I Sit and Look Out: Editorials from the Brooklyn Daily Times*. Ed. Emory Holloway and Vernolian Schwarz. New York: Columbia University Press, 1932.

———. *Leaves of Grass: Comprehensive Readers Edition*. Ed. Harold W. Blodgett and Sculley Bradley. New York: Norton, 1965.

———. *Leaves of Grass: The First (1855) Edition*. Ed. Malcolm Cowley. New York: Viking, 1959.

———. *New York Dissected*. Ed. Emory Holloway and Ralph Adimari. New York: Rufus Rockwell Wilson, 1936.

———. *Oeuvres choisies*. Ed. André Gide. Paris: Nouvelle Revue Française, 1918.

———. *Poèmes et proses*. Poitiers: Gallimard, 1960. Re-edition of Gide's *Walt Whitman: oeuvres choisies*.

———. *Prose Works 1892: Specimen Days, Collect, and Other Prose.* 2 vols. Ed. Floyd Stovall. New York: New York University Press, 1963. Volume 3 of *Collected Writings of Walt Whitman.*

———. *The Uncollected Poetry and Prose.* 2 vols. Ed. Emory Holloway. Garden City: Doubleday, 1921.

———. *Walt Whitman's Workshop.* Ed. Clifton J. Furness. Cambridge: Harvard University Press, 1928.

Willard, Charles. *Whitman's American Fame: The Growth of his Reputation in America After 1892.* Providence: Brown University, 1950.

Williams, William Carlos. *In the American Grain.* Norfolk: New Directions, 1925.

———. *Kora in Hell; improvisations.* Boston: The Four Seas Company, 1920.

———. *Selected Essays.* 1931; rpt. New York: Random House, 1954.

Wyzewa, Teodor de. "Notes sur les littératures étrangères—Walt Whitman, 1819-1892." *Revue Politique et Littéraire (Revue Bleu)*, 49, No. 17 (April 1892), 513-19.

INDEX

Library of Congress Cataloging in Publication Data

Erkkila, Betsy, 1944-
Walt Whitman among the French.

Bibliography: p.
Includes index.
1. Whitman, Walt, 1819-1892—Influence. 2. Whitman, Walt, 1819-1892—Sources. 3. French literature—20th century—History and criticism. 4. French literature—19th century—History and criticism. 5. Symbolism (Literary movement)—France. I. Title.
PS3236.E7 811'.4 79-3204
ISBN 0-691-06426-1